PREPARING FOR THE BIOLOGY
AP*EXAM

WITH
BIOLOGY, SEVENTH EDITION
CAMPBELL/REECE

*AP is a registered trademark of the College Board, which was not involved in the production of, and does not endorse, this product.

PEARSON

Benjamin
Cummings

San Francisco   Boston   New York   Cape Town   Hong Kong   London   Madrid   Mexico City
Montreal   Munich   Paris   Singapore   Sydney   Tokyo   Toronto

Editorial Director: Frank Ruggirello
Editor-in-Chief: Beth Wilbur
Project Editors: Amy Austin, Robin Heyden
Biology Marketing Manager: Jeff Hester
Managing Editor, Production: Erin Gregg
Production Supervisor: Vivian McDougal
Cover Designer: Stacy Wong
Manufacturing Buyer: Pam Augspurger
Production Service: TechBooks/GTS, Angie Armendarez
Printer: Command Web

Figures taken from:

Biology, Seventh Edition
by Neil A. Campbell and Jane B. Reece
Copyright © 2005 by Pearson Education, publishing as Benjamin Cummings
San Francisco, California 94111

Test Bank for *Biology,* Sixth Edition
Edited by William Barstow
Copyright © 2002 by Pearson Education, publishing as Benjamin Cummings

Student Study Guide for *Biology*, Sixth Edition
by Martha R. Taylor
Copyright © 2002 by Pearson Education, publishing as Benjamin Cummings

ISBN 0-8053-7187-7

7 8 9 10 – BRR– 07

www.aw-bc.com

Contents

CHAPTER 3

Genetics   75

CHAPTER 7
Animal Form and Function   173

CHAPTER 8
Ecology 207

Part III: *Sample Tests with Answers and Explanations* 221

About Your
Pearson AP* Guide

Pearson Education is the leading publisher of textbooks worldwide. With operations on every continent, we make it our business to understand the changing needs of students at every level, from Kindergarten to college. We think that makes us especially qualified to offer this series of AP test prep books, tied to some of our best-selling textbooks.

Our reasoning is that as you study for your course, you're preparing along the way for the AP test. If you can tie the material in the book directly to the test you're taking, it makes the material that much more relevant, and enables you to focus your time most efficiently. And that's a good thing!

The AP exam is an important milestone in your education. A high score means you're in a better position for college acceptance, and possibly puts you a step ahead with college credits. Our goal is to provide you with the tools you need to excel on the exam . . . the rest is up to you.

Good luck!

Part I

Introduction to the AP Biology Examination

This section gives an overview of the Advanced Placement* program and the AP Biology Examination. Part I introduces the types of questions you will encounter on the exam, explains the procedures used to grade the exam, and provides helpful test-taking strategies. A correlation chart shows where in Campbell and Reece, *BIOLOGY*, Seventh Edition, you will find key information that commonly appears on the AP Biology Examination. Finally, a thematic study grid will help you organize your thoughts as you prepare for the test. Review Part I carefully before trying the sample test items in Part II and Part III.

The Advanced Placement* Program

Probably you are reading this book for a couple of reasons. You may be a student in an Advanced Placement (AP) Biology class, and you have some questions about how the whole AP Program works and how it can benefit you. Also, perhaps, you will be taking an AP Biology Examination, and you want to find out more about it. This book will help you in several important ways. The first part of this book introduces you to the AP Biology course and the AP Biology Exam. You'll learn helpful details about the different question formats—multiple-choice and free-response—that you'll encounter on the exam. In addition, you'll find many test-taking strategies that will help you prepare for the exam. A correlation chart at the end of Part I shows how to use your textbook, Campbell and Reece *BIOLOGY*, to find the information you'll need to know to score well on the AP Biology Exam. By the way, this chart is useful, too, in helping you to identify any extraneous material that won't be tested. Following the correlation table, you will find a grid that connects the eight major AP Biology themes to the course topics. Part II of this book provides an extensive content review correlated to each unit of your textbook, along with sample multiple-choice and free-response questions. Finally, in Part III, you will find two full-length sample tests. These will help you practice taking the exam under real-life testing conditions. The more familiar you are with the AP Biology Exam ahead of time, the more comfortable you'll be on testing day.

The AP Program is sponsored by the College Board, a nonprofit organization that oversees college admissions examinations. (The College Board is composed of college and high school teachers and administrators.) The AP Program offers thirty-four college-level courses to qualified high school students. If you receive a grade of 3 or higher on an AP exam, you may be eligible for college credit, depending on the policies of the institution you plan to attend. Over 3,000 colleges and universities around the world grant credit to students who have performed well on AP exams. Some institutions grant sophomore status to incoming first-year students who have demonstrated mastery of several AP subjects. You can check the policies of specific institutions on the College Board's website (www.collegeboard.com). In addition, the College Board confers a number of AP Scholar Awards on students who score 3 or higher on three or more AP exams. Additional awards are available to students who receive very high grades on four or five AP exams.

Why Take an AP Course?

You may be taking an AP course simply because you like challenging yourself and you are thirsty for knowledge. Another reason may be that you know that colleges look favorably on applicants who have AP courses on their secondary school transcripts. AP classes involve rigorous, detailed lessons, a lot of homework, and numerous tests. College admissions officers may see your willingness to take these courses as evidence of your work ethic and commitment to your

3

education. Because AP course work is more difficult than average high school work, many admissions officers evaluate AP grades on a higher academic level. For example, if you receive a B in an AP class, it might carry the same weight as an A in a regular-level high school class.

Your AP Biology course prepares you for many of the skills you will need in college. For example, your teacher may assign a major research paper and require you to perform several challenging laboratory exercises using proper scientific protocol. AP Biology teachers routinely give substantial reading assignments, and students learn how to take detailed lecture notes and participate vigorously in class discussions. The AP Biology course will challenge you to gather and consider information in new—and sometimes unfamiliar—ways. You can feel good knowing that your ability to use these methods and skills will give you a leg up as you enter college.

Each college or university decides whether or not to grant college credit for an AP course, and each bases this decision on what it considers satisfactory grades on AP exams. Depending on what college you attend and what area of study you pursue, your decision to take the AP Biology Exam could save you tuition money. You can contact schools directly to find out their guidelines for accepting AP credits, or use the College Board's online feature, "AP Credit Policy Info."

Taking an AP Examination

The AP Biology Exam is given annually in May. Your AP teacher or school guidance counselor can give you information on how to register for an AP exam. Remember, the deadline for registration and payment of exam fees is usually in March, two months before the actual exam date in May. The cost of the exam is subject to change and can differ depending on the number of exams taken. However, in 2005 a single exam cost $82. For students who can show financial need, the College Board will reduce the price by $22, and your school might also waive its regular rebate of $8, so the lowest possible total price is $52. Moreover, schools in some states are willing to pay the exam fee for the student. If you feel you may qualify for reduced rates, ask your school administrators for more information.

The exams are scored in June. In mid-July the results will be sent to you, your high school, and any colleges or universities you indicated on your answer sheet. If you want to know your score as early as possible, you can get it (for an additional charge of $18) beginning July 1 by calling the College Board at (888) 308-0013. On the phone, you'll be asked to give your AP number or social security number, your birth date, and a credit card number.

If you decide that you want your score sent to additional colleges and universities, you can fill out the appropriate information on your AP Grade Report (which you will receive by mail in July) and return it to the College Board. There is an additional charge of $15 for each additional school that will receive your AP score.

On the other hand, if a feeling of disaster prevents you from sleeping on the nights following the exam, you could choose to withhold or cancel your grade. (Withholding is temporary, whereas canceling is permanent.) Each procedure carries a $10 charge per college or university. You'll need to write to (or email) the College Board and include your name, address, gender, birth date, AP number, the date of the exam, the name of the exam, a check for the exact amount due, and the name, city, and state of the college(s) from which you want the score withheld. You should check the College Board website for the deadline for withholding your score, but it's usually in mid-July. It is strongly suggested that you *do not* cancel your scores, since you won't know your score until mid-July. Instead, relax and try to assume that the glass is half full. At this point, you have nothing to lose and a lot to gain.

If you would like to get back your free-response booklet for a post-exam review, you can send another check for $7 to the College Board. You'll need to do this by mid-September. Finally, if you have serious doubts about the accuracy of your score for the multiple-choice section, the College Board will re-score it for an additional $25.

AP Biology: Course Goals

The two central goals of the AP Program in Biology are to help students develop a conceptual framework for modern biology and gain an appreciation of science as a process. AP Biology courses are built around topics, concepts, and themes. The College Board defines topics as the subject areas of biology. A concept is an important idea or principle that forms or enhances our current understanding of a particular topic. Themes are the overarching features of biology that recur, connect, and unify our understanding of topics. The College Board lists eight themes that should be stressed in AP Biology courses. The following outline is from "Topic Outline," page 5, *Course Description for AP Biology,* published by the College Board:

▌ Science as a process;
▌ Evolution;
▌ Energy transfer;
▌ Continuity and change;
▌ Relationship of structure to function;
▌ Regulation;
▌ Interdependence in nature;
▌ Science, technology, and society.

During the year, AP Biology students will be applying these themes to a wide range of topics. In fact, the College Board has created a topic outline to illustrate the topics that make up a typical college biology course—and so should form the basis for AP Biology courses. The percentages in parentheses show how much of the course should be spent on particular topics.

    I. Molecules and Cells (25% of the AP Biology course)
       A. Chemistry of Life (7%)
         Water
         Organic molecules in organisms

Free energy changes
Enzymes
B. Cells (10%)
Prokaryotic and eukaryotic cells
Membranes
Subcellular organization
Cell cycle and its regulation
C. Cellular Energetics (8%)
Coupled reactions
Fermentation and cellular respiration
Photosynthesis

II. Heredity and Evolution (25% of the AP Biology course)
A. Heredity (8%)
Meiosis and gametogenesis
Eukaryotic chromosomes
Inheritance patterns
B. Molecular Genetics (9%)
RNA and DNA structure and function
Gene regulation
Mutation
Viral structure and replication
Nucleic acid technology and applications
C. Evolutionary Biology (8%)
Early evolution of life
Evidence for evolution
Mechanisms of evolution

III. Organisms and Populations (50% of the AP Biology course)
A. Diversity of Organisms (8%)
Evolutionary patterns
Survey of the diversity of life
Phylogenetic classification
Evolutionary relationships
B. Structure and Function of Plants and Animals (32%)
Reproduction, growth, and development
Structural, physiological, and behavioral adaptations
Response to the environment
C. Ecology (10%)
Population dynamics
Communities and ecosystems
Global issues

No doubt, AP Biology courses vary somewhat from teacher to teacher and from school to school. For the most part, many high school teachers study the AP Biology course outline each year and meticulously customize their curriculum to fit it. In short, you may wish to consult the AP Biology course outline in order to take note of topics and concepts that might require further study.

Understanding the AP Biology Examination

You are probably aware that in general AP exams are long. The AP Biology Exam takes three hours. The exam probably looks like many other tests you've taken. It is made up of a multiple-choice section and a free-response (essay) section. At the core of the examination are questions designed to measure your knowledge and understanding of modern biology. You should be prepared to recall basic facts and concepts, to apply scientific facts and concepts to particular problems, to synthesize facts and concepts, and to demonstrate reasoning and analytical skills by organizing written answers to broad questions.

The AP Biology Exam is very challenging. When you sit down to take the test, exam administrators expect you not only to be fluent in the areas of biology that you find fascinating (the ones that probably inspired you to take a special interest in the subject originally), but they will expect you also to have an intimate knowledge of topics you don't find interesting at all. Whatever those topics might be—DNA replication, the dizzying details of animal and plant classification, or cell organization—you need to be comfortable with and knowledgeable about all of the AP Biology topics.

Section I: Multiple-Choice Questions

Section I contains 100 multiple-choice questions that test both scientific facts and their applications. You will have 80 minutes to complete Section I. This portion of the exam is followed by a 5–10 minute break—the only official break during the examination. The directions for the multiple-choice section of the test are straightforward and similar to the following:

> *Directions:* Each of the questions or incomplete statements below is followed by five suggested answers or completions. Select the choice that best answers the question or completes the statement.

It will probably not surprise you to know that not all multiple-choice questions are the same. In fact, the AP Biology Exam will contain the different types of multiple-choice questions listed and described below.

Factual Questions

The first type of multiple-choice question is your basic factual recall question, which will test whether you've mastered certain facts, processes, cycles, systems, etc. Here's an example of one of these:

1. In plants, which hormone is responsible for fruit ripening?
   (A) Auxin
   (B) Ethylene
   (C) Cytokinin
   (D) Phytochrome
   (E) Gibberellin

With a question like this, you either know the answer or you don't. It's what the College Board calls a "factual" question: They ask a question, and you're expected to know the answer. The best way to approach factual questions is to read the question and every one of the five choices carefully. If you are certain you know the answer, fill in the corresponding oval on the answer sheet. However, what if you're not certain? The next step is to see if you can eliminate one or more of the choices.

Let's look again at the question. Imagine that you don't recall that ethylene (choice *B*) is responsible for fruit ripening. You might realize that you can eliminate answer choice *D*, because the prefix phyto- suggests that the hormone phytochrome probably has something to do with plants' response to light and therefore phytochrome probably doesn't contribute to ripening. Now you have a one-in-four chance of making a correct guess. If you remember what any of the other three plant hormones do, your odds of guessing correctly increase even more. As a general rule on AP exams, if you can eliminate at least one answer choice, you are better off making an educated guess than you are leaving the question unanswered. We'll discuss this idea further in the section "Grading Procedures for the AP Biology Examination."

"Reverse" Multiple-Choice Questions

Sometimes the College Board question developers modify the format for factual questions slightly, and the result is a slightly more difficult type of multiple-choice question. This type of question features four answers that are correct and only one that is incorrect; you are asked to find the incorrect choice. Generally these questions contain the word *not* or the word *except*. Pay attention to the capitalization of these words in Section I of the exam to avoid making a careless mistake. Here is an example of a question you could expect to see on the AP Biology Exam.

2. All of the following statements about photosynthesis are true EXCEPT
   (A) the light reactions convert solar energy to chemical energy in the form of ATP and NADPH
   (B) the Calvin cycle uses ATP and NADPH to convert CO_2 to sugar
   (C) photosystem I contains P700 chlorophyll a molecules at the reaction center; photosystem II contains P680 molecules
   (D) in chemiosmosis, electron transport chains pump protons (H^+) across a membrane from a region of high H^+ concentration to a region of low H^+ concentration
   (E) the steps of the Calvin cycle are sometimes referred to as the dark reactions because they do not require light in order to take place

This question asks you not only to remember one simple fact (like the function of a plant hormone), but also to consider the results of cellular processes and how systems in the cell compare. The correct answer here is *D*, because the statement in choice *D* is not true (in fact, the electron transport chains pump protons across membranes from regions of low H^+ concentrations to regions of high H⁺ concentrations). Of course, the statements in choices *A*, *B*, *C*, and *E* are true. You may recall that this proton pumping occurs in both mitochondria and chloroplasts, and that the protons then diffuse—down the concentration gradient—back across the membrane (through ATP synthase), and that this drives the synthesis of ATP. However, you can also apply common sense to see that *D* doesn't look right. Why would a pump be needed to transport H⁺ down its concentration gradient?

Conceptual-Thematic Questions

Now let's look at another type of multiple-choice question that you'll encounter on the exam known as "conceptual-thematic" questions.

3. Which of the following groups is characterized by having a gastrovascular cavity, with a single opening acting as both mouth and anus, and existing in either polyp or medusa form?
   (A) Sponges
   (B) Cnidarians
   (C) Ctenophores
   (D) Platyhelminthes
   (E) Rotifers

Though it may be hard to see the difference between this question and a factual recall question, the difference is that this one asks you to use logic and synthesis to glean the sum of the organismal characteristics listed above. In other words, you're required to synthesize information rather than merely to recall a fact. In this case, the correct choice is *B*. The cnidarians you might encounter are hydras, jellies, sea anemones, and coral animals. They are simple, sac-like creatures with a gastrovascular cavity that contains a single opening.

Matching Questions

Another type of multiple-choice question you'll see in Section I of the AP Biology Exam is the matching question. Below is an example of how matching questions are presented.

Questions 4–8
   (A) Savanna
   (B) Chaparral
   (C) Rain forest
   (D) Coniferous forest
   (E) Tundra

4. Characterized by epiphytes, closed canopy, and pronounced vertical stratification

5. Characterized by cone-bearing trees, dominated by one or two species of trees, and receiving heavy snowfall in the winter

6. Dominated by spiny evergreen shrubs, which are dependent on seasonal shrub fires for growth

7. Characterized by having insects as the dominant herbivores, predominant grass growth, and large grazing mammals

8. Characterized by permafrost, very low temperatures, and low annual rainfall

(To satisfy your curiosity, the correct answers above are 4. *C*; 5. *D*; 6. *B*; 7. *A*; and 8. *E*.)

Lab-Based or Experimental Questions

The last type of multiple-choice question you'll see in Section I is the lab-based or experimental question. These questions either present you with a set of data in graph (or other) form, or they describe an experiment and ask you to make educated guesses and to form hypotheses. Take a look at the question below, for example. The graph shows the results of a study to determine the effect of soil air spaces on plant growth.

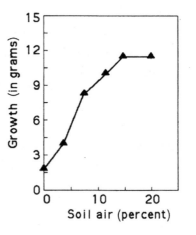

9. The data from the above graph show that the plant
   (A) grows fastest when the soil is 5–10% air
   (B) grows fastest when the soil is 15–20% air
   (C) grows at the same rate regardless of the soil air percentage
   (D) grows most slowly when the soil is 5–10% air
   (E) does not grow at all when the soil is 0–3% air

The correct choice is *A*. The graph shows the line with the greatest slope (the highest degree of change over the shortest amount of time) between the percentages 5 and 10. During this time, the plant grows by about 9 − 5 = 4 grams. Just to be sure, check the amount this plant grows when the soil is 15–20% air. At the start, when the air was 15% air, the plant weighed 12 grams. At the end, when the soil was 20% air, the plant weight is the same—12 grams. Virtually no growth occurred during this time.

Clearly this question requires you to be able to interpret a graph, but at this point in your biology education you should be quite capable of doing that. In order to brush up on the various ways that graphs present information, you might spend some time looking over Chapter 23 and Chapter 52 of Campbell and Reece, *BIOLOGY*, 7th Edition.

Section II: Free-Response Questions

Section II of the AP Biology Exam is made up of four free-response questions relating to the following topics: molecules and cells, heredity and evolution, and organisms and populations (two questions). One or more of the four free-response questions will be lab-based, because the test writers expect you to understand laboratory concepts and techniques. Many of the questions you encounter in Section II of the AP Biology Exam will require you to integrate material from across the topic outline. The free-response questions are often broken down into parts, and the parts vary in difficulty. Presenting free-response questions in this form is the College Board's way of making sure that you really understand the underlying concepts of biology—and that you aren't just a really lucky guesser.

At the beginning of Section II of the AP Biology Exam, you'll be given a 10-minute reading period to examine the questions and outline your response. After the reading period, you will be given a response booklet in which to write your essays. Following are some sample free-response questions.

BIOLOGY

Section II

Time—1 hour and 30 minutes

Directions: Answer all questions.

Answers must be in essay form. Outline form is NOT acceptable. Labeled diagrams may be used to supplement discussion, but in no case will a diagram alone suffice. It is important that you read each question completely before you begin to write.

1. Water comprises roughly 70% of the human body; cells are roughly 70–95% water, and water covers about three-quarters of the Earth's surface.
   (a) **Describe** the major physical properties of water that make it unique from other liquids.
   (b) **Explain** the properties of water that enable it to travel up through the roots and stems of plants to reach the leaves.
   (c) **Explain** why the temperature of the oceans can remain relatively stable and support vast quantities of both plant and animal life, when air temperature fluctuates so significantly throughout the year.

Like many free-response questions on the AP Biology Exam, this sample is broken into three distinct parts. Each contains a clear directive. In fact, they are printed in boldface to help you focus on exactly how you should answer the question. First you will need to explain the uniqueness of water by describing its major physical properties. (In your response to this first part of the question, you might wish to include a diagram of the structure of water, complete with electrons and bonds.) Then you must explain the properties of water that allow it to travel from root to leaf. Finally, you should explain the reason(s) why ocean water temperature remains stable and supports plant and animal life—even in the face of great air temperature variations. Of course, limiting your answer by addressing exactly what the question asks will make writing the essay easier for you and earn you a higher score. Always take the time to determine precisely what is being asked before you begin to formulate a concrete thesis and focus on writing your relevant supporting paragraphs.

Grading Procedures for the AP Biology Examination

The raw scores of the AP Biology Examination are converted to the following 5-point scale:

5—Extremely Well Qualified
4—Well Qualified
3—Qualified
2—Possibly Qualified
1—No Recommendation

Some colleges give undergraduate course credit to students who achieve scores of 3 or better on AP exams. Other colleges require students to achieve scores of 4 or 5. You may check the policy for individual colleges on the College Board website (www.collegeboard.com). Below is a breakdown of how the grading of the AP Biology Exam works.

Section I: Multiple-Choice Questions

The multiple-choice section of the exam is worth 60% of your total score. The raw score of Section I is determined by crediting one point for each correctly answered question and by deducting ¼ point for each question answered incorrectly. No points are gained or lost for unanswered questions. Consequently, if you are able to eliminate at least one choice as incorrect, it is to your advantage to make an educated guess rather than to leave the answer blank. As you take practice exams, determine your score with this equation (number right − ¼ number wrong). Some students find they are timid and leave too many blank, while others should be more cautious. Practice tests will reveal if you are too timid or too bold and allow you to adjust your test-taking strategy accordingly.

Section II: Free-Response Questions

Section II counts for 40% of your examination grade. Within Section II, each of the four essay responses is weighted equally. The free-response section is scored by several hundred faculty consultants, including high school teachers and college instructors from all over the country who work in a central location to grade the essays. This period of scoring exams is called the "Reading." To ensure that scoring of all exams is consistent, grading rubrics, or standards, are developed and then faculty consultants trained in their application. Because of this intense training, group discussion, and supervision, your essay should receive the same score regardless of who reads it. Ongoing internal checks during the Reading ensure this. Each of your four essays will be evaluated by a faculty consultant trained to score that single response.

Your answers to the free-response questions must be presented in essay form. Outlines or unlabeled and unexplained diagrams are not given credit. Each of the questions is scored on a scale from 0 to 10 points, and your performance on any single essay is evaluated independently of the other essays. Do not assume that information provided in one question will be considered during the grading of another essay. You should repeat information from question to question if it is necessary to illustrate your point.

Test-Taking Strategies for the AP Biology Examination

Here are a few tips for preparing yourself in the weeks leading up to the examination.

▌ The earlier you start studying for the AP Biology Exam, the better. Some students use this AP Biology prep book along with their textbook throughout the course, taking notes in the margin to supplement their teacher's lectures. You should definitely begin serious preparation for the test at least one month in advance.

▌ Each chapter in Part II is correlated to a unit in *BIOLOGY*, 7th Edition. For each unit, review your lecture notes, study the figures in your text that explain key concepts, and then make your way through the corresponding section of Part II of this book. If possible, retake your unit test on the topic, and also answer the questions in this guide for each unit. This will help you identify topics that will require further study. Do not try to reread your text; use it as a tool for those topics that need further study. You can use the correlation guide at the end of Part I of this book to link AP Biology topics to your textbook. Pace yourself!

AP Review: Lab Essays

The College Board suggests the following twelve labs for AP Biology courses, so you should be familiar with them. You can find more detailed descriptions of these labs in the *Course Description for AP Biology* or on the College Board's website.

1. Diffusion and Osmosis
2. Enzyme Catalysis
3. Mitosis and Meiosis
4. Plant Pigments and Photosynthesis
5. Cell Respiration
6. Molecular Biology
7. Genetics of Organisms
8. Population Genetics and Evolution
9. Transpiration
10. Physiology of the Circulatory System
11. Animal Behavior
12. Dissolved Oxygen and Aquatic Primary Productivity

▌ At least one essay on the exam will be based on an AP laboratory. To prepare for this question, review the objectives for all twelve laboratories. The College Board does not expect that you have done *the* lab, but that you have performed a lab that meets the same objectives. It is the objectives that you will be tested on. Go over the procedures and results obtained. You could also visit LabBench at www.biology.com as an additional review. The essay may ask you to "design an experiment to determine ...". In this case it is not necessary for you to create a new lab! If you preformed a lab in your AP class that would answer this question, it is fine to describe this lab. Here are the items that are generally required for a good response:

- **State a hypothesis** as an "**If** ... (conditions), **then** ... (results)" statement. Your hypothesis must be testable.
- **Identify the variable factor** for the experiment (e.g., temperature).
- **Identify a control.** You must explain the control for the experiment.
- **Hold all other variables constant.** Explain how you would do this.
- **Manipulate the variable** (e.g., one group at 10°C, one at 20°C, and one at 30°C).
- **Measure the results** (e.g., cm grown, grams increased in mass).
- **Discuss results expected** as related to hypothesis.
- **Replication or verification.** The experiment must be repeated or large sample sizes must be used.

If appropriate, you could also consider using statistical analysis of data (see Chi-square analysis, Lab 7) and review of the literature.

Graphing Data

Several recent exams have asked students to graph results. You will need to consider the type of graph that is appropriate for your data. Bar graphs are used when data points are discrete, that is, not related to each other, such as the number of girls in AP Biology vs. the number of boys in AP Biology. Line graphs are used when the data is continuous, such as the change in an individual's height at each birthday. Consider if there is a data point at 0 on the graph. Be sure to extend your line to 0 if there is, but do not take the line to 0 if there is no measurement for that data point. Also,

- Label the graph with a descriptive title.
- Label the *x*- and *y*-axes. Be sure you know which variable is independent and which is dependent.
- Keep all measurement units constant. Each division on the graph must be a unit equal to all the others.

Sample Tests

When you are ready to check your preparation, take the first sample exam in Part III of this book. Keep track of your time, and try to simulate test conditions. Score your responses as "number right – ¼ number wrong." Circle the items you get wrong, or could not answer, and keep a list of the subject matter of those questions. Then analyze the list to look for patterns—are you having a hard time with questions on animal physiology or the process of photosynthesis specifically? Spend the next week or so studying the topics in which you are weak. Then, perhaps a week or two before the AP Biology Exam, take the second sample exam. Once again, grade this exam and determine your weak areas. Then spend the final days before the test looking through this guide, your class notes, and textbook to fill in any remaining gaps.

The Day of the Exam

If you have followed this suggested study plan, you should feel well prepared by test day. Plan your schedule so that you get two very good nights of uninterrupted sleep before exam day. The night before the exam, relax, think positive thoughts, and focus on getting a good night's rest. Below is a brief list of basic tips and strategies to think about before you arrive at the exam site.

1. **Arrive early!** It's a good idea to arrive at the exam site thirty minutes before the start time. On the day of the exam, make sure that you eat a good, nutritious meal. These tips may sound corny or obvious, but your body must be in peak form in order for your brain to perform well. Remember, you are going to need ATP to fuel brain cells at peak efficiency for more than three hours.
2. **Bring a photo ID.** (It's essential if you are taking the exam at a school other than your own.) Carrying a driver's license or a student ID card will allow you to prove your identity.
3. **Bring at least two sharpened #2 pencils** for the multiple-choice section. Also, bring a clean pencil eraser with you. Many pencils today have cheap erasers that smudge. Invest in a good eraser. The machine that scores Section I of the exam recognizes only marks made by a #2 pencil. Poorly erased responses are often misscored.
4. **Bring two black ballpoint pens** for the free-response portion of the test. Felt-tip pens run and pencils and inks of other colors are harder to read.
5. **Bring a watch** with you to the exam. Most testing rooms do have clocks. Still, having your own watch makes it easy to keep close track of your own pace. Watches with calculators or alarms are not permitted in the exam room.

Several other items that are forbidden from the testing room are books, notes, laptops, beepers, cameras, and portable listening or recording devices. If you must bring a cellular phone with you, be prepared to turn it off and to give it to the test proctor until you are finished with your exam. For a complete list of what not to bring, see the College Board website.

Educational Testing Service prohibits the objects listed above in the interest of fairness to all test-takers. Similarly, the test administrators are very clear and very serious about what types of conduct are not allowed during the examination. Below is a list of actions to avoid at all costs, since each can result in your immediate dismissal from the exam room.

▌ Do not consult any outside materials during the three hours of the exam period. Remember, the break is technically part of the exam—you are not free to review any materials at that time either.

▌ Do not speak during the exam. If you have a question for the test proctor, raise your hand to get the proctor's attention.

- When you are told to stop working on a section of the exam, you must stop immediately.
- Do not open your exam booklet before the test begins.
- Never tear a page out of your test booklet or try to remove the exam from the test room.
- Do not behave disruptively—even if you're distressed about a difficult test question or because you've run out of time. Stay calm and make no unnecessary noise.

Section I: Strategies for Multiple-Choice Questions

Obviously, having a firm grasp of biology is, of course, the key to doing well on the AP Biology Examination. In addition, being well-informed about the exam itself increases your chances of achieving a high score. Below is a list of strategies that you can use to increase your comfort, your confidence, and your chances of excelling on the multiple-choice section of the exam.

- Become as familiar as possible with the format of Section I. The more comfortable you are with the multiple-choice format and with the kinds of questions you'll encounter, the easier the exam will be. Remember, Part II and Part III of this book provide you with invaluable practice on the kinds of multiple-choice questions you will encounter on the AP Biology Exam.
- Every question you answer correctly is a point, so pacing is important. If you have done all the suggested practice tests, you should have a good sense of how to pace yourself. You will have 80 minutes to answer 100 questions (about 48 seconds per question). Keep track of time!
- Some of the questions will require calculations. If you encounter a question that will require extra time, leave it blank and make a note. Your goal should be to reach the end of the test, picking up all the points from questions you can answer easily.
- The test is organized with three types of questions: standard multiple choice, matching, and lab sets. Lab sets are generally the most tedious. When a data table or graph is presented, proceed directly to the related questions. Determine what information is needed to answer the questions, and then return to the data table or graph and seek the information. Sometimes, although the data appear daunting, the questions are actually very easy.
- Make a light mark in your test booklet next to any questions you can't answer. Return to these questions after you reach the end of Section I. Sometimes questions that appear later in the test will refresh your memory on a particular topic, and you will be able to answer one or more of those earlier questions.
- Always read the entire question carefully, and underline key words or ideas. You might wish to double underline words such as NOT or EXCEPT in that type of multiple-choice question.
- Read each and every one of the answer choices carefully before you make your final selection.

- Use the process of elimination to help you arrive at the correct answer. Even if you are quite sure of an answer, cross out the letters of incorrect choices in your test booklet as you eliminate them. This cuts down on the incorrect choices and allows you to narrow the remaining choices even further.
- If you can eliminate even one answer choice, it is usually better to make an educated guess than to leave the answer blank.
- Become completely familiar with the instructions for the multiple-choice questions before you take the exam. By knowing the instructions cold, you'll save yourself the time of reading them carefully on exam day.

Section II: Strategies for Free-Response Questions

Below is a list of strategies that you can use to increase your chances of excelling on the free-response section of the exam.

- You will have a ten-minute period to review the essay questions before you receive a response book. During this time, you should organize your thoughts and outline your essays on the sheet provided. After the preparation time, you will be given the response book. Each essay question is repeated within the response book, and this is where you should record each answer. You have about twenty-two minutes to spend on each essay.
- Read the question, then read the question again. Be sure you answer the question that is asked and that you address each part of the question. As you read a question, underline any directive words (usually the first word in an essay) that indicate how you should answer and focus the material in your essay. Some of the most frequently used directives on the AP Biology Exam are listed below, along with descriptions of what you need to do in your writing to answer the question.

    - *Analyze* (show relationships between events; explain)
    - *Compare* (discuss similarities between two or more things)
    - *Contrast* (discuss points of difference or divergence between two or more things)
    - *Describe* (give a detailed account)
    - *Design* (create an experiment and convey its ideas)
    - *Explain* (clarify; tell the meaning)

- Make an outline of your response. Reread the question as many times as necessary to make sure that you will cover each aspect of the topic. Free-response questions frequently have several parts, so you will need to take this into account as you outline your ideas.
- Write an essay! As the exam states clearly in the directions to free-response questions, a diagram or graph by itself is never an acceptable way to answer a free-response question. However, you should think about whether you could use a labeled diagram or graph to develop your written answer in some useful way.

- The essay you craft for this exam is not the same type of essay you should write for an English course. Yes, it should be well-organized; however, introductory sentences and conclusions are absolutely not necessary. Readers are interested in what you know and how well you express your knowledge. Spend your time packing the essay with the biological information you have worked so hard to learn.

- If the question has several parts, answer the parts in the sequence given. Use a letter or some other indication for each part, so that the faculty consultant does not overlook a section of your response.

- If you are asked to perform a calculation, be sure to show the steps used to arrive at your answer. You have heard this before: show your work!

- If you cannot remember a specific term, describe the structure or process.

- Define any scientific term that you use that is directly related to your response. For example, if you discuss hydrogen bonding and how it relates to properties of water, be sure to explain what hydrogen bonds are, and then describe or define adhesion, cohesion, and so on.

- Your handwriting can affect your results. Although faculty consultants make every attempt to read each essay, sometimes it is impossible to decipher messy handwriting. When your handwriting is poor, the reader may lose concentration or patience and miss an important word or phrase.

- Don't leave any part of any essay blank. Every point made is worth twice as much as each multiple-choice point.

- If time allows, proofread your essays. Don't worry about crossing out material—readers understand that your responses are first drafts and that you are writing down ideas under the pressure of time.

The success of your four free-response essays will depend a great deal on how clearly and extensively you answer the questions posed. Of course, the structure of your essays will depend entirely on your knowledge of the subjects at hand. Take a look at an example of a free-response question below.

2. In cancer, the cell's reproductive machinery experiences a loss of control that makes cancer cells reproduce continually, and eventually form a tumor.
   (a) **Describe** three DNA-related cellular events that could lead to the loss of cell division control that contributes to cancer.
   (b) **Describe** why tumors are detrimental to the body.
   (c) **Discuss** several cell processes that you think should be studied more closely in finding a cure for cancer.

In order to answer this question, you should isolate exactly what it is that you must answer. You may want to underline the relevant information in the question to remind yourself of your focus:

2. In cancer, the cell's reproductive machinery experiences a loss of control that makes cancer cells reproduce continually, and eventually form a tumor.
   (a) **Describe** three DNA-related cellular events that could lead to the loss of cell division control that contributes to cancer.

(b) Describe why <u>tumors</u> are <u>detrimental</u> to the body.

(c) Discuss <u>several cell processes</u> that you think should be <u>studied more closely</u> in finding a <u>cure for cancer</u>.

In order to answer the first part of the question, you'll need to identify three appropriate DNA-related cellular events.

1. A mutation or change in the original DNA sequence
2. Errors in DNA replication that go undetected by the cell's proofreading devices
3. A translocation

Under each of the three events, you should list any and all details you remember about those events to use in your description. When you flesh out these details, you'll need to clearly connect them to the concept of the loss of cell division control leading to cancer.

To answer the second part of the question, you'll need to list as many reasons as you can think of as to why tumors are harmful to the body. These might include cancerous cells' ability to metastasize; tumors' ability to occur almost anywhere in the body; their tendency to block the flow of blood when they grow near blood vessels; disruption of the natural function of any organ in the body; and endangering of homeostasis. Of course, after you list reasons, you'll need to add details to each item in your list.

To answer the final part of the question, you'll need to consider first what causes cancer. Then you must think creatively in order to suggest possible approaches to dealing with each specific cause.

Part II of this book contains a review of everything that you learned in your textbook that could be on the AP Biology test. Many questions will be posed along the way so that you can get used to being tested on the concepts in the way that the College Board will test you. In Part III, there are two practice tests for you to try on your own, along with complete answers and explanations.

AP Topic Correlation to Campbell and Reece BIOLOGY, *Seventh Edition*

The following chart is intended to help you study for the AP Biology Exam. The left column includes a series of AP Biology topics with which you should be familiar before you take the AP Biology Exam. The right column includes a detailed breakdown of corresponding chapters and Key Concepts in your Campbell and Reece *BIOLOGY*, Seventh Edition, textbook. You may want to use this chart throughout the year to review what you've learned. It is also an excellent place to begin your pre-exam review of subjects.

AP BIOLOGY TOPICS	TEXTBOOK CORRELATIONS
I. Molecules and Cells	**Units 1 and 2**
A. Chemistry of Life	**Chapters 3, 5, 8**
1. Water	Concepts 3.1–3.3
2. Organic molecules in organisms	Concepts 5.1–5.5
3. Free energy changes	Concepts 8.1–8.3
4. Enzymes	Concepts 8.4, 8.5
B. Cells	**Chapters 6, 7, 11, 12**
1. Prokaryotic and eukaryotic cells	Concepts 6.1–6.3
2. Membranes	Concepts 6.4, 7.1–7.5, 11.1–11.4
3. Subcellular organization	Concepts 6.3–6.7
4. Cell cycle and its regulation	Concepts 12.1–12.3
C. Cellular Energetics	**Chapters 8, 9, 10**
1. Coupled reactions	Concepts 8.3, 9.1–9.4
2. Fermentation and cellular respiration	Concepts 9.1–9.6
3. Photosynthesis	Concepts 10.1–10.4
II. Heredity and Evolution	**Units 3, 4, and 5**
A. Heredity	**Chapters 13–15**
1. Meiosis and gametogenesis	Concepts 13.1–13.4
2. Eukaryotic chromosomes	Concepts 15.1–15.3
3. Inheritance patterns	Concepts 14.1–14.4, 15.3–15.5
B. Molecular Genetics	**Chapter 15–20**
1. RNA and DNA structure and function	Concepts 16.1, 16.2, 17.1–17.6, 18.3
2. Gene regulation	Concepts 18.4, 19.1–19.3
3. Mutation	Concepts 15.4, 17.7, 19.3, 19.5
4. Viral structure and replication	Concepts 18.1, 18.2
5. Nucleic acid technology and applications	Concepts 20.1–20.5

C. Evolutionary Biology   **Chapters 22–26**

   1. Early evolution of life   Concepts 26.1–26.5

   2. Evidence for evolution   Concepts 22.2, 22.3, 25.1–25.5

   3. Mechanisms of evolution   Concepts 22.1–22.3, 23.1–23.4, 24.1–24.3

III. Organisms and Populations   Units 4, 5, 6, 7, and 8

A. Diversity of Organisms   **Chapters 25–34**

   1. Evolutionary patterns   Concepts 29.1, 29.2, 32.1, 32.3

   2. Survey of the diversity of life   Concepts 26.3–26.6, 27.1, 27.3, 28.1–28.8, 29.1–29.4, 30.2–30.4, 31.4, 31.5, 32.1, 32.2, 33.3–33.8, 34.1–34.8

   3. Phylogenetic classification   Concepts 25.2, 26.3–26.6, 27.1, 27.3, 28.1–28.8, 29.1–29.4, 30.2–30.4, 31.4, 31.5, 32.1, 32.2, 33.1–33.8, 34.1–34.8

   4. Evolutionary relationships   Concepts 25.1–25.5

B. Structure and Function of Plants and Animals   **Chapters 29, 30, 35–39, 40–49, 51**

   1. Reproduction, growth, and development (plants)   Concepts 29.2–29.4, 30.1–30.3, 35.1–35.5, 38.1

   2. Reproduction, growth, and development (animals)   Concepts 21.1–21.4, 46.1–46.5, 47.1–47.3

   3. Structural, physiological, and behavioral adaptations (plants)   Concepts 35.1, 35.2, 36.1–36.5, 38.1–38.3, 39.1–39.5

   4. Structural, physiological, and behavioral adaptations (animals)   Concepts 40.1–40.5, 41.1–41.5, 42.1, 42.2, 42.5, 44.2–44.6, 48.1–48.5, 51.3, 51.5

   5. Response to the environment (plants)   Concepts 37.1, 37.4, 39.1–39.5

   6. Response to the environment (animals)   Concepts 40.4, 40.5, 41.5, 43.1–43.5, 44.1, 44.2, 44.5, 44.6, 45.1–45.5, 49.1–49.7, 51.3

C. Ecology   **Chapters 50, 52–55**

   1. Population dynamics   Concepts 50.2, 50.3, 52.1–52.6

   2. Communities and ecosystems   Concepts 53.1–53.5, 54.1–54.5

   3. Global issues   Concepts 50.1, 50.2, 54.5, 55.1–55.4

AP* Biology Thematic Study Grid

As you read in the Course Goals section, the College Board stresses eight themes that recur throughout the AP Biology Course. You will find these themes, along with a few others, in Chapter 1 of your textbook. This study tool connects the eight AP themes to the course topics (also listed in the Course Goals section). The topics are in the left column and the themes are listed along the top. On these pages, suggested examples of a theme applied to a topic are provided. Turn the page, and you will find an empty grid for you to fill in as you prepare for the exam. This exercise should help you develop your understanding of concepts and recognition of themes that are correlated to the major topics in biology.

	Science as a Process	Evolution	Energy Transfer	Continuity and Change	Relationships of Structure to Function	Regulation	Interdependence in Nature	Science, Technology, and Society
Chemistry of Life	X-ray crystallography helps scientists determine the 3-dimensional structure of proteins.	Chemical evolution of the young Earth set the stage for the origin of life.	Living systems rely on coupled exergonic and endergonic reactions.	DNA molecules carry biological information from one generation to the next.	Enzyme active sites have a shape that specifically matches the shape of the substrate.	In feedback inhibition, a metabolic pathway is switched off by its end product.	Prokaryotes play essential roles in chemical cycling for plants and animals.	DNA microarrays or chips provide powerful assays to analyze gene expression.
Cells	The discovery and early study of cells progressed with the invention and improvement of microscopes.	The matching machinery of all eukaryotic cilia provides evidence for a broad evolutionary connection among eukaryotes.	ATP powers cellular work.	Replicated DNA is packed in chromosomes that are separated at mitosis and meiosis.	The folded, membranous organization of the mitochondrion enhances the productivity of cellular respiration.	Freshwater protists, such as paramecium, have contractile vacuoles that maintain water balance.	Cells in a multicellular organism are coordinated by various modes of cell-cell communication.	Advances in cancer research depend on progress in our basic understanding of how cells work.
Cellular Energetics	The Calvin cycle and its intermediate products were determined by using radioactive isotopes.	According to endosymbiotic theory, mitochondria and chloroplasts are the ancestors of ancient independent bacteria.	A proton gradient across membranes powers the synthesis of ATP in cells.	Mitochondrial inheritance patterns are different than Mendelian patterns of inheritance. They follow a maternal pattern.	The arrangement of the electron transport chain components within the inner membrane of the mitochondria facilitates energy transfer during cellular respiration.	With the controlled opening and closing of stomata, plants balance water loss with CO_2 intake for photosynthesis.	Most of the ecosystems of the biosphere are powered by energy captured by chloroplasts and "burned" by mitochondria	Ethanol produced from crops is used as a fuel additive.
Heredity	Beadle and Tatum developed the "one gene–one enzyme hypothesis" by using mutations as a tool to investigate metabolic pathways.	Many quantitative traits display polygenetic inheritance patterns.	Mitochondrial myopathy, a disorder that affects ATP production, is inherited in mtDNA.	DNA molecules carry biological information from one generation to the next.	Chromosomes are a marvel of packaging.	Alleles can show different degrees of dominance and recessiveness in relation to each other.	Interaction of genes and their environment produces the phenotype.	DNA technology has provided new treatments for genetic diseases.
Molecular Genetics	The Hershey-Chase experiment used radioactive labels to determine that the genetic material in phages is DNA.	Genomes provide a written history to life.	Extremophiles have a diversity of energy metabolism. These unique metabolic pathways are rich areas of study.	The continuity of life depends on the inheritance of information encoded in the nucleotide sequences of DNA molecules.	The structure of tRNA molecules fits their function as readers/translators of genetic code.	Mutations that cause deficiencies in signaling pathways that regulate the cell cycle can lead to cancer.	The universal genetic code makes genetic recombination possible.	Automatic DNA sequencing machines accelerated the completion of the Human Genome Project.

Evolutionary Biology	Reznick and Endler designed experiments that demonstrated natural selection in wild populations of guppies.	Natural selection is the mechanism of evolutionary adaptation.	Stromatolites provide evidence of the rise of photosynthetic organisms about 2.8 billion years ago.	Evolution can be defined as a change in gene frequency.	The whale fossil record provides evidence of key structural adaptations for locomotion in an aquatic lifestyle.	Peter and Rosemary Grant documented natural selection as finch populations in the Galápagos adapted to cyclical environmental changes.	The coevolution of flowering plants and their pollinators has created mutually dependent relationships such as the Yucca moth and the yucca plant.	Molecular phylogenies are increasingly important tools for identifying emergent diseases.
Diversity of Organisms	Evolutionary theory itself evolves as new methods and data refine our view of phylogenetic relationships among organisms.	Life on Earth shares a common history that is the basis of phylogenies.	Plants transform the light energy from the sun into chemical energy stored in the bonds of carbohydrates.	Multicellular organisms have a diversity of life cycles. Some, such as mosses, have distinctly different generations that alternate between haploid and diploid stages.	Key adaptations, such as the amniotic egg, have enabled vertebrates to colonize terrestrial environments.	Diverse groups have adapted to hypotonic, freshwater environments.	The symbiotic relationship of mycorrhizae and plants is vital to ecosystems.	Destruction of tropical rain forests has led to a great loss of biodiversity.
Structure and Function of Plants and Animals	Recent work suggests that some redwoods may be very near the limit for maximum height that water can be transported by plant vascular systems.	Natural selection can refine and fine tune adaptations such as wings.	The shape and stacks of grana in chloroplasts maximize the collection of photon energy by photosystems.	Samaras are winged seeds that enhance seed dispersal in trees, such as the maples.	The honeycombed construction of a bird's bones provides a lightweight skeleton of great strength that makes flight possible.	Countercurrent heat exchange between out-going and in-coming blood vessels in whale flippers helps to conserve internal body temperature.	Consumers acquire their energy in chemical form by eating plants, by eating animals that ate plants, or by decomposing organic refuse.	Natural models such as the wing structure of dragonflies can sometimes inform human engineering.
Ecology	Long-term ecological reserves are established to monitor critical ecosystems throughout North America.	A very significant portion of Earth's biodiversity is concentrated in just a few "hot spots."	Energy flows from sunlight to producers to consumers.	Life cycles of species are adapted for different environments—"r-species" are often species of disturbed areas whereas "K-species" predominate in stable ecosystems.	Parasites have evolved adaptations that enhance their survival in their specific hosts.	Life on Earth is dependent on biogeochemical nutrient cycles.	The energy that enters an ecosystem as sunlight exits as heat, which all organisms dissipate to their surroundings.	Genetic engineering is used to improve certain species of bioremediators that detoxify polluted ecosystems.

	Science as a Process	Evolution	Energy Transfer	Continuity and Change
Chemistry of Life				
Cells				
Cellular Energetics				
Heredity				
Molecular Genetics				
Evolutionary Biology				
Diversity of Organisms				
Structure and Function of Plants and Animals				
Ecology				

Relationships of Structure to Function	Regulation	Interdependence in Nature	Science, Technology, and Society

Part II

Topical Review with Sample Questions and Answers and Explanations

Part II is keyed to Biology, Seventh Edition, by Campbell and Reece. It gives an overview of important information in bulleted form and provides sample multiple-choice and free-response questions, along with answers and explanations. Use the topical review and the Summary of Key Concepts sections at the end of each chapter in your textbook before attempting the practice questions. Be sure to review the answers thoroughly to prepare yourself for the range of test items you will encounter on the AP Biology Examination.

CHAPTER 1

The Chemistry of Life

Concept 2.1 Matter consists of chemical elements in pure form and in combinations called compounds

▊ **Matter** is anything that takes up space and has mass.

▊ An **element** is a substance that cannot be broken down to other substances by chemical reactions.

▊ A **compound** is a substance consisting of two or more elements combined in a fixed ratio.

▊ About 25 of the 92 natural elements are known to be essential to life. **Trace elements** are those required by an organism in only minute quantities (e.g., iron and iodine).

Concept 2.2 An element's properties depend on the structure of its atoms

▊ **Atoms** are the smallest unit of an element that still retains the property of the element. Atoms are made up of neutrons, protons, and electrons.

▊ **Neutrons** and **protons** are close together in the nucleus of the atom, and **electrons** move quickly in a cloud around the nucleus.

▊ The number of protons an element possesses is referred to as its **atomic number,** and this number is unique to every element. The **mass number** of an element is the sum of its protons and neutrons.

Concept 2.3 The formation and function of molecules depend on chemical bonding between atoms

▊ **Chemical bonds** are defined as interactions between the valence electrons of different atoms. Atoms are held together by chemical bonds to form molecules.

▊ A **covalent bond** occurs when valence electrons are shared by two atoms. **Nonpolar covalent bonds** occur when the electrons being shared are shared equally between the two atoms. In **polar covalent bonds,** one atom has greater electronegativity than the other, resulting in an unequal sharing of the electrons (e.g., H_2O).

▊ **Ionic bonds** are ones in which the two bonded atoms attract the shared electrons so unequally that the more electronegative atom steals the electron away from the less electronegative atom. Ionic bonds form ionic compounds, or salts.

▊ A charged atom or molecule is called an **ion.** If the charge is positive, the ion is called a **cation.** If the charge is negative, it is called an **anion.**

▊ **Hydrogen bonds** are relatively weak bonds that form between molecules, as in water. In hydrogen bonds, the positively charged hydrogen atom of one molecule is attracted to the negatively charged atom of another molecule.

Concept 3.1 **The polarity of water molecules results in hydrogen bonding**

▌ The **structure of water** is the key to its special properties. Water is made up of one atom of oxygen and two atoms of hydrogen, bonded to form a molecule that is depicted like this:

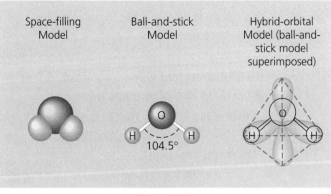

Water (H₂O)

▌ The fact that water molecules are **V-shaped** means that the opposite ends of the individual molecules have opposite charges—they are polar. The end bearing the oxygen atom has a slightly negative charge, whereas the end bearing the hydrogen atoms has a slightly positive charge. This is why water molecules form **hydrogen bonds**—the slightly negative oxygen atom from one water molecule is attracted to the slightly positive hydrogen end of another water molecule. Each water molecule can form a maximum of four hydrogen bonds at a time.

Concept 3.2 **Four emergent properties of water contribute to Earth's fitness for life**

▌ Water molecules stay close to each other as a result of hydrogen bonding. When water is in its liquid form, its hydrogen bonds are very fragile. They break and re-form with great frequency. Thus, at any instant, a substantial percentage of all the water molecules are bonded to their neighbors, making water more structured than most other liquids. Collectively, the hydrogen bonds hold the substance together, a phenomenon called **cohesion.** Cohesion due to hydrogen bonding contributes to the transport of xylem sap from the roots to the leaves of plants. **Adhesion** is the clinging of one substance to another. Water is very adhesive because of its hydrogen bonds. It is this property of adhesion that allows water to travel up the stems of plants. Adhesion of water to the walls of the cells helps counter the downward pull of gravity.

▌ Because of its high specific heat, water insulates Earth and **moderates temperature. Specific heat** is the amount of heat required to raise or lower the temperature of a substance by 1 degree Celsius. The specific heat of water is 1 cal/g/°C. Relative to other materials, the temperature of water changes less when a given amount of heat is lost or absorbed. This high specific heat makes the temperature of Earth's oceans relatively stable and able to support vast quantities of both plant and animal life.

- Water's **solid state** is less dense than its liquid state, whereas the opposite is true of most other substances. Solid water forms a regular crystal lattice structure, in which each water molecule is hydrogen bonded to four other water molecules. Because ice is less dense than liquid water, ice floats.

- Water is also an important **solvent.** (The substance that something is dissolved in is called the solvent, while the substance being dissolved is called the solute. Together they are called the solution.) Solutions in which water is the solvent are called aqueous solutions. Substances that are water-soluble are **hydrophilic** substances. These include ionic compounds, polar molecules (e.g., sugars), and some proteins. Oils, however, are **hydrophobic** and nonpolar, meaning they do not dissolve in water.

Concept 3.3 Dissociation of water molecules leads to acidic and basic conditions that affect living organisms

- When a hydrogen atom is transferred from one water molecule to another, it leaves its electron and is transferred as a **hydrogen ion,** which is a proton with a charge of +1. This transfer, or disassociation, makes the water molecule that lost its proton the **hydroxide ion** (depicted as OH^-) and the molecule that gains the proton is a **hydronium ion,** H_3O^+. Hydronium and hydroxide ion quantities are about equal in pure water. But if acids or bases are added to water, this equilibrium shifts. Water has a pH of 7, which means it is neutral.

- **Buffers** are substances that minimize changes in pH. They accept H^+ from solution when they are in excess and donate H^+ when they are depleted.

Concept 4.2 Carbon atoms can form diverse molecules by bonding to four other atoms

- Organic molecules have different properties as a result of their different structures. More specifically, the behavior of organic molecules is dependent on the identity of their functional groups.

- Some common functional groups are listed below:

Functional Group	Organic Molecules with the Functional Group	Chemical Properties of Functional Group
Hydroxyl, —OH	alcohols such as ethanol, methanol, etc.	hydrophilic and polar
Carboxyl, —COOH	carboxylic acids such as fatty acids and sugars	hydrophilic and polar
Carbonyl, $>CO$	ketones, and aldehydes such as sugars	hydrophilic and polar
Amino, —NH_2	amines such as amino acids	hydrophilic and polar
Phosphate, PO_3	organic phosphates, including ATP, DNA, and phospholipids	hydrophilic and polar
Sulfhydryl, —SH	thiols	hydrophobic

Concept 5.1 Most macromolecules are polymers, built from monomers

- Most large organic molecules (macromolecules) are **polymers.** Polymers are long chain molecules made of repeating units that are either the same as or very similar to each other. The small units that make up polymers are called **monomers.** What distinguishes polymers is the different identity of their monomers.

▌The reaction that creates polymers from monomers is called a **condensation, or dehydration reaction.** In this reaction, two monomers are combined, and one water molecule is released. The reverse reaction, in which a polymer is broken down into monomers after the addition of water, is called **hydrolysis.**

Concept 5.2 Carbohydrates serve as fuel and building material

▌There are four basic kinds of macromolecules that are biologically important: carbohydrates, lipids, proteins, and nucleic acids. The term *carbohydrates* refers both to simple sugars (glucose, fructose, galactose, etc.) and to the polymers made from these and other subunits. All carbohydrates exist in a ratio of 1 carbon:2 hydrogen:1 oxygen or $C:H_2:O$.

▌The simplest sugars are **monosaccharides.** Monosaccharides are simple ring structures such as **glucose** and **fructose.** Both glucose and fructose have the same chemical formula $C_6H_{12}O_6$, but the way their atoms are arranged gives each one a different molecular formula and different chemical properties.

▌**Disaccharides** are made up of two monosaccharides that have undergone a condensation reaction. Three examples of these are **sucrose, maltose,** and **lactose.**

▌**Polysaccharides** are basically polymers of monosaccharides. Polysaccharides are involved in the storage of carbohydrates in organisms (both plant and animal). In plants, carbohydrates are stored in the form of **starch,** which is made of glucose monomers. In animals, carbohydrates are stored as **glycogen.** This, too, is a polysaccharide made up of glucose, but its structure is more branched than is the structure of starch.

▌Polysaccharides are also found in structural components of organisms. **Cellulose** (a polysaccharide) makes up the thick cell walls of plants. Cellulose is a polymer of glucose, but again its identity differs from that of starch and glycogen because of the way the glucose molecules are joined.

▌In arthropods (lobsters, insects, and related animals), **chitin** is an important structural polysaccharide. Chitin is made up of a variation of glucose with a nitrogenous arm.

Concept 5.3 Lipids are a diverse group of hydrophobic molecules

▌Unlike the four other major groups of biological molecules, lipids aren't polymers. They are grouped together because they are hydrophobic. There are many different kinds of lipids, some of which are **waxes, oils, fats,** and **steroids.**

▌**Fats** are large molecules that are created by dehydration reactions between smaller molecules. Fats (also called triacylglycerols or triglycerides) are made up of a **glycerol** molecule and three **fatty acid** molecules.

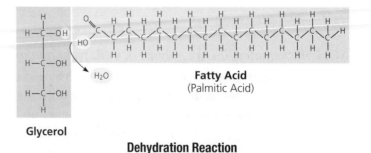

Glycerol

Fatty Acid
(Palmitic Acid)

Dehydration Reaction

- Fats differ in the length of their hydrocarbon backbones and also in the presence and positions of the double bonds they contain between carbon atoms. **Saturated fatty acids** contain no double bonds; **unsaturated fatty acids** contain at least one double bond. The process of hydrogenation—adding hydrogen molecules to unsaturated fats—produces fats with *trans* double bonds. Recent studies indicate that these fats, often found in processed foods such as crackers and cookies, may be a greater contributor to atherosclerosis and other health problems than saturated fats.
- In animals, fat is an important storage molecule. In humans and other mammals, fat is stored in **adipose cells.**
- Lipids are a very important part of **phospholipids,** which make up cell membranes. Phospholipids have a glycerol backbone and two fatty acid tails; the glycerol head is hydrophilic, and the fatty acid tails are hydrophobic. In forming the cell membrane, they are arranged in a bilayer, with their hydrophobic ends sandwiched in between the outer portion and inner portion of the cell membrane. The hydrophilic ends point toward the watery cytosol and extracellular environment.
- **Steroids** are made up of four rings that are fused together. One common type of steroid is cholesterol, an important component of cell membranes. Steroids are also found in certain hormones such as estrogen and testosterone.

Concept 5.4 *Proteins have many structures, resulting in a wide range of functions*

- Proteins are a very important component of the cell; in fact, they make up about 50% of the cell.
- **Proteins** are polymers made up of amino acid monomers.
- **Amino acids** are organic molecules that contain a carboxyl group, an amino group, a hydrogen atom, and an R group (variable group or side chain) that gives each amino acid its identity and properties. You should be able to recognize the names of amino acids, because they usually end with *-ine*.
- In proteins, amino acids are joined by **peptide bonds** in dehydration reactions. The function of proteins depends on how many amino acids and what type of amino acids are joined together.
- There are four levels of protein structure. The most basic is the **primary structure**—the sequence in which the amino acids are joined.
- The **secondary structure** refers to one of two three-dimensional shapes that the protein can have due to its hydrogen bonding. One shape, called an α helix, is coiled. The second shape is an accordion shape called a β pleated sheet.
- The **tertiary structure** of a protein refers to interactions between side chains of the protein. These interactions involve hydrophobic interactions, van der Waals interactions, and disulfide bridges.
- The **quaternary structure** of a protein refers to the association of two or more polypeptide chains into one giant macromolecule, or functional protein.
- Heat, a change in pH, or some other disturbance, can cause a protein to **denature** and become inactive. Denaturation causes the protein to lose its shape, or conformation.

Concept 5.5 *Nucleic acids store and transmit hereditary information*

▌ The last group of important biological molecules we'll discuss is the nucleic acids. The two nucleic acids are **DNA** (deoxyribonucleic acid) and **RNA** (ribonucleic acid).

▌ DNA is the molecule of heredity. It is inherited from cell to cell, parent organism to offspring. DNA molecules are very long; they are polymers of **nucleotide** monomers. Nucleotides are made up of three parts: a **nitrogenous base,** a five-carbon sugar called a **pentose,** and a phosphate group.

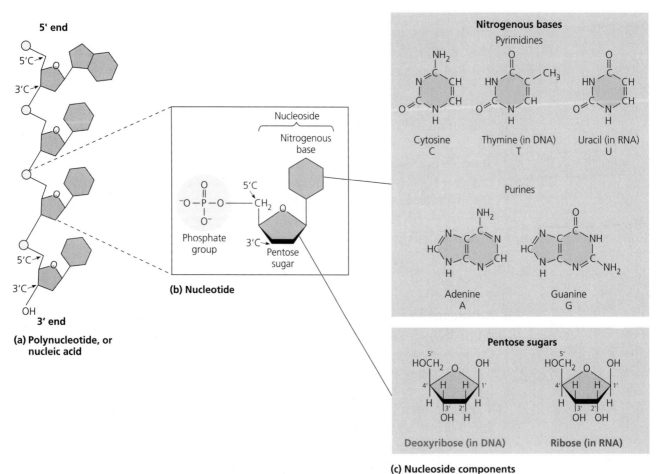

Figure 5.26   The components of nucleic acids

▌ There are two types of nitrogenous bases, **purines** and **pyrimidines.** The purines are **adenine** (A), and **guanine** (G), and the pyrimidines are **cytosine** (C), **thymine** (T), and **uracil** (U). Thymine is found only in DNA, and uracil is found only in RNA. In DNA, adenine always pairs with thymine, and cytosine always pairs with guanine. In RNA adenine pairs with uracil.

▌ In DNA, the pentose sugar is **deoxyribose,** and in RNA the pentose sugar is **ribose.** Deoxyribose has one less oxygen molecule than ribose.

▌ In DNA and RNA, the nucleotides are joined by **phosphodiester bonds.** In DNA, two polynucleotide chains wrap around each other in a helical shape, whereas RNA consists of a single polynucleotide.

For Additional Review

For the four major types of biological macromolecules you just reviewed (carbohydrates, lipids, proteins, and nucleic acids), consider how the atoms of which they consist fit together and determine the shape of the molecule, as well as how the shape of the molecule fits its function in the cell.

Multiple-Choice Questions

1. Which list of components characterizes RNA?
   (A) a PO_3 group, deoxyribose, and uracil
   (B) a PO_3 group, ribose, and uracil
   (C) a PO_3 group, ribose, and thymine
   (D) a PO_2 group, deoxyribose, and uracil
   (E) a PO_2 group, deoxyribose, and thymine

2. Which of the following molecules would contain a polar covalent bond?
   (A) Cl_2
   (B) NaCl
   (C) H_2O
   (D) KBr
   (E) $C_6H_{12}O_6$

3. Which of the following compounds would NOT be water-soluble?
   (A) potassium chloride
   (B) fatty acids
   (C) fructose
   (D) cellulose
   (E) hydrogen bromide

4. Three terms associated with the travel of water from the roots up through the vascular tissues of plants are
   (A) adhesion, cohesion, and translocation.
   (B) adhesion, cohesion, and transcription.
   (C) cohesion, hybridization, and transpiration.
   (D) cohesion, adhesion, and transpiration.
   (E) transpiration, neutralization, and adhesion.

Directions: The group of questions below consists of five lettered choices followed by a list of numbered phrases or sentences. For each numbered phrase or sentence, select the one choice that is most closely related to it. Each choice may be used once, more than once, or not at all.

Questions 5–9
   (A) Lipids
   (B) Peptide bonds
   (C) Alpha helix
   (D) Unsaturated fatty acids
   (E) Cellulose

5. Contain one or more double bonds

6. The major class of biological molecules that are not polymers

7. Linkages between the monomers of proteins

8. A secondary structure of proteins

9. A structural carbohydrate found in plants

10. The process by which protein conformation is lost or broken down is
    (A) decondensation.
    (B) deconstruction.
    (C) denaturation.
    (D) hydrolysis.
    (E) hybridization.

11. An organic compound that is composed of carbon, hydrogen, and oxygen in a 1:2:1 ratio is known as a
    (A) lipid.
    (B) carbohydrate.
    (C) salt.
    (D) nucleic acid.
    (E) protein.

12. Lactose and sucrose are examples of
    (A) monosaccharides.
    (B) nucleic acids.
    (C) unsaturated fatty acids.
    (D) disaccharides.
    (E) glucose polymers.

13. Which of the macromolecules below could be structural parts of the cell, enzymes, or involved in cell movement or communication?
    (A) nucleic acids
    (B) proteins
    (C) lipids
    (D) carbohydrates
    (E) minerals

14. Which macromolecule is the main component of all cell membranes?
    (A) DNA
    (B) phospholipids
    (C) carbohydrates
    (D) steroids
    (E) glucose

15. The partial negative charge at one end of a water molecule is attracted to a partial positive charge of another water molecule. What is the cause of this attraction?
    (A) a polar covalent bond
    (B) an ionic bond
    (C) a hydration shell
    (D) a hydrogen bond
    (E) a hydrophobic bond

16. Polymers of carbohydrates and proteins are all synthesized from monomers by
    (A) the joining of monosaccharides.
    (B) hydrolysis.
    (C) dehydration reactions.
    (D) ionic bonding of monomers.
    (E) cohesion.

17. When a water molecule loses an H^+ in solution, and another water molecule accepts the proton, what is the water molecule that accepts the proton called?
    (A) a hydroxide ion
    (B) crystal lattice structure
    (C) a solution not in equilibrium
    (D) a hydronium ion
    (E) a basic solution

18. Which of the following is NOT considered to be an emergent property of water?
    (A) cohesion
    (B) transpiration
    (C) moderation of temperature
    (D) insulation of bodies of water by floating ice
    (E) a versatile solvent

Free-Response Question

1. *Phospholipids are a critical component of the cell wall. The cell wall is selectively permeable, allowing only certain substances in and out, and in certain amounts.*

   (a) Describe why phospholipids are important components of cell membranes, based on their structure and properties.
   (b) Explain why proteins are an important component of the cell membrane, based on their structure and properties.
   (*Note:* A strong response to this item requires an understanding of topics from Units One and Two of the textbook.)

ANSWERS AND EXPLANATIONS

Multiple-Choice Questions

▌ **1. (B) is correct.** RNA is made up of a phosphate group, a ribose sugar, and one of the following four nitrogenous bases: cytosine, guanine, uracil, and adenine. The phosphate group of RNA contains a phosphate atom and three atoms of oxygen, not two. DNA is similar to RNA in many ways but different in two important ones. First, it contains deoxyribose as its sugar, instead of ribose, and it contains the base thymine instead of uracil.

▌ **2. (C) is correct.** The answer is water, H_2O. Polar covalent bonds are those in which valence electrons are shared between atoms, but unequally. (The more electronegative atom will attract the electrons more strongly, and that end of the molecule will have a slightly negative charge, whereas the less electronegative atom will attract them less strongly and be slightly positive.) The two atoms involved in the bond must differ in electronegativity in order to form a polar covalent bond.

▌ **3. (B) is correct.** Water dissolves polar and ionic compounds, but it doesn't dissolve oils and nonpolar compounds as well. Potassium chloride (KCl) looks a lot like table salt, NaCl. Potassium is positively charged, and chlorine is negatively charged—this is an ionic compound. HBr is also an ionic compound; therefore, you can eliminate answer choices (A) and (E). Sugars dissolve in water (and fructose is a sugar), so you can eliminate (C). Cellulose (D) molecules do not dissolve in water because they are too large. They are hydrophilic compounds, however, and thus are categorized as water-soluble. Now look at (B), and think back to the cell membrane. The phospholipids that make up the cell membrane consist of hydrophobic fatty acid chains, and hydrophilic head groups, which (among other variable components) contain glycerol. The fact that phospholipids have a hydrophilic end and a hydrophobic end makes them able to form the plasma membranes of cells, which are responsible for selectively allowing substances to enter and exit the cell. Fatty acids comprise the hydrophobic end of the phospholipid and are not water-soluble.

▌ **4. (D) is correct.** The three terms you should keep in mind as you think of water traveling up through the xylem of a plant are transpiration (in which water evaporates from the plant's leaves); cohesion, in which the water molecules stick together due to the hydrogen bonds; and adhesion, whereby the water molecules stick to plant cell walls and resist the downward pull of gravity.

▌ **5. (D) is correct.** Unsaturated fatty acids contain one or more carbon-carbon double bonds, whereas saturated fatty acids contain no double bonds.

▌ **6. (A) is correct.** Lipids are the only one of the four major classes of biological molecules that are not polymers. They are grouped together because they are hydrophobic. Nucleic acids are polymers of nucleotide monomers, proteins are polymers of amino acid monomers, and carbohydrates are polymers of monosaccharide monomers.

7. (B) is correct. The linkages between the amino acids of proteins are peptide bonds. Peptide bonds are covalent bonds formed in dehydration reactions. The carboxyl group of one amino acid is joined to the amino group of an adjacent amino acid, resulting in the loss of one molecule of water.

8. (C) is correct. One common secondary structure of proteins is the α helix; another is the β pleated sheet. The secondary structure of a protein refers to a section of the polypeptide chain that is repeatedly folded or coiled in a regular pattern. The patterns are the result of regular hydrogen bonding between segments of the polypeptide backbone.

9. (E) is correct. Cellulose is the polysaccharide that forms the strong cell walls of plant cells. It is a polymer of glucose.

10. (C) is correct. Denaturation is the process by which proteins lose their overall structure, or conformation, as a result of changes in pH, temperature, or salt concentration. Denatured proteins are biologically inactive.

11. (B) is correct. The ratio of carbon, hydrogen, and oxygen atoms in monosaccharides is 1:2:1.

12. (D) is correct. Lactose, the sugar found in milk, is a disaccharide consisting of glucose and galactose. Sucrose is a disaccharide consisting of glucose and fructose.

13. (B) is correct. Proteins have many functions, which encompass most of a cell's metabolic activity.

14. Phospholipids are unique macromolecules. Their hydrophilic heads and hydrophobic tails contribute to the semipermeability of cell membranes.

15. Polar covalent bonds are found in water molecules because of the unequal sharing of electrons among the atoms in water. The oxygen end of a water molecule has a slightly negative charge, while the hydrogen end has a slightly positive charge.

16. The monomers in macromolecules are joined when a molecule of water is removed during dehydration, or condensation reactions.

17. (D) is correct. In this situation, the water that donated the H^+ would become a hydroxide ion (OH^-), whereas the water that accepted the H^+ would become a hydronium ion, H_3O^+.

18. (B) is correct. Transpiration refers to the evaporation of water from pores in leaves. Transpiration is possible because of cohesion and adhesion, but it is not an emergent property of water.

Free-Response Question

(a) A phospholipid molecule contains a negatively charged hydrophilic "head" (containing a glycerol molecule and a phosphate group) and two hydrophobic fatty acid tails. In cell membrane surfaces, phospholipids are arranged in a bilayer, in which the hydrophilic heads are in contact with the cell's watery interior and exterior, while the tails are pointed away from water and toward each other in the interior of the membrane. The fatty acid chains of phospholipids can contain double bonds, which makes them unsaturated. Because of the kinks in the tails, phospholipids aren't packed together tightly, which contributes to the fluidity of the membrane. The fluidity of the cell membrane is very important in its function; the less fluid the membrane is, the more impermeable it is. There is an optimum permeability for the cell membrane, at which all the substances necessary for metabolism can pass into and out of the cell.

The fluidity of cell membranes enables hydrophobic molecules such as hydrocarbons, carbon dioxide, and oxygen to dissolve in the bilayer and easily cross the membrane. However, ions and polar molecules (including water, glucose, and other sugars) cannot pass through, because of the hydrophobic interior. Protein channels and transport proteins allow these required substances to cross membranes.

(b) Proteins function as cell membrane transporters because they act as channels; substances that bind to them can help alter their conformation to permit the passage of molecules through them, and into the cell interior.

There are many different ways by which proteins can permit the passage of ionic and polar molecules through the lipid bilayer. Proteins associated with the membrane are either integral proteins, which actually penetrate the lipid bilayer (ones that completely go through the bilayer are called transmembrane proteins), or they are "peripheral proteins" that are associated with the outside of the membrane. Transmembrane proteins can form hydrophilic channels that permit the passage of certain hydrophilic substances that otherwise would not be able to get across. Other functions that membrane proteins serve are to attach the cell to the extracellular matrix, to stabilize it, and to function in cell-cell recognition. Membrane proteins are also important in cell-cell signaling; some have enzyme function and carry out important metabolic reactions, and they aid in joining adjacent cells.

This response shows thorough knowledge of the processes of the structure of phospholipids, cell membrane structure and components, and movement across membranes. A strong response to this item requires an understanding of topics from Units One and Two of the textbook. Note that the response includes the following key terms in context, showing the writer's knowledge of their meanings and relatedness:

phospholipids	*metabolism*
hydrophilic head	*protein channels*
glycerol	*transporters*
phosphate	*conformation*
hydrophobic tails	*integral proteins*
lipid bilayer	*transmembrane proteins*
double bonds	*extracellular matrix*
unsaturated	*cell-cell signaling*
permeability	

CHAPTER 2

The Cell

Concept 6.1   To study cells, biologists use microscopes and the tools of biochemistry

▪ **Light microscopes** (LMs) are used to observe most plant and animal cells, bacteria, and some organelles such as mitochondria and nuclei. Most other cell organelles are too small to be seen with a light microscope, which cannot resolve detail finer than about 0.2 μm.

▪ Electron microscopes are used to study objects from about 2 nm to 100 μm in size. They function by focusing a beam of electrons either through the specimen or onto its surface. There are two kinds of EMs: **transmission electron microscopes** (TEMs) and **scanning electron microscopes** (SEMs). Electron microscopes cannot be used to observe living cells.

Concept 6.2   Eukaryotic cells have internal membranes that compartmentalize their functions

The table below organizes the major characteristics of prokaryotic and eukaryotic cells.

Characteristics	Prokaryotic Cells	Eukaryotic Cells
Plasma membrane	yes	yes
Cytosol with organelles	yes	yes
Ribosomes	yes	yes
Nucleus	no	yes
Size	1μm–10 μm	10 μm–100 μm
Internal membranes	no	yes

Prokaryotic cells include bacteria and archaea, whereas eukaryotic cells are animal, fungi, plant, and protist cells. Some details to remember about prokaryotes include:

▪ chromosomes are grouped together in a region called the nucleoid
▪ no membrane-bounded organelles
▪ smaller than eukaryotes

Some details to remember about eukaryotic cells include:

▪ membrane-enclosed nucleus, which contains cell's chromosomes
▪ membrane-bounded organelles in cytoplasm
▪ much larger than prokaryotes

Figure 6.9 Exploring Animal and Plant Cells

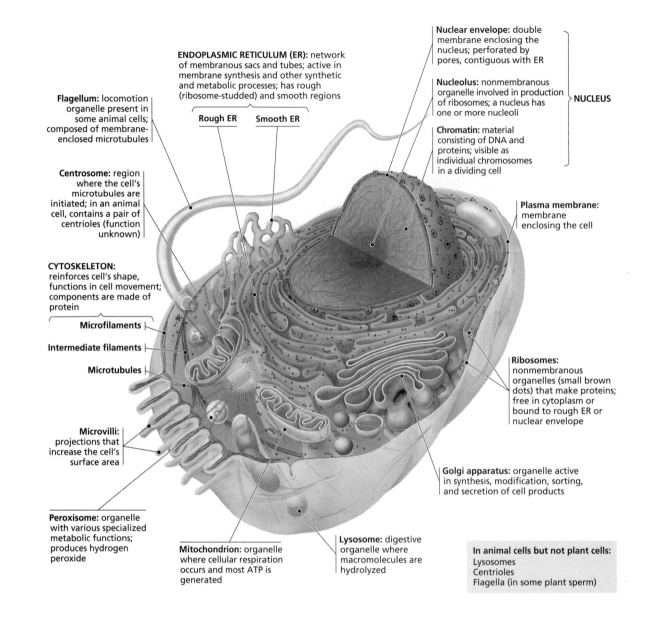

Flagellum: locomotion organelle present in some animal cells; composed of membrane-enclosed microtubules

ENDOPLASMIC RETICULUM (ER): network of membranous sacs and tubes; active in membrane synthesis and other synthetic and metabolic processes; has rough (ribosome-studded) and smooth regions

Rough ER   Smooth ER

Nuclear envelope: double membrane enclosing the nucleus; perforated by pores, contiguous with ER

Nucleolus: nonmembranous organelle involved in production of ribosomes; a nucleus has one or more nucleoli

Chromatin: material consisting of DNA and proteins; visible as individual chromosomes in a dividing cell

NUCLEUS

Centrosome: region where the cell's microtubules are initiated; in an animal cell, contains a pair of centrioles (function unknown)

Plasma membrane: membrane enclosing the cell

CYTOSKELETON: reinforces cell's shape, functions in cell movement; components are made of protein

Microfilaments

Intermediate filaments

Microtubules

Ribosomes: nonmembranous organelles (small brown dots) that make proteins; free in cytoplasm or bound to rough ER or nuclear envelope

Microvilli: projections that increase the cell's surface area

Golgi apparatus: organelle active in synthesis, modification, sorting, and secretion of cell products

Peroxisome: organelle with various specialized metabolic functions; produces hydrogen peroxide

Mitochondrion: organelle where cellular respiration occurs and most ATP is generated

Lysosome: digestive organelle where macromolecules are hydrolyzed

In animal cells but not plant cells:
Lysosomes
Centrioles
Flagella (in some plant sperm)

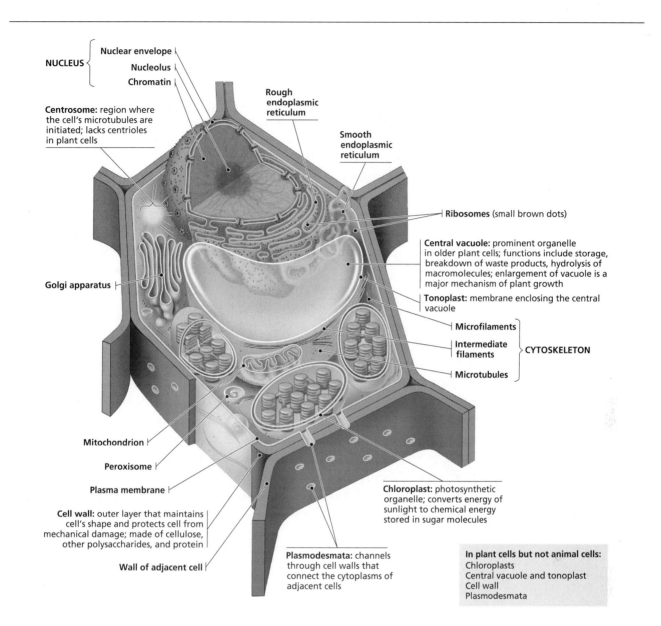

NUCLEUS
- Nuclear envelope
- Nucleolus
- Chromatin

Centrosome: region where the cell's microtubules are initiated; lacks centrioles in plant cells

Rough endoplasmic reticulum

Smooth endoplasmic reticulum

Golgi apparatus

Ribosomes (small brown dots)

Central vacuole: prominent organelle in older plant cells; functions include storage, breakdown of waste products, hydrolysis of macromolecules; enlargement of vacuole is a major mechanism of plant growth

Tonoplast: membrane enclosing the central vacuole

Microfilaments

Intermediate filaments | CYTOSKELETON

Microtubules

Mitochondrion

Peroxisome

Plasma membrane

Cell wall: outer layer that maintains cell's shape and protects cell from mechanical damage; made of cellulose, other polysaccharides, and protein

Wall of adjacent cell

Chloroplast: photosynthetic organelle; converts energy of sunlight to chemical energy stored in sugar molecules

Plasmodesmata: channels through cell walls that connect the cytoplasms of adjacent cells

In plant cells but not animal cells:
Chloroplasts
Central vacuole and tonoplast
Cell wall
Plasmodesmata

These cell structures are found in both plant and animal cells

▮ The **plasma membrane** forms the boundary for a cell, selectively permits the passage of materials into and out of the cell, and is made up of phospholipids, proteins, and associated carbohydrates.

▮ The **nucleus** contains most of the cell's DNA; it is the most noticeable organelle in the cell because of its relative size; surrounded by a double membrane, mRNA is transcribed here and then sent out to the cytoplasm; it is considered the control center of the cell.

▮ **Chromatin** is the complex of DNA and protein housed in the nucleus; as a cell gets ready for cell division, chromatin condenses into chromosomes; each species has a characteristic number of chromosomes (humans have 46 chromosomes in their somatic cells).

- The **nucleolus** is associated with chromatin, the nucleolus exists in a nondividing nucleus; ribosomal RNA (rRNA) is produced here and is not enclosed by a membrane.
- **Ribosomes** consist of rRNA and protein. They are sites of protein synthesis in the cell; they consist of two subunits and are not enclosed by a membrane; there are two types of ribosomes—those free-floating in cytosol and those bound to endoplasmic reticulum; both produce proteins.
- **Endoplasmic reticulum** (ER) makes up more than half the total membrane structure in many cells; it is a network of membranes and sacs called cisternae; its internal component is called the cisternal space; there are two types of ER—rough and smooth ER; smooth ER is involved in synthesis of lipids and metabolism of carbohydrates; rough ER is so called because of its associated ribosomes; ribosomes associated with ER synthesize important proteins secreted by the cell; as these proteins are created on the ER-bound ribosomes, the polypeptide chains travel through ER membrane into cisternal space, where they are kept separate from proteins created at free-floating ribosomes, which will not be secreted; rough ER proteins are then excreted from the cell through transport vesicles.
- **Golgi apparatus**—when transport vesicles from the rough ER leave the ER, they next travel to the Golgi apparatus, where their contents are modified, stored, and sent on their way; Golgi apparatus consists of flattened sacs of membranes, again called cisternae arranged in stacks; Golgi stacks have polarity—one face is called the *cis* face, and the other is called the *trans* face; the *cis* face receives vesicles, and *trans* face ships vesicles out.
- **Mitochondria** are organelles in which cellular respiration takes place; in cellular respiration, ATP is created, so mitochondria are often referred to as the powerhouses of the cell; they are enclosed by a double membrane; the inner membrane has infolds called cristae.
- **Peroxisomes** are single-membrane-bound compartments in the cell responsible for various metabolic functions, such as breakdown of purines; they produce hydrogen peroxide as a byproduct of their actions.
- **Cytoskeleton** is a network of fibers that runs through the entire cytoplasm; it is responsible for organizing cell structures and activities; it is involved in cell motility, including actual locomotion of the cell, and movement of structures within the cell; three types of fibers make up cytoskeleton—**microtubules** (which are made up of the protein **tubulin**), **microfilaments,** and **intermediate filaments.**
- **Centrosomes** are a region located near the nucleus, from which microtubules grow. They contain centrioles in animal cells.

These are the cell structures associated with animal cells

- **Lysosomes** are membrane-bound sacs of hydrolytic enzymes that can digest large molecules, such as proteins, polysaccharides, fats, and nucleic acids; they have a low internal pH; they can break down macromolecules for organic monomers to be excreted back into cytosol and recycled by the cell; as a cell ages, the lysosomal membrane can break, thus digesting its cellular contents and destroying the cell—hence the nickname "the suicide bag."

- **Centrioles** are located within the centrosome of animal cells; they replicate before cell division.
- **Flagella** are appendages used for cell locomotion, protruding from cell surface; most cells with flagella possess only one, but a few possess more than one (note that the sperm of some plants also have flagella).
- **Extracellular matrix** of animal cells is situated just external to plasma membrane; it is composed of glycoproteins secreted by the cell (most prominent of which is collagen).
- **Tight junctions** are sections of animal cell membrane where two neighboring cells are fused.
- **Desmosomes** fasten adjacent animal cells together; they are made of intermediate filaments.
- **Gap junctions** provide channels between adjacent animal cells through which ions, sugars, and other small molecules can pass.

These are the cell structures associated with plant cells

- **Central vacuoles** are membrane-bounded organelles whose functions include storage and breakdown of some waste products; in plants, a vacuole can make up about 80% of the cell.
- **Chloroplasts** are found in both plant and algae cells; they are sites of photosynthesis; here, solar energy is converted to chemical energy; inside chloroplasts are flattened membranes called thylakoids; a stack of thylakoids is called a granum (plural, grana).
- The **cell wall** of a plant protects the plant and helps maintain its shape.
- **Plasmodesmata** are channels that perforate adjacent plant cell walls and allow cytosol to pass through from cell to cell.

Concept 7.1 Cellular membranes are fluid mosaics of lipids and proteins

- Membranes are of utmost importance to the cell as a whole, and to many of the organelles contained in the cell, because they act as selective barriers to let in only the substances that each cell or specific organelle needs to function properly.
- Membranes are primarily made up of phospholipids and proteins (though carbohydrates are crucial to membranes, too) held together by weak interactions that cause the membrane to be fluid. The fluid mosaic model of the cell membrane describes the membrane as fluid with proteins embedded in or associated with the phospholipid bilayer.
- There are both integral proteins and peripheral proteins in the cell membrane. **Integral proteins** are those that are completely embedded in the membrane, some of which are transmembrane proteins that span the membrane completely. **Peripheral proteins** are loosely bound to the membrane's surface.
- **Carbohydrates** on the membrane are crucial in cell-cell recognition (which is necessary for proper immune function) and in developing organisms (for tissue differentiation). Cell surface carbohydrates—many of which are oligosaccharides—vary from species to species and are the reason that blood transfusions must be type-specific.

Concept 7.3 Passive transport is diffusion of a substance across a membrane with no energy investment

▌ **Hydrocarbons, carbon dioxide,** and **oxygen** are hydrophobic substances that can pass easily across the cell membrane by passive diffusion. In **passive diffusion,** a substance travels from where it is more concentrated to where it is less concentrated, diffusing down its **concentration gradient.** This type of diffusion requires that no work be done, and it relies only on the thermal motion energy intrinsic to the molecule in question. The term "passive diffusion" is used because the cell expends no energy in moving the substances.

▌ The term for the passive transport of water is **osmosis.** In osmosis, water flows from a **hypotonic solution** (the solution with lower solute concentration) to a **hypertonic solution** (one with higher solute concentration).

▌ **Ions** and **polar molecules** cannot pass easily across the membrane. The process by which ions and hydrophilic substances diffuse across the cell membrane with the help of transport proteins is called **facilitated diffusion.** Transport proteins are specific for the substances they transport. They work in one of two ways:

1. They provide a hydrophilic channel through which the molecules in question can pass.
2. They bind loosely to the molecules in question and carry them through the membrane.

Concept 7.4 Active transport uses energy to move solutes against their gradients

▌ In **active transport,** substances can be moved against their concentration gradient. Not surprisingly, in this type of transport, the cell must expend energy. This type of transport is crucial for cells to maintain sufficient quantities of substances that are relatively rare in their environment.

▌ Specific transmembrane proteins are responsible for active transport, and ATP supplies the energy for this type of transport. ATP transfers one of its phosphates to the transport protein, which might be responsible for making the protein change its shape to allow for the passage of the substance.

▌ Ions have both a chemical and a voltage gradient across the membrane, and this causes an **electrochemical gradient.** The inside of the cell is slightly more negative than the outside, so that membrane potential favors the movement of cations (positively charged ions) into the cell.

▌ The sodium-potassium pump works by exchanging sodium (Na^+) for potassium (K^+) across the cell membrane; it exchanges three Na^+ for two K^+, so for each round of the pump, there is a net transfer of one positive charge from the cell interior to the exterior. This type of pump, called an **electrogenic pump,** generates voltage across the membrane.

▌ In **cotransport,** an ATP pump that transports a specific solute indirectly drives the active transport of other substances. In this process, the substance that was initially pumped across the membrane can do work as it moves back across the membrane by diffusion. This process is analogous to water that has been pumped uphill and performs work as it flows back down.

Concept 7.5 Bulk transport across the plasma membrane occurs by exocytosis and endocytosis

▌ Large molecules are moved across the cell membrane through exocytosis and endocytosis. In **exocytosis,** vesicles from the cell's interior fuse with the cell membrane, expelling their contents to the exterior. In **endocytosis,** the cell forms new vesicles from the plasma membrane; this is basically the reverse of exocytosis, and this process allows the cell to take in macromolecules. There are three types of endocytosis.

1. **Phagocytosis** occurs when the cell wraps pseudopodia around the substance and packages it within a large vesicle formed by the membrane.
2. In **pinocytosis,** the cell takes in small droplets of extracellular fluid within small vesicles. Pinocytosis is not specific, because any and all included solutes are taken into the cells.
3. **Receptor-mediated endocytosis** is a very specific process. Certain substances (ligands) bind to specific receptors on the cell's surface (these receptors are usually clustered in **coated pits**), and this causes a vesicle to form around the substance and then to pinch off into the cytoplasm.

Concept 8.1 An organism's metabolism transforms matter and energy, subject to the laws of thermodynamics

▌ **Metabolism** is the totality of an organism's chemical reactions. Metabolism as a whole manages the material and energy resources of the cell.

▌ A **catabolic pathway** leads to the release of energy by the breakdown of complex molecules to simpler compounds. **Anabolic pathways** consume energy to build complicated molecules from simpler ones.

▌ **Energy** is defined as the capacity to do work. Anything that is moving is said to possess **kinetic energy.** An object at rest can possess **potential energy** if it has stored energy as a result of its position or structure. **Chemical energy**, a form of potential energy, is stored in molecules, and the amount of chemical energy a molecule possesses depends on its chemical bonds.

▌ The study of energy transformations that occur in matter is called thermodynamics. The **first law of thermodynamics** states that the energy of the universe is constant and that energy can be transferred and transformed, but it cannot be created or destroyed. The **second law of thermodynamics** states that every energy transfer or transformation increases the **entropy,** or the amount of disorder or randomness, in the universe.

Concept 8.2 The free-energy change of a reaction tells us whether the reaction occurs spontaneously

▌ **Free energy** is defined as the part of a system's energy that is able to perform work when the temperature of a system is uniform. Free energy is depicted as G. The symbol for the total energy of a system is H, and the symbol for entropy is S. The relationship between the change in free energy, change in energy, change in entropy, and temperature is as follows:

$$\Delta G = \Delta H - T\Delta S$$

- In order for a chemical reaction to occur spontaneously, the system must experience either a decrease in H (energy) or an increase in S (entropy).
- An **exergonic reaction** is one in which energy is released (ΔG is negative). An **endergonic reaction** is one that requires energy in order to proceed. Endergonic reactions absorb free energy (ΔG is positive).
- Reactions in a closed system eventually reach equilibrium and can then do no work. Living cells are never in a state of equilibrium. The fact that metabolism as a whole is never at equilibrium is one of the defining features of life.

Concept 8.3 *ATP powers cellular work by coupling exergonic reactions to endergonic reactions*

- The primary source of energy for cells is **ATP (adenosine triphosphate).** ATP is made up of the nitrogenous base adenine, bonded to ribose and a chain of three phosphate groups. When a phosphate group is hydrolyzed, energy is released in an exergonic reaction.
- Work in the cell is done by the release of a phosphate group from ATP. When ATP transfers one phosphate group through hydrolysis, it becomes **ADP (adenosine diphosphate).**

Concept 8.4 *Enzymes speed up metabolic reactions by lowering energy barriers*

- **Catalysts** are substances that can change the rate of a reaction without being altered themselves in the process. **Enzymes** are proteins that are biological catalysts.
- The **activation energy** of a reaction is the amount of energy it takes to start a reaction—the amount of energy it takes to break the bonds in the reactant molecules.
- Enzymes speed up reactions by lowering the activation energy of the reaction—but without changing the free energy change of the reaction. The reactant that the enzyme acts on is called a **substrate.**
- A certain region in the enzyme, known as the **active site,** is the part of the enzyme that binds to the substrate. The enzyme and substrate form a complex called an **enzyme-substrate complex** that is held together by weak interactions. The substrate is then converted into **products,** and the products are released from the enzyme.
- There are some substances that inhibit the actions of enzymes. **Competitive inhibitors** are reversible inhibitors that compete with the substrate for the active site on the enzyme. **Noncompetitive inhibitors** bind to another site on the enzyme, other than the active site; this causes the enzyme to change its shape, preventing the substrate from binding to the active site.
- Many enzyme regulators bind to an allosteric site on the enzyme, which is a specific receptor far from the active site. Once bound, they can either stimulate or inhibit enzyme activity.

Oxidation-reduction reactions, fermentation, cellular respiration, and photosynthesis are covered in one of the most technically challenging sections of your textbook. Here we will focus on the major steps of each of the processes, as well as the results. Questions on the AP* Biology Exam are likely to focus on the net results of photosynthesis and respiration—not on the exact reactions that create the products.

Concept 9.1 Catabolic pathways release energy by oxidizing organic fuels

▌ **Energy** in a cell is stored in the chemical bonds between atoms, and this energy is released when the bonds are broken. The cell uses some of the released energy for work, and the rest is given off as heat.

▌ **Catabolism** is the process by which molecules are broken down and their energy is released. Two types of catabolism are

1. **Fermentation**—the partial degradation of sugars that occurs without the use of oxygen.
2. **Cellular respiration**—the most prevalent and efficient catabolic pathway, in which oxygen is consumed as a reactant along with the organic fuel.
   • Carbohydrates, fats, and proteins can all be broken down to release energy in cellular respiration. However, glucose is the primary nutrient molecule that is used in cellular respiration. The standard way of representing the process of cellular respiration shows glucose being broken down in the following reaction:

   $$C_6H_{12}O_6 + 6\,O_6 \rightarrow 6\,CO_2 + 6\,H_2O + \text{Energy (in the form of chemical bonds in ATP and heat)}$$

   • As you can see from the reaction, the breakdown of glucose is exergonic—that is, energy is given off in this reaction, in the form of heat and ATP. This ATP is used to power all cellular activities.

▌ Energy is released from ATP when enzymes in the cell transfer one of its three phosphate groups to another molecule (exergonic reaction). The dephosphorylated ATP is called ADP (adenosine diphosphate), and the ADP can be rephosphorylated by the cell to form ATP again.

▌ To fully understand how energy is exchanged in these molecular reactions in the cell, we need to look at exactly how energy moves. As you learned earlier in this course, electrons are exchanged in the course of chemical reactions. When electrons are transferred from one reactant to another, the reaction is called an **oxidation-reduction reaction,** or **redox reaction.**

▌ The loss of an electron from a substance is called **oxidation;** the substance that gives up the electron is said to be **oxidized.** The gain of an electron by a substance is called **reduction;** the substance that accepts the electron is said to be **reduced.**

Concept 9.2 Glycolysis harvests chemical energy by oxidizing glucose to pyruvate

▌ In **glycolysis** (which occurs in the cytosol), the degradation of glucose begins as it is broken down into two pyruvate molecules. The six-carbon glucose molecule is split into two three-carbon sugars through a long series of steps.

▌ In the course of glycolysis, there is an ATP-consuming phase and an ATP-producing phase. In the ATP-consuming phase, two ATP molecules are consumed, but later 4 ATP molecules are produced. Therefore, glycolysis results in a net gain of 2 ATP. Two NADH are also produced, which are used to make more ATP during oxidative phosphorylation, in the presence of oxygen.

Concept 9.3 *The citric acid cycle completes the energy-yielding oxidation of organic molecules*

▌ In the **citric acid cycle** (which occurs in the mitochondrial matrix), the job of breaking down glucose is completed and the final product is CO_2.

▌ In the presence of oxygen, the two pyruvate molecules produced by glycolysis travel to a mitochondrion to take part in the citric acid cycle. In the citric acid cycle, the chemical energy in the pyruvate molecules is released.

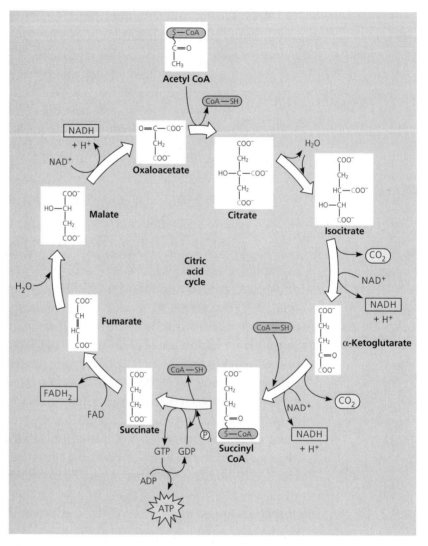

Figure 9.12   A closer look at the citric acid cycle

- The citric acid cycle has many steps, and as with glycolysis, each of the steps is catalyzed by a different enzyme. Since glycolysis results in the production of two pyruvate molecules (which are converted to acetyl CoA) and each turn of the citric acid cycle requires the input of one acetyl CoA. The citric acid cycle must make two turns before you get the products from the breakdown of the two pyruvate molecules. The **net results of the citric acid cycle** are:

  4 CO_2
  2 ATP
  6 NADH
  2 $FADH_2$

Concept 9.4 During oxidative phosphorylation, chemiosmosis couples electron transport to ATP synthesis

- So far, glycolysis and the citric acid cycle have produced a total of 4 molecules of ATP for each glucose molecule that was degraded. The rest of the ATP produced from the breakdown of glucose is produced in the next steps of cellular respiration, through the electron transport chain and oxidative phosphorylation.
- The NADH and $FADH_2$ that were produced during the citric acid cycle are used in the course of the electron transport system and oxidative phosphorylation to create relatively large amounts of ATP.
- The **electron transport chain** produces energy that drives the synthesis of ATP in **oxidative phosphorylation.** The electron transport chain consists of molecules (mostly proteins) that are embedded in the inner mitochondrial membrane. There are millions of such electron transport chains in the inner mitochondrial membrane.
- Sitting atop these embedded proteins are associated molecules that are alternately reduced and oxidized as they accept and donate electrons.
- The initial electron acceptor in the electron transport chain is a flavoprotein called flavin mononucleotide, or FMN, which accepts an electron from NADH. The electron is passed down a series of molecules to oxygen, which is the final electron acceptor. Then it is combined with two hydrogen atoms to form a molecule of water.
- The electron transport chain doesn't make ATP. Instead these reactions are coupled to others to produce ATP in a process called chemiosmosis.
- The **net result** of the electron transport chain is:

  1. the movement of free energy down a series of steps from $FADH_2$ and NADH to oxygen.
  2. a source of energy for the production of ATP through chemiosmosis.

- Also embedded in the mitochondrial inner membrane are protein complexes called **ATP synthases.** ATP synthases phosphorylate ATP out of ADP plus inorganic phosphate. ATP synthases use the energy from a proton gradient built up by the electron transport system to power the synthesis of ATP.
- The flow of electrons in the electron transport chain is exergonic, and the energy given off is used to pump H^+ across the membrane against its concentration gradient. The H^+ flows back across the membrane into the mitochondrial matrix with the concentration gradient, and since the H^+ can flow only back through the ATP synthases (they are the only regions in this membrane permeable to H^+), their flow drives the **oxidative phosphorylation** of ADP to ATP. This is how the H^+ gradient built up by the electron transport chain is coupled to ATP synthesis, in **chemiosmosis.**

Concept 9.5 *Fermentation enables some cells to produce ATP without the use of oxygen*

- Remember that oxygen is the final electron acceptor in the electron transport chain, and without it this chain will not function. Fermentation allows a cell to continue to produce ATP without the use of oxygen.
- Fermentation can take place under **anaerobic** conditions—that is, when there is no oxygen present. At times, it also takes place when oxygen is present but not in adequate amounts, such as in working human muscle cells. Cellular respiration takes place under **aerobic** conditions (when oxygen is present). Fermentation consists of glycolysis and reactions that regenerate NAD^+ (so that it can be reused during glycolysis).
- The two common types of fermentation are alcohol fermentation and lactic acid fermentation.

    - In **alcohol fermentation,** pyruvate is converted to ethanol, releasing CO_2 and oxidizing NADH in the process to create more NAD^+.
    - In **lactic acid fermentation,** pyruvate is reduced by NADH (and NAD^+ is created in the process), and lactate is formed as a waste product.

- **Facultative anaerobes** can make enough ATP to survive using fermentation or respiration.

Concept 9.6 *Glycolysis and the citric acid cycle connect to many other metabolic pathways*

- In addition to organic molecules that can be oxidized as fuel, food must also provide materials for anabolic pathways. For example, amino acids from food can be incorporated into the consumer's own proteins. Compounds formed as intermediates of glycolysis and the citric acid cycle can be diverted into anabolic pathways.

Concept 10.1 *Photosynthesis converts light energy to the chemical energy of food*

- **Chloroplasts** are plant cell organelles that are mostly located in the cells that make up the **mesophyll** tissue in leaves. The exterior of the lower epidermis of a leaf cell contains many tiny pores called **stomata,** through which carbon dioxide enters and oxygen and water exit the leaf.

- Chloroplasts have an outer membrane and an inner membrane. Inside the inner membrane is the **stroma,** which is a dense fluid-filled area. Within the stroma is a vast network of interconnected membranous sacs called **thylakoids.** Within the thylakoids is a compartment known as the **thylakoid space.**
- **Chlorophyll** is located in the thylakoid membranes and is the light-absorbing pigment that drives photosynthesis and gives plants their green color. The overall reaction of photosynthesis looks like this:

$$6\ CO_2 + 12\ H_2O + \text{Light energy} \rightarrow C_6H_{12}O_6 + 6\ O_2 + 6\ H_2O$$

    Basically, plants produce organic compounds using light energy, carbon dioxide, and water. Oxygen is released in the process. The two main parts of photosynthesis are the light reactions and the Calvin cycle.
- In the **light reactions** of photosynthesis, solar energy is converted to chemical energy. Light is absorbed by chlorophyll and drives the transfer of electrons from water to NADP$^+$, forming NADPH. Water is split during these reactions, and O_2 is released. Photophosphorylation during the light reactions leads to the production of ATP from ADP. The net products of the light reactions are **NADPH** (which stores electrons), **ATP,** and **oxygen.**
- In the **Calvin cycle,** CO_2 from the air is incorporated into organic molecules in **carbon fixation.** The fixed carbon is then used to make carbohydrates. NADPH is used to power carbon fixation. The Calvin cycle also uses ATP in the course of its reactions.

Concept 10.2 *The light reactions convert solar energy to the chemical energy of ATP and NADPH*

- Light is electromagnetic energy, and it behaves as though it is made up of discrete particles, called **photons**—each of which has a fixed quantity of energy.
- Substances that absorb light are called **pigments,** and different pigments absorb light of different wavelengths. Chlorophyll is a pigment that absorbs violet-blue and red light while transmitting and reflecting green light. This is why we see summer leaves as green.
- Photons of light are absorbed by certain groups of pigment molecules in the thylakoid membrane of chloroplasts. These groups are called photosystems. Photosystems have a light-harvesting complex made up of chlorophyll molecules and carotenoid molecules (accessory pigments in the thylakoid membrane); this allows them to gather light effectively. When chlorophyll absorbs light energy in the form of photons, one of the molecule's electrons is raised to an orbital of higher potential energy. The chlorophyll is then said to be in an "excited" state.
- Thylakoid membranes contain two photosystems that are important to photosynthesis—**photosystem I** (PS I) and **photosystem II** (PS II). Each of these photosystems has a reaction center (the site of the first light-driven chemical reaction of photosynthesis).

■ Following are the major steps of the light reactions of photosynthesis.

1. Photosystem II absorbs light in the 680-nanometer wavelength range. An electron in the reaction center chlorophyll (called P680) becomes excited and is captured by a primary electron acceptor. The reaction center chlorophyll is oxidized and needs an electron.

2. An enzyme splits a water molecule into two hydrogen ions, two electrons, and an oxygen atom. The electrons are supplied to the needy P680 molecules. The oxygen combines with another oxygen molecule.

3. The original excited electron passes from the primary electron acceptor of photosystem II to photosystem I through an electron transport chain.

4. The energy from the transfer of electrons down the electron transport chain is used to phosphorylate ADP to ATP in the thylakoid membrane, in a process called **noncyclic electron flow.** This process is similar to chemiosmosis. Later, this ATP will be used as energy in the formation of carbohydrates, in the Calvin cycle.

5. The electrons that reach the end of the electron transport chain are donated to the chlorophyll in P700 of photosystem I. (This need for an electron by PS I is created when light energy excites an electron in P700, and that electron is taken up by the primary acceptor of photosystem I).

6. The primary electron acceptor of photosystem I passes the excited electrons along to another electron transport chain, which transmits them to ferredoxin, and then finally to $NADP^+$, which is reduced to NADPH, the second of the two important light-reaction products.

■ An alternative to noncyclic electron flow is **cyclic electron flow.** While noncyclic electron flow produces nearly equal quantities of ATP and NADPH, the Calvin cycle reactions use more ATP than NADPH. In cyclic electron flow, only photosystem I is used. The electrons from ferredoxin cycle back to chlorophyll via the cytochrome complex and plastocyanin (Pc). Neither NADPH nor oxygen is produced, but ATP is still a product.

Concept 10.3 *The Calvin cycle uses ATP and NADPH to convert CO_2 to sugar*

■ In the course of the **Calvin cycle,** CO_2 is converted to a carbohydrate called glyceraldehyde-3-phosphate (G3P), and ATP and NADPH are both consumed. But in order to make one molecule of G3P, the cycle must go through three rotations and fix three molecules of CO_2. Here is an outline of what the cycle looks like:

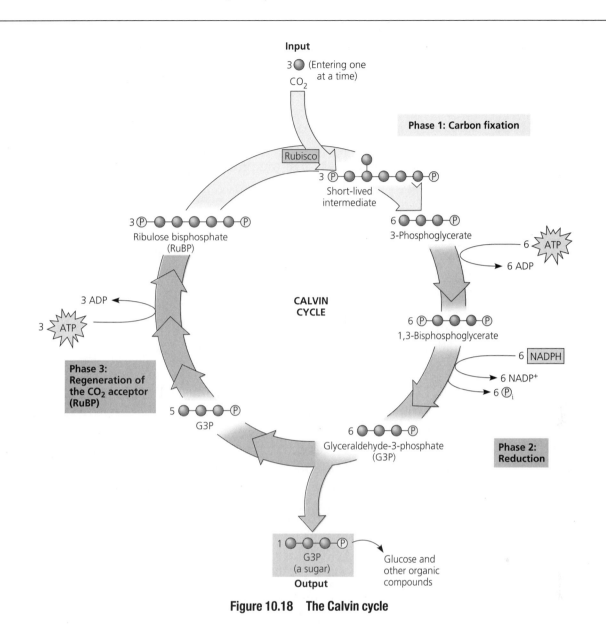

Figure 10.18   The Calvin cycle

▌ These are the major steps of the Calvin cycle:

1. Three CO_2 molecules are attached to three molecules of **ribulose bisphosphate (RuBP);** these reactions are catalyzed by **rubisco** and produce an unstable product that immediately splits into two three-carbon compounds called **3-phosphoglycerate.**

2. The 3-phosphoglycerate molecules are phosphorylated to become **1, 3-bisphosphoglycerate.**

3. Next, 6 NADPH reduce the six 1, 3-bisphosphoglycerates to six **glyceraldehyde-3-phosphate (G3P).**

4. One G3P leaves the cycle to be used by the plant cell.

5. Finally, RuBP is regenerated as the 5 G3Ps are reworked into 3 of the starting molecules, with the expenditure of 3 ATP molecules.

The results of the Calvin cycle (which produces one G3P molecule for each trip through the cycle) are that

- nine molecules of ATP are consumed (to be replenished by the light reactions).
- six molecules of NADPH are consumed (also to be replenished by the light reactions).
- one of the six G3P that was produced is later metabolized into larger carbohydrates.

Concept 10.4 Alternative mechanisms of carbon fixation have evolved in hot, arid climates

- Many plants living in hot, dry climates use C_4 **fixation** instead of C_3 fixation (the standard Calvin cycle). In C_4 fixation, the first carbon compound formed in the Calvin cycle contains four carbons instead of three.
- C_4 plants have two kinds of photosynthetic cells: bundle-sheath cells and mesophyll cells. The **bundle-sheath cells** are grouped around the leaf's veins, and the mesophyll cells are dispersed elsewhere around the leaf.
- The steps of C_4 photosynthesis are as follows:

  1. CO_2 is added to **phosphoenolpyruvate** (PEP) to form the four-carbon compound **oxaloacetate.** This reaction is catalyzed by **PEP carboxylase.**
  2. The mesophyll cells export the oxaloacetate to the bundle-sheath cells, which break down the oxaloacetate back into CO_2.
  3. The CO_2 is converted into carbohydrates through the Calvin cycle.

- In C_4 plants, the mesophyll cells pump CO_2 into the bundle-sheath cells, keeping the CO_2 concentration high enough so that rubisco will bind to CO_2 rather than O_2. Therefore, we could say that C_4 photosynthesis minimizes photorespiration and enhances sugar production.

- **CAM photosynthesis** is another adaptation to hot, dry climates. These plants keep their stomata closed during the day to prevent excessive water loss. Of course, this also prevents gas exchange. At night, the stomata open and CO_2 is taken in. Cells convert the CO_2 into various organic compounds and store it in vacuoles. In the morning when the stomata close, the plant cells release the stored CO_2 needed for photosynthesis.
- In both C_4 and CAM photosynthesis, CO_2 is first transformed into an organic intermediate before it enters the Calvin cycle. All of the processes—C_3, C_4, and CAM photosynthesis—use the Calvin cycle; they just have different methods for getting there.

Concept 11.1 External signals are converted into responses within the cell

- In signaling, animal cells communicate by direct contact or by secreting local regulators, such as growth factors or neurotransmitters. There are three stages of cell signaling: reception, transduction, and response.

Concept 11.2 Reception: A signal molecule binds to a receptor protein, causing it to change shape

▌ The binding between a signal molecule (**ligand**) and a **receptor** is highly specific. A conformational change in a receptor is often the initial transduction of the signal. Intracellular receptors are cytoplasmic or nuclear proteins.

▌ Receptors in the plasma membrane—a **G-protein-linked receptor** is a membrane receptor that works with the help of a **cytoplasmic G protein.** Receptor **tyrosine kinases** react to the binding of signal molecules by forming dimers and then adding phosphate groups to tyrosines on the cytoplasmic side of the other subunit of the receptor. Specific signal molecules cause **ligand-gated ion channels** in a membrane to open or close, regulating the flow of specific ions.

Concept 11.3 Transduction: Cascades of molecular interactions relay signals from receptors to target molecules in the cell

▌ At each step in a pathway, the signal is **transduced** into a different form, commonly a conformational change in a protein. Many signal transduction pathways include **phosphorylation cascades,** in which a series of different molecules in a pathway are phosphorylated in turn, each molecule adding a phosphate group to the next one in line.

Concept 11.4 Response: Cell signaling leads to regulation of cytoplasmic activities or transcription

▌ In the cytoplasm, signaling pathways regulate, for example, enzyme activity and cytoskeleton rearrangement. Other pathways regulate genes by activating **transcription factors**—proteins that turn specific genes on or off. Each catalytic protein in a signaling pathway amplifies the signal by activating multiple copies of the next component of the pathway; for long pathways, the total amplification may be a millionfold or more.

Concept 12.1 Cell division results in genetically identical daughter cells

▌ Before the cell can divide, the cell's genome (its complete complement of DNA, in the form of chromosomes) must be copied. All eukaryotic organisms have a characteristic number of chromosomes in their cell nuclei. Human somatic cells (all body cells except gametes), have 46 chromosomes, which is the diploid chromosome number. Human gametes—sperm and egg cells—are haploid and have 23 chromosomes. Mitosis is the process by which somatic cells divide, forming daughter cells that contain the same diploid chromosome number as the parent cell.

▌ When the chromosomes are replicated, just prior to mitosis, each duplicated chromosome consists of two sister **chromatids** attached by a **centromere.**

▌ Mitosis is the division of the cell's nucleus. It is followed by **cytokinesis,** which is the division of the cell's cytoplasm. During the cell cycle the chromosomes are doubled, but then mitosis reduces the chromosome number back to the diploid 46.

■ Conversely, gametes are produced by a process called meiosis, which in humans occurs only in the ovaries and testes. In meiosis, daughter cells have half as many chromosomes (23) as the parent cell.

Concept 12.2 *The mitotic phase alternates with interphase in the cell cycle*

■ The cell cycle consists of

■ the **mitotic phase** (10% of the total cycle, consisting of mitosis and cytokinesis).

■ **interphase** (90% of the cell cycle, consisting of G_1 phase, S phase, and G_2 phase).

■ During interphase, the cell prepares for division by increasing in volume, duplicating cell organelles, replicating histones and other proteins associated with DNA, and replicating its DNA.

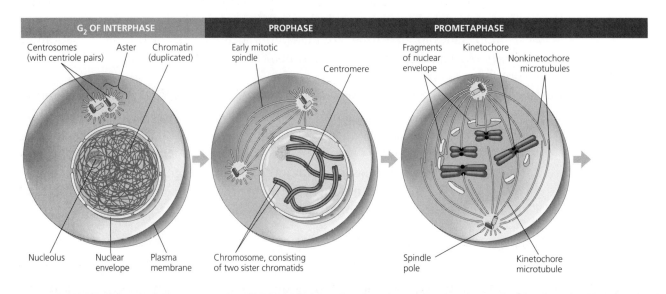

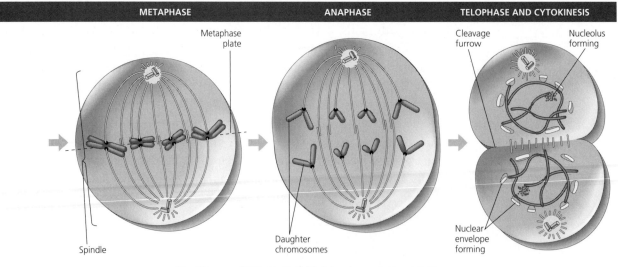

The Stages of Mitotic Cell Division in an Animal Cell

Mitosis can be broken down into five phases, not including cytokinesis. It might be helpful to think of a good mnemonic device for these steps.

▌ **Prophase:** In this phase, the chromatin becomes more tightly coiled into discrete chromosomes, the nucleoli disappear, and the mitotic spindle (consisting of microtubules extending from the two centrosomes) begins to form in the cytoplasm.

▌ **Prometaphase:** The nuclear envelope begins to fragment and the microtubules can begin to attach to the chromosomes, which have further condensed. Each of the two chromatids from a chromosome pair now has a kinetochore at its centromere region, to which the microtubules will begin to attach.

▌ **Metaphase:** In this phase, the centrioles have now migrated to opposite poles in the cell. The chromosomes line up on the metaphase plate at the equator of the cell. All of the kinetochores have attached microtubules, and all the microtubules together are called the spindle.

▌ **Anaphase:** In this phase, the sister chromatids begin to separate, pulled apart by the retracting microtubules. The cell also elongates at this time, as the poles elongate. By the end of anaphase, the opposite ends of the cell both contain complete and equal sets of chromosomes.

▌ **Telophase:** At this point, nuclear envelopes re-form around the sets of chromosomes located at opposite ends of the cell. The chromatin fiber of the chromosomes becomes less condensed. Cytokinesis begins, during which the cytoplasm of the cell is divided. In animal cells, a **cleavage furrow** forms that eventually pinches off as two new cells form; in plant cells, a cell plate forms that eventually leads to two daughter cells.

▌ You will want to be familiar with how the microtubules reel in the chromosomes. Kinetochores are equipped with protein motors that "walk" along the microtubule, breaking off tubulin subunits as they go, thereby shortening the microtubules and effectively reeling in the chromosomes. This process is ATP-dependent.

Concept 12.3 *The cell cycle is regulated by a molecular control system*

▌ The steps of the cycle are controlled by a cell cycle control system. This control system moves the cell through its stages by a series of checkpoints, during which signals tell the cell either to continue dividing or to stop.

▌ The major cell cycle checkpoints include the **G_1 phase checkpoint, G_2 phase checkpoint,** and **M phase checkpoint.** The G_1 phase checkpoint is thought of as the most important checkpoint. If the cell gets the go-ahead signal at this checkpoint, it usually will complete the whole cell cycle and divide. If it does not receive the go-ahead signal, it enters a nondividing phase called G_0 phase.

▌ **Kinases** are the proteins that control the cell cycle. They exist in the cells at all times but are active only when they are connected to cyclin proteins. Thus, they are called **cyclin-dependent kinases (Cdk).** As you might guess, the levels of cyclin and Cdk activity rise and fall simultaneously in the cell cycle.

▌ **MPF,** or **maturation-promoting factor,** is a Cdk. MPF triggers the cell to pass from the G_2 checkpoint into M phase.

For Additional Review

Compare the process of meiosis with the process of mitosis. In your comparison, include a study of the change in chromosomal number through the cell, the purposes of each process within an organism, and the starting material and product for each. *Note:* The details of meiosis are covered in Chapter 13, Unit 3 of the text.

Multiple-Choice Questions

1. Which structure could you observe with a light microscope?
   (A) a ribosome
   (B) a Golgi apparatus
   (C) a nucleus
   (D) an endoplasmic reticulum
   (E) a peroxisome

2. Prokaryotic and eukaryotic cells have all of the following structures in common EXCEPT
   (A) a plasma membrane.
   (B) protein-complexed DNA.
   (C) a nucleoid region.
   (D) ribosomes.
   (E) cytoplasm.

Directions: Questions 3–7 below consist of five lettered choices followed by a list of numbered phrases or sentences. For each numbered phrase or sentence, select the one choice that is most closely related to it. Each choice may be used once, more than once, or not at all in each group.

Questions 3–7
   (A) Peroxisomes
   (B) Golgi apparatus
   (C) Lysosomes
   (D) Endoplasmic reticulum
   (E) Mitochondria

3. An organelle that is characterized by extensive, folded membranes and is often associated with ribosomes

4. An organelle with a *cis* and *trans* face, which act as the packaging and secreting center of the cell

5. The sites of cellular respiration

6. Single-membrane structures in the cell that perform many metabolic functions and produce hydrogen peroxide

7. Large membrane-bound structures that contain hydrolytic enzymes and that are found predominantly in animal cells

8. Which of the following molecules is a typical component of an animal cell membrane?
   (A) starch
   (B) glucose
   (C) nucleic acids
   (D) carbohydrates
   (E) vitamin K

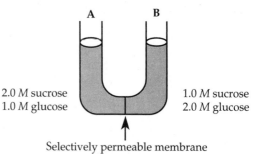

2.0 *M* sucrose
1.0 *M* glucose

1.0 *M* sucrose
2.0 *M* glucose

Selectively permeable membrane
U-Tube Setup

9. The drawing above shows two solutions of glucose and sucrose in a U-tube containing a semipermeable membrane (which allows the passage of sugars). Which of the following accurately describes what will take place next?
   (A) Glucose will diffuse from side A to side B.
   (B) Sucrose will diffuse from side B to side A.
   (C) No net movement of molecules will occur.
   (D) Glucose will diffuse from side B to side A.
   (E) There will be a net movement of water from side B to side A.

10. Which of the following is an example of passive transport across the cell membrane?
    (A) the stimulation of a muscle cell
    (B) the uptake of glucose by the microvilli of cells lining the stomach
    (C) the movement of insulin across the cell membrane
    (D) the movement of carbon dioxide across the cell membrane
    (E) the selective uptake of hormones across the cell membrane

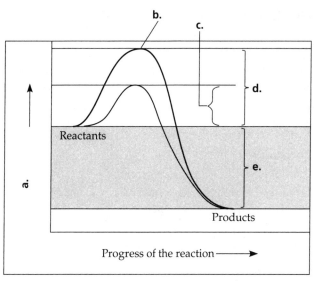

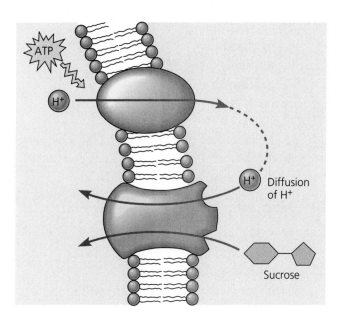

11. The figure above illustrates the process of
    (A) cotransport.
    (B) passive diffusion.
    (C) receptor-mediated endocytosis.
    (D) phagocytosis.
    (E) pinocytosis.

12. Large molecules are moved out of the cell by which of the following processes?
    (A) pinocytosis
    (B) phagocytosis
    (C) receptor-mediated endocytosis
    (D) cytokinesis
    (E) exocytosis

13. The above graph most accurately depicts the energy changes that take place in which of the following types of reaction?
    (A) hypothermic
    (B) hyperthermic
    (C) endergonic
    (D) exergonic
    (E) free range

14. Which of the following theories or laws states that every energy transfer increases the amount of entropy in the universe?
    (A) the free energy law
    (B) the first law of thermodynamics
    (C) the second law of thermodynamics
    (D) evolutionary theory
    (E) the law of increased chaos

15. Catalysts speed up chemical reactions by
    (A) decreasing the free energy change of the reaction.
    (B) increasing the free energy change of the reaction.
    (C) degrading the competitive inhibitors in a reaction.
    (D) lowering the activation energy of the reaction.
    (E) raising the activation energy of the reaction.

Directions: The group of questions below consists of five lettered choices followed by a list of numbered phrases or sentences. For each numbered phrase or sentence, select the one choice that is most closely related to it. Each choice may be used once, more than once, or not at all.

Questions 16–20
- (A) Allosteric inhibition
- (B) Feedback inhibition
- (C) Competitive inhibitor
- (D) Noncompetitive inhibitor
- (E) Cooperativity

16. Describes inhibition by an enzyme that is capable of either activating or inhibiting a metabolic pathway

17. A reversible inhibitor that looks similar to the normal substrate and competes for the active site of the enzyme

18. The process by which the binding of the substrate to the enzyme triggers a favorable conformation change, which causes a similar change in all of the proteins' subunits

19. The process by which a metabolic pathway is shut off by the product it produces

20. Binds to the enzyme at a site other than the active site, causing the enzyme to change shape and be unable to bind substrate

21. $A + B \rightarrow AB + Energy$
    Which of the following best characterizes the reaction represented above?
    - (A) metabolism
    - (B) anabolism
    - (C) catabolism
    - (D) endergonic reaction
    - (E) exergonic reaction

22. The purpose of cellular respiration in a eukaryotic cell is to
    - (A) synthesize carbohydrates from CO_2.
    - (B) synthesize fats and proteins from CO_2.
    - (C) break down carbohydrates to provide energy for the cell in the form of ATP.
    - (D) break down carbohydrates to provide energy for the cell in the form of ADP.
    - (E) provide oxygen to the cell.

$$2 K + Br_2 \rightarrow 2 K^+ + 2 Br^-$$

23. In the course of the above reaction, potassium is
    - (A) neutralized.
    - (B) oxidized.
    - (C) reduced.
    - (D) sublimated.
    - (E) recycled.

24. The net result of glycolysis is
    - (A) 4 ATP and 4 NADH.
    - (B) 4 ATP and 2 NADH.
    - (C) 2 ATP and 4 NADH.
    - (D) 2 ATP and 2 NADH.
    - (E) 4 ATP and 8 NADH.

25. In the course of the citric acid cycle, how many molecules of ATP are produced?
    - (A) 1
    - (B) 2
    - (C) 3
    - (D) 4
    - (E) 5

26. The process that produces the greatest amount of ATP during respiration is
    - (A) glycolysis.
    - (B) fermentation.
    - (C) the citric acid cycle.
    - (D) the electron transport chain.
    - (E) chemiosmosis and oxidative phosphorylation.

Directions: The group of questions below consists of five lettered choices followed by a list of numbered phrases or sentences. For each numbered phrase or sentence, select the one choice that is most closely related to it. Each choice may be used once, more than once, or not at all in each group.

Questions 27–31
   (A) Chemiosmosis
   (B) Electron transport chain
   (C) The citric acid cycle
   (D) Glycolysis
   (E) Fermentation

27. The process by which glucose is split into pyruvate

28. The process by which a hydrogen ion gradient is used to produce ATP

29. A process that makes a small amount of ATP and can produce lactic acid as a byproduct

30. A series of membrane-embedded electron carriers that ultimately create the hydrogen ion gradient to drive the synthesis of ATP

31. The process by which the breakdown of glucose is completed and CO_2 is produced

32. Muscle fatigue is caused when the process of fermentation in oxygen-depleted cells produces which of the following?
   (A) ADP
   (B) Ethanol
   (C) Lactic acid
   (D) Uric acid
   (E) Pyruvate

33. Groups of photosynthetic pigment molecules situated in the thylakoid membrane are called
   (A) photosystems.
   (B) carotenoids.
   (C) chlorophyll.
   (D) grana.
   (E) CAM plants.

34. The main products of the light reactions of photosynthesis are
   (A) NADPH and $FADH_2$.
   (B) NADPH and ATP.
   (C) ATP and $FADH_2$.
   (D) ATP and CO_2.
   (E) ATP and H_2O.

35. The process in photosynthesis that bears the most resemblance to chemiosmosis and oxidative phosphorylation in cell respiration is called
   (A) cyclic phosphorylation.
   (B) noncyclic photophosphorylation.
   (C) ATP synthase coupling.
   (D) preemptive photophosphorylation.
   (E) dark reaction phosphorylation.

36. The reactions of the Calvin cycle are also known as the dark reactions because these reactions
   (A) occur in plants only at night.
   (B) occur in dark-staining cells of plant leaves.
   (C) must absorb black light from the spectrum in order to proceed.
   (D) do not require light directly in order to proceed.
   (E) take place only during the day.

37. The major product of the Calvin cycle is
   (A) rubisco.
   (B) oxaloacetate.
   (C) ribulose bisphosphate.
   (D) pyruvate.
   (E) glyceraldehyde-3-phosphate.

38. All of the following statements are false EXCEPT
    (A) C_3 plants grow better in hot, arid conditions than do C_4 plants.
    (B) C_4 plants grow better in cold, moist conditions than do C_3 plants.
    (C) C_3 plants grow better in hot, arid conditions than do CAM plants.
    (D) CAM plants grow better in cold, moist conditions than do C_3 plants.
    (E) CAM plants and C_4 plants both grow better in hot, arid conditions than do C_3 plants.

39. All of the following statements about photosynthesis are true EXCEPT
    (A) the light reactions convert solar energy to chemical energy in the form of ATP and NADPH.
    (B) the Calvin cycle uses ATP and NADPH to convert CO_2 to sugar.
    (C) photosystem I contains P700 chlorophyll *a* molecules at the reaction center; photosystem II contains P680 molecules.
    (D) in chemiosmosis, electron transport chains pump protons (H^+) across a membrane from a region of high H^+ concentration to a region of low H^+ concentration.
    (E) the steps of the Calvin cycle are sometimes referred to as the dark reactions because they do not directly require light in order to take place.

40. In cell signaling, how is the flow of specific ions regulated?
    (A) opening and closing of ligand-gated ion channels
    (B) transduction
    (C) cytoskeleton rearrangement
    (D) endocytosis
    (E) phosphorylation cascades

Directions: The group of questions below consists of five lettered choices followed by a list of numbered phrases or sentences. For each numbered phrase or sentence, select the one choice that is most closely related to it. Each choice may be used once, more than once, or not at all in each group.

Questions 41–45
    (A) Telophase
    (B) Interphase
    (C) Cytokinesis
    (D) Prometaphase
    (E) Anaphase

41. Cytokinesis begins during this final stage of mitosis.

42. Division of the cytoplasm of the cell

43. Sister chromatids begin to separate.

44. The genetic material of the cell replicates to prepare for cell division.

45. Microtubules begin to attach to the centromeres of the sister chromatids.

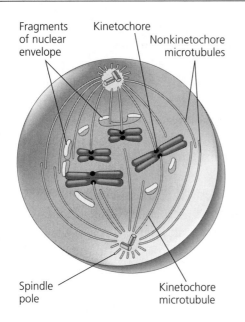

Fragments of nuclear envelope

Kinetochore

Nonkinetochore microtubules

Kinetochore

Spindle pole

Kinetochore microtubule

46. What stage of mitosis is represented in this figure?
(A) prophase
(B) prometaphase
(C) metaphase
(D) anaphase
(E) telophase

47. After which of the following checkpoints in the cell cycle is the cell most likely fated to divide?
(A) G_2 phase checkpoint
(B) M phase checkpoint
(C) interphase checkpoint
(D) G_1 phase checkpoint
(E) MPF checkpoint

Free-Response Question

1. *Prokaryotic and eukaryotic cells are physiologically different in many ways, but both represent functional collections of living matter.*

   (a) It has been theorized that the organelles of eukaryotic cells evolved from prokaryotes living symbiotically within a larger cell. Compare and contrast the structure of the prokaryotic cell with eukaryotic cell organelles, and make an argument for or against this theory.

   (b) Trace the path of a protein in a eukaryotic cell from its formation to its excretion from the cell.

ANSWERS AND EXPLANATIONS

Multiple-Choice Questions

▌ **1. (C) is correct.** Light microscopes are good for viewing objects that are 0.2 μm or larger. With a light microscope, you can observe animal and plant cells, some bacterial cells, and some larger organelles such as nuclei and mitochondria. To see the other organelles in the list of choices you would need an electron microscope.

▌ **2. (C) is correct.** The nucleoid region is the only cell structure on this list not found in both prokaryotes and eukaryotes. Eukaryotic cells have a true nucleus, which is surrounded by a membrane called a nuclear envelope. The genetic material of prokaryotes is localized in a clump in one particular region of the cell that is not enclosed by a membrane. Both prokaryotes and eukaryotes contain a plasma membrane, cytoplasm, DNA associated with proteins, and cilia (although not all eukaryotes and prokaryotes possess all the cell structures listed).

▌ **3. (D) is correct.** The endoplasmic reticulum (ER) is an organelle characterized by extensive, folded membranes, and it is often associated with ribosomes. It is a site of protein synthesis, because the ribosomes associated with rough ER are protein-producing.

4. (B) is correct. The Golgi apparatus is the organelle that has a *cis* and *trans* face, and it acts as the packaging and secreting center of the cell. It consists of a series of flattened sacs of membranes called cisternae.

5. (E) is correct. Mitochondria are the powerhouses of the cell; cellular respiration takes place in the mitochondria, forming ATP, the cell's energy currency. Mitochondria are bound by double membranes, and the proteins involved in ATP production are embedded in the inner membranes of the mitochondria.

6. (A) is correct. Peroxisomes perform many metabolic functions in the cell, including the production of hydrogen peroxide.

7. (C) is correct. Lysosomes are characteristic of animal cells but not most plant cells. They are large membrane-bound structures that contain hydrolytic enzymes, and they are responsible for the breakdown of proteins, polysaccharides, fats, and nucleic acids. They function best at a low pH (around 5), so they pump hydrogen ions from the cytosol into their lumen to maintain this acidic pH.

8. (D) is correct. The only answer choice listed that names a molecule typically found in the plasma membranes of animal cells is *D*, carbohydrates. The major components of animal cell membranes are phospholipids, integral and peripheral proteins, and carbohydrates. One of the main functions of carbohydrates in the cell membrane is cell-cell recognition, which means carbohydrates are an important component of the immune system. Cell surface carbohydrates are unique to each organism.

9. (D) is correct. Substances will move down their concentration gradient until their concentration is equal on either side of a membrane. For this reason, because the concentration of glucose on side B of the tube is 2.0 *M*, while the concentration of glucose on the A side of the tube is 1.0 *M*, glucose will move to side A.

10. (D) is correct. The only substance listed that can passively diffuse through the cell membrane is carbon dioxide. Remember that passive diffusion occurs without the cell doing any work, and that the substances that can passively diffuse across the membrane are small nonpolar molecules, such as carbohydrates, carbon dioxide, and oxygen. Other substances need the processes of facilitated diffusion and the help of transport proteins to cross the membrane. This is true of all of the answer choices listed except for *D*.

11. (A) is correct. This figure illustrates the process of cotransport. In cotransport, a pump that is powered by ATP transports a specific solute—in this case protons—out of the cell. The protons then travel down their concentration gradient back into the cell, passing through another transport protein and indirectly providing energy for the movement of another substance (sucrose in this case) against its concentration gradient and out of the cell.

12. (E) is correct. Large molecules are moved out of the cell by exocytosis. In exocytosis, vesicles that are to be exported from the cell (usually coming from the Golgi apparatus) fuse with the plasma membrane, and their contents are expelled into the extracellular matrix. Pinocytosis, phagocytosis, and receptor-mediated endocytosis are types of endocytosis; cytokinesis is cell division.

13. (D) is correct. The shape of the curve in the art shown most closely depicts an exergonic reaction. The potential energy of the products is lower than that of the reactants—meaning that in the course of the reaction, energy is given off. This is characteristic of exergonic reactions. Conversely, in an endergonic reaction, energy is taken in during the course of the reaction.

14. (C) is correct. The second law of thermodynamics states that every energy transfer that occurs increases the amount of entropy in the universe. The first law of thermodynamics states that the amount of energy in the universe is constant, and therefore energy can be neither created nor destroyed. Evolutionary theory refers to the myriad changes that have taken place to transform living organisms from the beginning of life on Earth until today.

15. (D) is correct. Catalysts speed up chemical reactions by providing an alternate reaction pathway that lowers the activation energy of the reaction. Less energy is required to start the reaction, so it runs more quickly.

16. (A) is correct. In allosteric regulation, the enzyme is usually composed of more than one polypeptide chain with more than one allosteric site (remote from the active site), and the enzyme usually oscillates between an inactive conformation and an active one. When an allosteric activator binds to the allosteric site, the protein assumes a stable conformation with a functional active site, and the reaction can proceed. When an allosteric inhibitor binds, this stabilizes the inactive conformation of the protein.

17. (C) is correct. Competitive inhibitors bind to the active site of the enzyme through covalent bonds. They are able to bind because they closely resemble the normal substrate. One way to overcome the effects of competitive inhibitors is to increase the amount of substrate so that chances are greater that a substrate molecule (rather than the competitive inhibitor) will bind.

18. (E) is correct. In cooperativity, the enzyme in question has more than one subunit with more than one active site, and it is able to bind more than one substrate—so multiple reactions can be taking place at once in the enzyme. The binding of one substrate molecule to the enzyme causes a conformation change that makes the binding of other substrate molecules, at the other active sites, more favorable.

19. (B) is correct. In feedback inhibition, the product of a metabolic pathway switches off the pathway by binding to and inhibiting an enzyme involved somewhere along the pathway.

20. (D) is correct. In noncompetitive inhibition, the inhibitor binds to a site other than the active site of the enzyme, and this causes the enzyme to change shape. The change in conformation makes the substrate unable to bind to the active site of the enzyme, and this prevents the reaction from taking place.

21. (E) is correct. The reaction shown here is an exergonic reaction. An exergonic reaction is a spontaneous chemical reaction in which there is a net release of free energy. Energy is given off in the course of the reaction shown.

22. (C) is correct. The purpose of cellular respiration in eukaryotes is to produce energy for cellular work in the form of ATP. Respiration is an aerobic process, meaning that it requires oxygen. Answer choices *A* and *B* are incorrect because respiration involves the breakdown (not the synthesis) of carbohydrates, fats, and proteins. Choice *D* is wrong because ADP is the product of the dephosphorylation of ATP—it is left over after the energy from ATP has been released. Choice *E* is wrong because oxygen is required for cellular respiration.

23. (B) is correct. In the course of the reaction shown, potassium (K) is oxidized. Oxidation involves the loss of an electron. Reduction is the gain of an electron by an atom or molecule. In this reaction, potassium is the reducing agent; it reduces bromide and becomes oxidized. Bromide is the oxidizing agent; it becomes reduced when it receives an electron from potassium.

24. (D) is correct. The net energy result of glycolysis is the production of two molecules of ATP and two molecules of NADH. Glycolysis is the first of the three stages of respiration—the second being the citric acid cycle and the third being chemiosmosis and oxidative phosphorylation. During glycolysis, glucose is broken down and oxidized to form pyruvate. Glycolysis occurs in the cytosol, and the pyruvate it produces travels to the mitochondria where it is used in the citric acid cycle.

25. (D) is correct. In the citric acid cycle, 2 ATP are produced. The citric acid cycle takes in a molecule called acetyl CoA (pyruvate is converted into acetyl CoA before it enters the citric acid cycle), and this is joined to a four-carbon molecule of oxaloacetate to form a six-carbon compound citrate that is then broken down again to produce oxaloacetate; the oxaloacetate reenters the cycle. In the course of the citric acid cycle, the following are produced: 4 CO_2, 2 ATP, 6 NADH, and 2 $FADH_2$.

26. (E) is correct. The process that produces the most ATP during cellular respiration is chemiosmosis and oxidative phosphorylation. $FADH_2$ and NADH donate electrons to the electron transport chain, which is coupled to ATP synthesis by chemiosmosis; the movement of electrons down the electron transport chain creates an H^+ gradient across the mitochondrial membrane, which drives the synthesis of ATP from ADP. About 34 ATP are produced per glucose molecule.

27. (D) is correct. In glycolysis, glucose is oxidized to two molecules of pyruvate. This is the first step in cellular respiration, and it also produces 2 ATP and 2 NADH.

28. (A) is correct. In chemiosmosis, the hydrogen ion gradient created by the transfer of electrons in the electron transport chain provides the power to synthesize ATP from ADP.

29. (E) is correct. Fermentation is an anaerobic alternative to cellular respiration. It consists of glycolysis and several reactions that serve to regenerate NAD^+; electrons are transferred from NADH to pyruvate or its derivatives, and the NAD^+ oxidizes sugar in glycolysis. There are two main types of fermentation—alcohol fermentation (which creates ethanol as a product) and lactic acid fermentation (which creates lactate).

30. (B) is correct. The electron transport chain is a series of inner mitochondrial matrix membrane-embedded molecules that are capable of being oxidized and reduced as they pass along electrons. The energy produced from the passage of these electrons down the chain is used to create an H^+ gradient across the membrane, and the flow of H^+ down the gradient and back across the membrane powers the phosphorylation reaction of ADP to form ATP.

31. (C) is correct. The citric acid cycle includes the final reactions for the breakdown of glucose that began in glycolysis. The pyruvate from glycolysis is converted into acetyl CoA, which enters the cycle and is joined to oxaloacetate to create citrate, which is then converted to oxaloacetate again and reused. This cycle gives off CO_2, and forms 1 ATP, 3 NADH, and 1 $FADH_2$. The cycle goes through one rotation to break down each of the molecules of pyruvate produced in glycolysis (which of course is first converted to acetyl CoA), so the net result of the breakdown of one glucose molecule is 2 ATP, 6 NADH, and 2 $FADH_2$.

32. (C) is correct. When muscle cells in the body are depleted of oxygen, they switch from cellular respiration to lactic acid fermentation. In lactic acid fermentation, NADH reduces pyruvate directly, and lactate is formed as a waste product. This lactic acid fermentation occurs when all of the cell's metabolic machinery is using available oxygen to break down sugars in the cell. The lactate that builds up in the cell as the waste product from fermentation is broken down again when it is filtered through the liver.

33. (A) is correct. Groups of photosynthetic pigment molecules in the thylakoid membrane are called photosystems. The two photosystems involved in photosynthesis are photosystem I and photosystem II. Both contain chlorophyll molecules and many proteins and other organic molecules, and both have a light-harvesting complex that harnesses incoming light. Each of these photosystems contains a reaction center, where chlorophyll *a* and the primary electron acceptor are located. Photosystem II is the site of the first redox reaction of photosynthesis.

34. (B) is correct. The main products of the light reactions of photosynthesis are NADPH and ATP. This ATP and NADPH is used to convert CO_2 to sugar in the Calvin cycle; the enzyme rubisco combines the CO_2 with ribulose bisphosphate (RuBP), and electrons from NADPH and energy from ATP are used to synthesize a three-carbon molecule called glyerceralde-3-phosphate—some of which leaves the cycle and is used to make various carbohydrates for the plant.

35. (B) is correct. The process in the dark reactions of photosynthesis that bears the closest resemblance to chemiosmosis and oxidative phosphorylation in cellular respiration is noncyclic photophosphorylation. In this process, energy from the transfer of electrons down the electron transport chain is generated with the help of proteins embedded in the thylakoid membrane wall. Later, the energy stored in this ATP is used during the formation of carbohydrates in the Calvin cycle.

36. (D) is correct. The Calvin cycle reactions are also called dark reactions because they do not need light directly. In fact, the Calvin cycle works mainly during the day in plants because the products of the light reactions (which are necessary for the Calvin cycle to proceed) are created during the day. The two sets of reactions are coordinated in the chloroplast.

37. (E) is correct. The organic product of the Calvin cycle, which is later used to build large carbohydrates in the cell, is glyceraldehyde-3-phosphate, or G3P. This molecule is created as a result of the fixation of three molecules of CO_2, which costs the cell ATP and NADPH that were created in the light reactions of photosynthesis.

38. (E) is correct. C_4 and CAM plants both grow better than do C_3 plants under conditions of increased median air temperature and decreased relative humidity. Both C_4 and CAM plants use an alternative method of carbon fixation that enables them to fix carbon into an acid intermediate for later deposit into the Calvin cycle.

39. (D) is correct. The electron transport chains pump protons across membranes from regions of low H^+ concentrations to regions of high H^+ concentrations. This proton pumping occurs in both mitochondria and chloroplasts, and the protons then diffuse (with the concentration gradient) back across the membrane (through ATP synthases); this drives the synthesis of ATP.

40. (A) is correct. When a signal molecule binds to the receptor protein, the gate of the ion channel opens or closes, allowing or blocking the flow of specific ions.

41. (A) is correct. In telophase, nuclear envelopes begin to form around the sets of chromosomes, which are now located at opposite ends of the cell. The chromatin becomes less condensed, and cytokinesis begins—the cytoplasm of the cell is divided.

42. (C) is correct. During cytokinesis, the cytoplasm of the cell is divided approximately equally as the cell membrane pinches off (in animal cells), forming two daughter cells; a cell plate forms in plant cells.

43. (E) is correct. In anaphase, the sister chromatids, which were lined up along the equator of the cell, begin to separate, pulled apart by the retracting microtubules. By the end of anaphase, the opposite ends of the cell contain complete and equal sets of chromosomes.

44. (B) is correct. Interphase is not a part of mitosis; rather it is the part of the cell cycle when the cell gets ready to divide by replicating its DNA. There are three stages in interphase—G_1 phase, S phase, and G_2 phase.

45. (D) is correct. Prometaphase is the phase of mitosis in which the nuclear envelope begins to fragment so that the microtubules can begin to attach to the kinetochores of the chromatids, which by this time are very condensed.

46. (B) is correct. The depicted cell is in prometaphase. As you can see, the nuclear envelope is fragmenting, and the microtubules have already attached to some of the kinetochores at the centromeres of the chromosomes. The chromosomes are condensed and beginning to line up along the cell's equator.

47. (D) is correct. The most crucial checkpoint of the cell cycle is the G_1 checkpoint. In the cell cycle, a checkpoint is a point at which there can be a signal to stop or to go ahead with division. If a cell receives the signal to go ahead at the G_1 checkpoint, it will usually complete the cycle and divide. If it does not receive the go-ahead signal, it will enter the (nondividing) G_0 phase for an indeterminate period of time.

Free-Response Question

(a) Some eukaryotic cell organelles might have evolved from free-living prokaryotic organisms. First of all, prokaryotic cells are much smaller than eukaryotic cells—they range from 100 nm to 10 µm, compared to the average size of eukaryotic cells: 10 µm–100 µm. However, mitochondria (organelles unique to eukaryotic cells, and functioning in the creation of ATP in cellular respiration) and eukaryotic cell nuclei are comparable in size to prokaryotic cells, ranging from about 1 µm–10 µm.

Another interesting characteristic of organelles that may tie them to prokaryotes is their structure and cell contents. To illustrate this, let's consider the structure of mitochondria. With few exceptions, mitochondria are found in all animal cells, plant cells, fungi, and protists. They can exist in great numbers in these cells, or cells can contain just one mitochondrion (depending on the metabolic activity of the cell). It has been observed that mitochondria can move around, alter their shape, and even divide in two—all of which are characteristic of living cells. Their structure consists of a double membrane exterior (the membrane is a typical combination of phospholipids and proteins, like the membrane of the cell itself); the outer membrane is relatively smooth, but the interior membrane has infoldings called cristae. This creates two different compartments in mitochondria: the inner compartment is the mitochondrial matrix, and the compartment in between the two membranes is called the intermembrane space. Mitochondria also contain mitochondrial DNA. Not very much DNA is contained in mitochondria, but the presence of DNA could be evidence that they were independent organisms at some time. Also similar to prokaryotes, mitochondria do not contain many interior structures other than their genetic material (which is not enclosed in a nucleus) and their cell membranes. All of the above indicates a close evolutionary relationship between prokaryotic cells and mitochondria.

(b) In order to trace the path of proteins in the cell from their creation to their expulsion, we must start in the nucleus. The nucleus can be thought of as the brain of the cell because it directs the actions of the cell. In the nucleus, mRNA is created from the transcription of DNA, and mRNA travels out of the nucleus to the cytoplasm, ending up at ribosomes, some of which are associated with the endoplasmic reticulum (called rough endoplasmic reticulum because of this association). Here they are translated into proteins, which then undergo folding to assume their final shape, or conformation. Proteins then either carry out their metabolic function in the cell, whether they act as structural components, enzymes, etc., or they are packaged for secretion from the cell.

Secretory proteins travel from the endoplasmic reticulum to the series of flattened membranous sacs known as the Golgi apparatus. They enter at the *cis* face, where they bud off in vesicles from fold to fold through the length of the Golgi, to eventually bud from the *trans* face, after undergoing a series of modifications to prepare them for secretion. The vesicles may then fuse with the cell membrane, and the contents are exocytosed to the cell's exterior.

This response shows that the writer used the following key terms in context, showing the writer's knowledge of their meanings and relatedness:

organelles	*mRNA*
prokaryote	*ribosomes*
eukaryote	*endoplasmic reticulum*
mitochondria	*conformation*
phospholipids	*enzymes*
proteins	*secretory proteins*
cristae	*Golgi apparatus*
mitochondrial matrix	cis/trans *face*
DNA	*vesicle*

The response also contains an explanation of the following subjects and processes:

—*size comparison of prokaryotes and eukaryotes (with data)*
—*structure, content, and behavior of prokaryotes versus mitochondria*
—*location of transcription and translation*
—*pathway of proteins*

CHAPTER 3

Genetics

Concept 13.1 Offspring acquire genes from parents by inheriting chromosomes

▌ **Heredity,** or inheritance, is defined as the transmission of traits from one generation to the next.

▌ **Genetics** is the study of heredity and variation. **Variation** is the genetic differences between siblings or other members of the same species.

▌ **Genes** are segments of DNA—the basic units of heredity that are transmitted from one generation to the next. In animals and plants, reproductive cells that transmit genes from one generation to the next are called **gametes.**

▌ The location of a gene on the chromosome is called its **locus** (plural, loci).

▌ **Asexual reproduction** is a form of reproduction in which a single parent is involved in passing on all of its genes to its offspring. Some organisms capable of reproducing asexually are some single-celled eukaryotes and hydra (which are related to the jellyfish). Asexually produced organisms are similar in appearance.

▌ In **sexual reproduction,** two individuals (parents) contribute genes. This form of reproduction results in greater genetic variation in the offspring than asexual reproduction.

Concept 13.2 Fertilization and meiosis alternate in sexual life cycles

▌ A **life cycle** is the generation-to-generation sequence of stages in the reproductive history of an organism, from conception to production of its own offspring.

▌ **Somatic cells** are any cells in the body that are not gametes. They are the body cells of an organism. Each somatic cell in humans has 46 chromosomes.

▌ The **karyotype** of an organism refers to a picture of its complete set of chromosomes, arranged in pairs of homologous chromosomes from the largest pair to the smallest pair. **Homologous chromosomes** are those that carry the genes that control the same traits. They are similar in length and centromere position, and they have the same staining pattern. One homologous chromosome from each pair is inherited from each parent; in other words, half of the set of 46 chromosomes in your somatic cells was inherited from your mother, and the other half was inherited from your father.

▌ Exceptions to the rule that all chromosomes are part of a homologous pair are the sex chromosomes—in humans, it is the **X and Y.** Human females have a homologous pair of chromosomes, XX, but males have one X chromosome and one Y chromosome. Nonsex chromosomes are called **autosomes.**

- Gametes—meaning sperm and ova (eggs)—are **haploid cells.** That is, they contain half the number of chromosomes of somatic cells. They contain 22 autosomes plus a single sex chromosome (either X or Y) giving them a haploid number of 23. The haploid number of chromosomes is symbolized by n.
- During **fertilization** (a combination of a sperm cell and an egg cell), one haploid gamete from each parent fuse. The result is a fertilized egg called a **zygote.** It is **diploid** (has two sets of chromosomes), as are all the somatic cells of an organism, which are derived from the zygote. The diploid number of chromosomes is symbolized by $2n$.
- **Meiosis** is the process by which, in the course of gamete production, the chromosome number is halved so haploid gametes are formed. Fertilization restores the diploid number as the gametes are combined. Fertilization and meiosis alternate in the life cycles of sexually reproducing organisms. There are three types of sexual life cycles:

  1. In humans and most animals, meiosis occurs during gamete production, and the diploid zygote divides by mitosis to produce a diploid multicellular organism.
  2. In fungi, some protists, and algae, after gametes fuse to form the diploid zygote, meiosis occurs to produce haploid cells. These cells then divide by mitosis, forming a haploid, multicellular organism.
  3. In plants and some algae, **alternation of generations** occurs, including a haploid and diploid stage in the life cycle. The diploid stage is the **sporophyte.** Meiosis in the diploid phase creates haploid spores, which divide mitotically to produce a **gametophyte.** The gametophyte produces haploid gametes through mitosis, and the fertilization occurs, producing a diploid zygote.

Concept 13.3 Meiosis reduces the number of chromosome sets from diploid to haploid

- Meiosis and mitosis look similar—both are preceded by the replication of the cell's DNA, for instance, but in meiosis this replication is followed by two stages of cell division, meiosis I and meiosis II.
- The final result of meiosis is four **daughter cells,** each of which has half as many chromosomes as the parent cell.

The stages of meiosis are as follows:

- **Interphase:** Each of the chromosomes replicate, resulting in two sister chromatids attached at their centromeres. The centrosomes also replicate during this phase.
- **Prophase I:** The chromosomes condense, and the homologues (consisting of two sister chromatids) pair up. Synapsis occurs—that is, the joining of two pairs of homologous chromosomes along their length. This newly formed structure is called a tetrad. It has four chromatids. Parts of the homologous chromosomes undergo crossing over at chiasmata (places at which homologous

chromosomes overlap during synapsis). The centrioles move away from each other, the nuclear envelope disintegrates, and spindle microtubules attach to the kinetochores forming on the chromosomes that begin to move to the metaphase plate of the cell.

- **Metaphase I:** The homologous pairs of chromosomes are lined up at the metaphase plate, and microtubules from each pole attach to each member of the homologous pairs in preparation for pulling them to opposite ends of the cell.
- **Anaphase I:** The spindle apparatus helps to move the chromosomes toward opposite ends of the cell; sister chromatids stay connected and move together toward the poles.
- **Telophase I** and **cytokinesis:** The homologous chromosomes move until they reach the opposite poles. Each pole, then, contains a haploid set of chromosomes, with each chromosome still consisting of two sister chromatids. Cytokinesis occurs at the same time as telophase—a **cleavage furrow** occurs in animal cells, and **cell plates** occur in plant cells. Both result in the formation of two haploid cells.
- **Prophase II:** A spindle apparatus forms, and sister chromatids move toward the metaphase plate.
- **Metaphase II:** The chromosomes are lined up on the metaphase plate, and the kinetochores of each sister chromatid prepare to move to the opposite poles.
- **Anaphase II:** The centromeres of the sister chromatids separate, and individual chromosomes move to opposite ends of the cell.
- **Telophase II** and **cytokinesis:** The chromatids have moved all the way to opposite ends of the cell, nuclei reappear, and cytokinesis occurs. Each of the four daughter cells has the haploid number of chromosomes and is genetically different from the other daughter cells and from the parent cell.
- Three events occur during meiosis I that do not occur during mitosis.
  - Synapsis and crossing over normally do not occur during mitosis.
  - At metaphase I, paired homologous chromosomes (tetrads) are positioned on the metaphase plate, rather than individual replicated chromosomes, as in mitosis.
  - At anaphase I, duplicated chromosomes of each homologous pair move toward opposite poles, but the sister chromatids of each duplicated chromosome stay attached. In mitosis, the chromatids separate.

Concept 13.4 Genetic variation produced in sexual life cycles contributes to evolution

Following are some processes that contribute to variation in the offspring of sexually reproducing organisms:

- **Independent assortment of chromosomes**—In metaphase I, when the homologous chromosomes are lined up on the metaphase plate, they can pair up in any combination, with any of the homologous pairs facing either pole. This means that there is a 50-50 chance that a particular daughter cell will get a maternal chromosome or a paternal chromosome from the homologous pair.

■ **Crossing over**—After prophase I, homologous chromosomes synapse and the homologous chromosomes exchange homologous parts of two nonsister chromatids. Then during metaphase II, chromosomes that now have recombinant chromatids can face either of two poles with respect to each other, which further increases variation in reproduction.

■ **Random fertilization**—Fertilization is random. Because each egg and sperm is different, as a result of independent assortment and crossing over, each combination of egg and sperm is unique.

Concept 14.1 Mendel used the scientific approach to identify two laws of inheritance

■ In genetics, a **character** is a heritable feature, such as flower color. Each variant for a character, such as purple or white flowers, is called a **trait.**

■ **True-breeding** refers to a phenomenon such as this one: When a pea plant is self-pollinated, all the offspring are of the same type. In other words, a true-breeding white pea plant would produce only white pea plant offspring. The crossing (or mating) of two true-breeding varieties of an organism is called **hybridization.**

■ The true-breeding parents in a hybridization are called the **P (parental) generation;** their offspring are called the **F$_1$ (first filial) generation.** If the F$_1$ population is crossed, their offspring are called the **F$_2$ (second filial) generation.**

The following are four related concepts that make up Mendel's model explaining the 3:1 inheritance pattern that he observed among F$_2$ offspring.

- **Alternative versions of genes cause variations in inherited characteristics among offspring.** For example, consider flower color in peas. The gene for flower color in pea plants comes in two versions: white and purple. These alternative versions of the gene, called **alleles,** are the result of slightly different DNA content at homologous loci on chromosomes.

- **For each character, every organism inherits one allele from each parent.**

- **If the two alleles are different, then the** *dominant allele* **will be fully expressed in the offspring, while the** *recessive allele* **will have no noticeable effect on the offspring.**

- **The two alleles for each character separate during gamete production.** If the parent has two of the same alleles, then the offspring will all get that version of the gene, but if the parent has two different alleles for a gene, each offspring has a 50% chance of getting one of the two alleles. This is Mendel's **law of segregation.**

■ Another of Mendel's laws is the **law of independent assortment.** It states that each pair of alleles will segregate (separate) independently during gamete formation.

■ **Homozygous** organisms have two of the same alleles for a particular trait. If the dominant allele for a trait is designated as *R* (dominant traits are generally capitalized), and the recessive allele is designated *r* (recessive traits are generally not capitalized), then an individual homozygous for the dominant trait would be *RR*.

■ A **heterozygous** organism has two different alleles for a trait (*Rr*).

■ **Phenotype** refers to an organism's expressed physical traits.

■ **Genotype** refers to an organism's genetic makeup.

■ **Testcross** refers to the crossing of a recessive homozygote with an individual exhibiting the dominant phenotype, in order to find out if the organism is homozygous dominant or heterozygous.

■ A **monohybrid cross** is a cross involving the study of only one character (e.g., flower color).

■ A **dihybrid cross** is a cross intended to study two characters (e.g., seed color and seed shape).

The following diagram shows the results of a monohybrid cross between two plants: one with white flowers that is homozygous recessive (*pp*), and one with purple flowers that is homozygous dominant (*PP*).

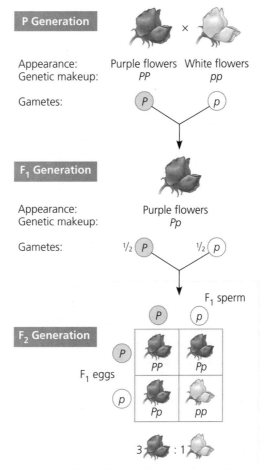

Figure 14.5   Mendel's law of segregation

The diagram below shows the results of a dihybrid cross. In this case, in the parental generation two homozygous plants are crossed: one homozygous dominant for purple flowers and yellow seeds (*PPYY*) and one homozygous recessive for white flowers and green seeds (*ppyy*). The only gamete type the first parent can produce is *PY*, and the only gamete the second parent can produce is *py*. The F$_1$ generation, therefore, is composed of individuals with genotype *PpYy*. This gene combination is called a dihybrid genotype. Crossing *PpYy* gives an F$_2$ generation that looks like this:

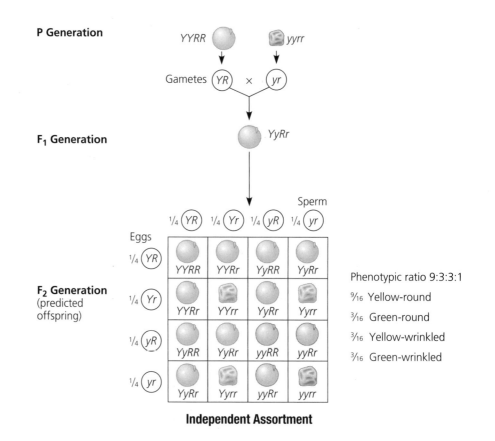

Independent Assortment

Concept 14.2 *The laws of probability govern Mendelian inheritance*

Understanding how to predict genetic crosses involves familiarity with the basic laws of probability. There are two laws that you will use directly in solving genetics problems.

▌ **The rule of multiplication:** When calculating the probability that two or more independent events will occur together in a specific combination, multiply the probabilities of each of the two events. Thus, the probability of a coin landing face up two times in two flips is: ½ × ½ = ¼. If you cross two organisms with the genotypes *AABbCc* and *AaBbCc*, the probability of an offspring having the genotype *AaBbcc* is ½ × ½ × ¼ = ⅟₁₆.

- **The rule of addition:** When calculating the probability that any of two or more mutually exclusive events will occur you need to add together their individual probabilities. For example if you are tossing a die, what is the probability that it will land on either the side with 4 spots or the side with 5 spots?

$$\tfrac{1}{6} + \tfrac{1}{6} = \tfrac{1}{3}.$$

Concept 14.3 Inheritance patterns are often more complex than predicted by simple Mendelian genetics

- **Complete dominance** is dominance in which the heterozygote and the homozygote for the dominant allele are indistinguishable.
- **Codominance** occurs when two alleles are dominant and affect the phenotype in two different but equal ways. The traditional example for this type of dominance is human blood types.
- **Incomplete dominance** is a type of dominance in which the F_1 hybrids have an appearance that is in between that of the two parents. For example, if two plants, one with white flowers and one with red flowers, were crossed and all of the offspring had pink flowers, one could conclude that the trait for flower color exhibits incomplete dominance. Breeding two of the hybrids with incomplete dominance gives a flower ratio of 1 red:2 pink:1 white.
- Most genes exist in different forms—that is, **multiple alleles.** Again, a good example of this is seen in human blood types. The chart below will help you familiarize yourself with blood types.

Phenotype	Genotype	Antibodies Expressed
A	$I^A I^A$ or $I^A i$	Anti-B
B	$I^B I^B$ or $I^B i$	Anti-A
AB	$I^A I^B$	None
O	ii	Anti-A, Anti-B

- **Pleiotropy** is the property of a gene that causes it to have multiple phenotypic effects.
- In **epistasis,** a gene at one locus alters the effects of a gene at another locus.
- In **polygenic inheritance,** two or more genes have an additive effect on a single character in the phenotype (such as height or skin color in humans).

Concept 14.4 Many human traits follow Mendelian patterns of inheritance

- A **pedigree** is a diagram—basically a family tree—that shows the relationship between parents and offspring across two or more generations. In a typical pedigree, circles represent women, and squares represent men. White open circles or squares indicate that the individual did not or does not express a particular trait, whereas black indicates that the individual expresses or expressed that trait. Through the patterns they reveal, pedigrees can help determine the genome of individuals that comprise them; pedigrees can also help predict the genome of future offspring.

- Genes that cause **recessively inherited disorders** are inherited as any other recessive genes. For example, alleles that cause genetic disorders may code for a dysfunctional protein or for no protein at all. Heterozygotes that inherit one copy of the mutant allele and one copy of the normal allele usually have a normal phenotype, because the normal allele can usually code for the production of enough protein to make up for the mutant allele's function, or lack thereof. Heterozygotes with the normal phenotype but who carry one mutant allele are called **carriers.**
- **Cystic fibrosis** is caused by a mutation in an allele that codes for a certain cell membrane protein that functions in the transport of chloride ions into and out of cells.
- **Tay-Sachs** disease is caused by an allele that codes for a dysfunctional enzyme, which is unable to break down certain lipids in the brain.
- **Sickle-cell disease** is caused by an allele that codes for a mutant hemoglobin molecule that forms long rods when the oxygen levels in the blood are low.
- **Lethal dominant alleles** are much less common than lethal recessive alleles. Because the lethal allele usually kills offspring before they are mature and can reproduce, the lethal allele is not passed on to the next generation.
- Usually, only late-acting lethal alleles are passed on. One example of this is the allele for Huntington's disease, which usually doesn't affect the individual until he or she is over 40 years old.

Concept 15.1 *Mendelian inheritance has its physical basis in the behavior of chromosomes*

- In the early 1900s, the **chromosome theory of inheritance** was formed. It stated that genes have specific locations (called loci) on chromosomes and that it is chromosomes that segregate and assort independently.
- After the chromosome theory of inheritance was formed, Thomas Hunt Morgan discovered the existence of sex-linked genes. A **sex-linked gene** is one located on a sex chromosome (X or Y in humans).

Concept 15.2 *Linked genes tend to be inherited together because they are located near each other on the same chromosome*

- **Linked genes** are those located on the same chromosome that tend to be inherited together during cell division.
- **Genetic recombination** is the production of offspring with a new combination of genes inherited from the parents.
- **Parental types** receive nonrecombinant genes, and their phenotype matches that of one of the parents. **Recombinants** are individuals who receive new combinations of genes from their parents.
- During meiosis, unlinked genes follow independent assortment because they are located on different chromosomes. Linked genes are located on the same chromosome and would not seem to follow independent assortment. However, recombinations of linked genes are explained by crossing over. The farther apart two genes are on a chromosome, the higher the probability that a crossover event will occur between them and, therefore, the higher the recombination frequency.

- Geneticists use recombination data to construct a **genetic map,** which is an ordered list of the genes and their loci along a particular chromosome.
- A **linkage map** is a genetic map that is based on recombination frequencies, and map units are used to express distances along the chromosome. One **map unit** is equal to a 1% recombination frequency.

Concept 15.3 Sex-linked genes exhibit unique patterns of inheritance

- In humans, there are two types of sex chromosomes, X and Y. Normal females have two X chromosomes, whereas normal males have one X and one Y chromosome.
- In the testes and ovaries, the sex chromosomes segregate as any other chromosome pair would, into separate gametes during meiosis. Each ovum contains an X chromosome; there are two types of sperm—those with an X chromosome and those with a Y chromosome. In fertilization, there is a 50-50 chance that a sperm carrying an X or Y will reach and penetrate the egg first. Thus, gender is determined by chance and by the male sperm cell in humans.
- Sex-linked genes carry genes for many characters that are not related to sex. This is especially true of the X chromosome, so the term "sex-linked" is usually used for genes that are found on the X chromosome, rather than the Y.
- Fathers pass sex-linked genes on to their daughters but not to their sons.
- Females will express a sex-linked trait only if they are homozygous for it, but because males have only one X chromosome, if they have the sex-linked gene, there will be no other normal X chromosome allele to mask the effects of the mutant, and so they will express the trait.
- **Duchenne muscular dystrophy** is a sex-linked disorder characterized by a progressive weakening of muscle tissue, caused by the absence of a muscle protein called dystrophin.
- **Hemophilia** is a sex-linked disorder characterized by having blood with an inability to clot normally, caused by the absence of proteins required for blood clotting.
- Although female mammals inherit two X chromosomes, one of the X chromosomes (randomly chosen) in each cell of the body becomes inactivated during embryonic development. As a result, males and females have the same effective dose of genes with loci on the X chromosome.
- The inactive chromosome condenses into a Barr body, which lies along the inside of the nuclear envelope. Still, females are not affected as heterozygote carriers of problematic alleles, because half of their sex chromosomes are normal and produce the necessary protein.

Concept 15.4 Alterations of chromosome number or structure cause some genetic disorders

- When the members of a pair of homologous chromosomes do not separate properly during meiosis I, or sister chromatids don't separate properly during meiosis II, **nondisjunction** occurs.

- As a result of nondisjunction, one gamete receives two copies of the gene, while the other gamete receives none. In the next step, if the faulty gametes engage in fertilization, the offspring will have an incorrect chromosome number. This is known as **aneuploidy.**
- Fertilized eggs that have received three copies of the chromosome in question are said to be **trisomic;** those that have received just one copy of a chromosome are said to be **monosomic** for the chromosome.
- If nondisjunction occurs during mitosis during early embryonic development, the error will be passed on to a large number of the organism's cells and have a significant effect on the organism.
- **Polyploidy** is the condition of having more than two complete sets of chromosomes, and this is somewhat common in plants.
- **Deletion** occurs when a chromosomal fragment lacking a centromere is lost. The affected chromosome is then missing certain genes.
- If the chromosome fragment that broke off (causing the deletion above) becomes attached to its sister chromatid, this causes a **duplication.** In this case, the zygote will get a double dose of the genes located on that chromosome.
- An **inversion** occurs when a chromosome fragment breaks off and reattaches to its original position—but backward, so that the part of the fragment that was originally at the attachment point is now at the end of the chromosome.
- A **translocation** occurs when the deleted chromosome fragment joins a nonhomologous chromosome. This moves a segment of one chromosome to a nonhomologous chromosome. A translocation can be reciprocal—that is, the nonhomologous chromosome can exchange segments.

Human disorders caused by chromosome alterations include:

- **Down syndrome**—an aneuploid condition that is the result of having an extra chromosome 21. (People affected are trisomic for 21.)
- **Klinefelter syndrome**—an aneuploid condition in which a male possesses the sex chromosomes XXY (an extra X).
- **Turner syndrome**—a monosomic condition in which those affected have just one sex chromosome, an X.

Concept 16.1 DNA is the genetic material

- X-ray crystallography is a process used to visualize molecules three-dimensionally. X-rays are diffracted as they pass through the molecule, and they bounce back to produce patterns that can be interpreted through mathematical equations. Through this technique, the structure of DNA was first visualized.
- DNA is a double helix, which can be described as a twisted ladder with rigid rungs. The side, or backbone, is made up of sugar-phosphate components, whereas the rungs are made up of pairs of nitrogenous bases.

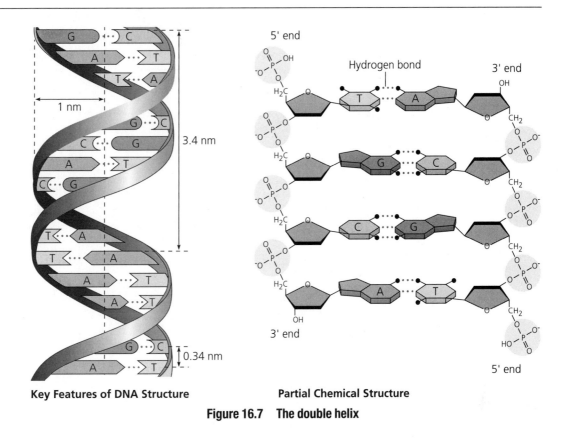

Key Features of DNA Structure **Partial Chemical Structure**

Figure 16.7 The double helix

▮ The nitrogenous bases of DNA are adenine (A), thymine (T), guanine (G), and cytosine (C). In DNA, adenine pairs only with thymine, and guanine pairs only with cytosine. Two hydrogen bonds form between adenine and thymine; three hydrogen bonds form between cytosine and guanine.

Concept 16.2 *Many proteins work together in DNA replication and repair*

▮ DNA replication is semiconservative. At the end of its replication, each of the daughter molecules has one old strand, derived from the parent strand of DNA, and one strand that is newly synthesized.

▮ The replication of DNA begins at sites called the origins of replication.

▮ Initiation proteins bind to the origin of replication and separate the two strands, forming a replication bubble. DNA replication then proceeds in both directions along the DNA strand until the molecule is copied.

▮ A group of enzymes called DNA polymerases catalyzes the elongation of new DNA at the replication fork.

▮ DNA polymerase adds nucleotides to the growing polypeptide chain one by one. Each nucleotide loses two phosphate groups, which are subsequently hydrolyzed in an exergonic reaction to fuel the process of polymerization.

▮ The strands of DNA are antiparallel, meaning that their sugar phosphate backbones run in opposite directions. This means that DNA replication occurs continuously along one strand, which is called the **leading strand,** and in a series of segments along the other strand, the **lagging strand.**

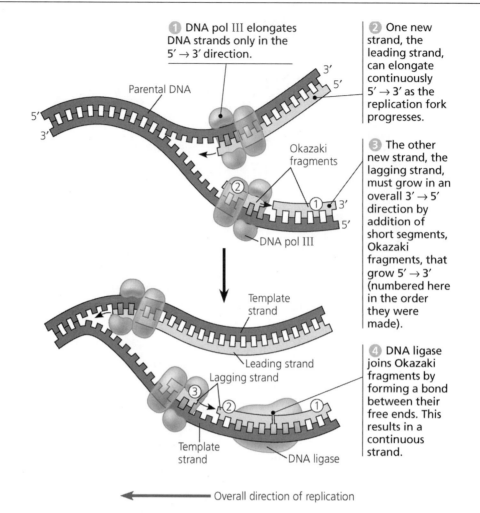

1 DNA pol III elongates DNA strands only in the 5′ → 3′ direction.

2 One new strand, the leading strand, can elongate continuously 5′ → 3′ as the replication fork progresses.

3 The other new strand, the lagging strand, must grow in an overall 3′ → 5′ direction by addition of short segments, Okazaki fragments, that grow 5′ → 3′ (numbered here in the order they were made).

4 DNA ligase joins Okazaki fragments by forming a bond between their free ends. This results in a continuous strand.

Parental DNA

Okazaki fragments

DNA pol III

Template strand

Leading strand

Lagging strand

Template strand

DNA ligase

⟵ Overall direction of replication

Figure 16.14   Synthesis of leading and lagging strands during DNA replication

▌ The lagging strand is synthesized in separate pieces called **Okazaki fragments,** which are then sealed together by **DNA ligase,** forming a regular DNA strand.

▌ DNA polymerases do not initiate DNA replication. The initial nucleotide chain is a short one called a **primer,** which is a short stretch of RNA with an available 3′ end. **Primase** starts an RNA chain that is complementary to the template strand at the location where initiation of the new DNA strand will occur.

▌ **Helicases** are enzymes that are responsible for unwinding the DNA helix as replication proceeds. **Single-strand binding proteins** hold the strands apart for the duration of replication.

▌ There are several different factors contributing to the accuracy of DNA replication:

  ▪ The specificity of base pairing.
  ▪ **Mismatch repair,** in which special repair enzymes fix incorrectly paired nucleotides.
  ▪ **Nucleotide excision repair,** in which incorrectly placed nucleotides are excised by an enzyme called **nuclease,** and the gap left over is filled in with the correct nucleotides.

The fact that DNA polymerase can add nucleotides only to the 3′ end of a molecule means that it would have no way to complete the 5′ end of the molecule. Thus, the linear ends of eukaryotic chromosomes are "capped" with **telomeres,** short nucleotide sequences that do not contain genes but protect the chromosome from being degraded.

Concept 17.1 Genes specify proteins via transcription and translation

- The **one gene–one polypeptide hypothesis** states that each gene codes for a polypeptide, which can be—or can constitute a part of—a protein.
- **Transcription** is the synthesis of RNA using DNA as a template. It takes place in the nucleus of eukaryotic cells.
- Messenger RNA, or mRNA, is produced during transcription. It carries the genetic message of DNA to the protein-making machinery of the cell in the cytoplasm.
- In eukaryotes, transcription results in pre-mRNA, which undergoes **RNA processing** to yield the final mRNA that participates in **translation**—the synthesis of polypeptides in the cytoplasm.
- The instructions for building a polypeptide chain are written as a series of three-nucleotide groups; this is called a triplet code, or **codon.**
- During transcription, only one strand of the DNA is transcribed, and it is called the **template strand.** The mRNA that is produced is said to be complementary to the original DNA strand. The mRNA base triplets are also called codons. They are written in the 5′ to 3′ direction.
- The genetic code is redundant, meaning that more than one codon codes for each of the 20 amino acids. The codons are read based on a consistent reading frame—the groups of 3 must be read in the correct groupings in order for translation to be successful.

Concept 17.2 Transcription is the DNA-directed synthesis of RNA

- The enzyme **RNA polymerase** separates the two DNA strands and connects the RNA nucleotides as they base-pair along the DNA template strand.
- The RNA polymerases can add RNA nucleotides only to the 3′ end of the strand, so RNA elongates in the 5′ to 3′ direction.
- The DNA sequence at which RNA polymerase attaches is called the **promoter.**
- The DNA sequence that signals the end of transcription is called the **terminator.**
- The entire stretch of DNA that is transcribed into mRNA is called a **transcription unit.**

There are three main stages of transcription:

1. **Initiation:** A group of proteins plus RNA polymerase, bound to the promoter region of a DNA sequence, is collectively known as a transcription initiation complex.

2. **Elongation:** RNA polymerase moves along the DNA, continuing to untwist the double helix. RNA nucleotides are continually added to the 3′ end of the growing chain, and as the complex moves down the DNA strand, the double helix re-forms, with the new RNA molecule straggling away from the DNA template.

3. **Termination:** This occurs after RNA polymerase transcribes a terminator sequence in the DNA, and the transcribed RNA sequence is the actual termination signal.

Concept 17.3 *Eukaryotic cells modify RNA after transcription*

▌ In eukaryotes, there are a couple of key post-transcription modifications to RNA—the addition of a **5′ cap,** and the addition of a **poly-A tail.**

▌ Another process, called **RNA splicing,** also takes place in eukaryotic cells. In RNA splicing, large portions of the newly synthesized RNA strand are removed. The sections of the mRNA that are spliced out are called **introns,** and the sections that remain—and subsequently spliced together by a spliceosome—are called **exons.**

Concept 17.4 *Translation is the RNA-directed synthesis of a polypeptide*

▌ Translation is the synthesis of a polypeptide, under the direction of a ribosome.

▌ **tRNA** functions in transferring amino acids from a pool of amino acids in the cell's cytoplasm to a ribosome. The ribosome accepts the amino acid from tRNA and incorporates the amino acid into a growing polypeptide chain.

▌ Each type of tRNA is specific for a particular amino acid; at one end it loosely binds the amino acid, and at the other end it has a nucleotide triplet called an anticodon, which allows it to pair specifically with a complementary codon on the mRNA.

▌ The mRNA is read codon by codon, and one amino acid is added to the chain for each codon read.

▌ The rules for base-pairing between the third base of a codon and the corresponding base of a tRNA anticodon are not as strict as those for DNA and mRNA codons. This relaxation of base-pairing rules is called **wobble.**

▌ Ribosomes are made up of two subunits made up of proteins and RNA molecules called ribosomal RNA (rRNA).

▌ Ribosomes have three binding sites for mRNA:

  ▪ a **P site,** which holds the tRNA that carries the growing polypeptide chain.
  ▪ an **A site,** which holds the tRNA that carries the amino acid that will be added to the chain next.
  ▪ an **E site,** which is the exit site.

▌ Translation, like transcription, can be divided into three stages:

1. **Initiation:** mRNA, a tRNA that has the first amino acid of the polypeptide, and the two ribosomal subunits come together to form a translation initiation complex. Initiation factors (proteins) are also required in order for translation to begin.

2. **Elongation:** Amino acids are added one by one to the growing polypeptide chain with the participation of proteins called elongation factors. Elongation involves the recognition of codons by anticodons, the formation of peptide bonds between amino acids added to the chain, and translocation—in which the tRNA in the A site is moved to the P site, and the tRNA in the P site is moved to the E site.
3. **Termination:** A stop codon in the mRNA is reached and translation stops. UAA, UAG, and UGA are all stop codons. A protein called release factor binds to the stop codon, and the polypeptide is freed from the ribosome.

▌ Polypeptides then fold to assume their specific conformation, and they are sometimes modified further to render them functional.

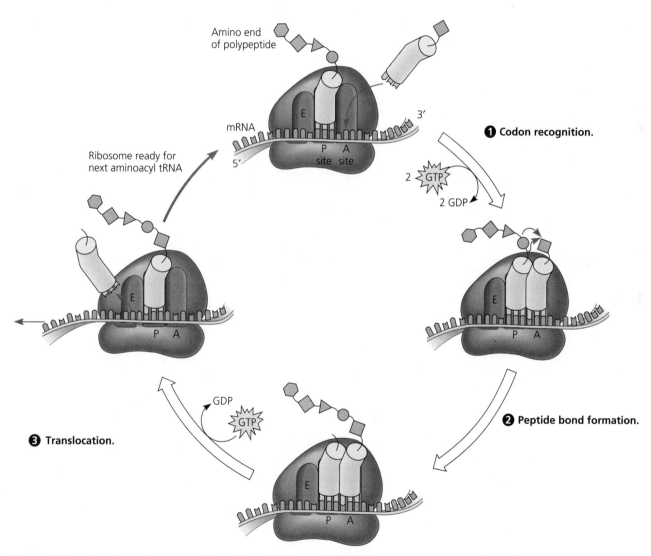

Figure 17.18   The elongation cycle of translation. Not shown in this diagram are the proteins called elongation factors. The hydrolysis of GTP drives the elongation process.

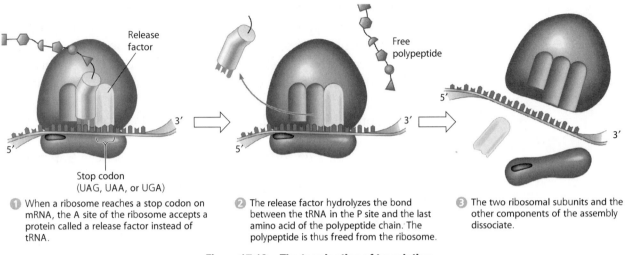

① When a ribosome reaches a stop codon on mRNA, the A site of the ribosome accepts a protein called a release factor instead of tRNA.

② The release factor hydrolyzes the bond between the tRNA in the P site and the last amino acid of the polypeptide chain. The polypeptide is thus freed from the ribosome.

③ The two ribosomal subunits and the other components of the assembly dissociate.

Figure 17.19   The termination of translation

Concept 17.6 Comparing gene expression in prokaryotes and eukaryotes reveals key differences

Difference	Prokaryotic Cells	Eukaryotic Cells
Ribosomes	Smaller than ribosomes in eukaryotic cells and differ in molecular composition. Difference is important because certain antibiotics that interfere with protein synthesis in prokaryotic cells do not affect eukaryotic cells.	Subunits of rRNA are made in the nucleus. Ribosomes are larger than prokaryotic ribosomes.
Promoter binding	RNA polymerase recognizes and binds to the promoter.	Transcription factors mediate the binding of RNA polymerase to the promoter.
The end of transcription	A terminator signals the end of transcription.	Pre-mRNA is cleaved from the growing RNA chain while RNA polymerase II continues transcription until the polymerase eventually falls off the DNA.
Signal sequences	Prokaryotes use signal sequences to target proteins for secretion after transcription.	Some proteins are targeted for movement to endomembrane system organelles during transcription.

Concept 17.7 Point mutations can affect protein structure and function

▌ Mutations are alterations in the genetic material of the cell; **point mutations** are alterations of just one base pair of a gene. They come in two basic types:

▪ **Base-pair substitution** refers to the replacement of one nucleotide and its complementary base pair in DNA with another pair of nucleotides. **Missense mutations** are those substitutions that enable the codon to still code for an amino acid, although it might not be the correct one. **Nonsense mutations** are those substitutions that change a regular amino acid codon into a stop codon, ceasing translation.

▪ **Insertions** and **deletions** refer to the additions and losses of nucleotide pairs in a gene. If they interfere with the codon groupings, they can cause a **frameshift mutation,** which causes the mRNA to be read incorrectly.

▌ **Mutagens** are substances or forces that interact with DNA in ways that cause mutations. X-rays and other forms of radiation are known mutagens, as are certain chemicals.

Concept 18.1 A virus has a genome but can reproduce only within a host cell

▌ Smaller than ribosomes, the tiniest viruses are about 20 nm across. The genetic material of viruses can be double- or single-stranded DNA or double- or single-stranded RNA. The viral genome is enclosed by a protein shell called a **capsid.** Some viruses also have **viral envelopes** that surround the capsid and aid the viruses in infecting their hosts.

▌ **Bacteriophages,** or **phages,** are viruses that infect bacterial cells.

▌ Some viruses (called virulent phages) have a reproductive cycle that ends in the death of the host cell, and this is called the **lytic cycle.** In the course of the lytic cycle, the phage attaches to receptors on the cell surface, injects its DNA into the host, and directs the replication of its own DNA. In the last stage of infection, the bacterium lyses (breaks open), and the new phages are released to infect other cells.

▌ Some viruses undergo what is called the **lysogenic cycle,** in which the host cell is not killed. In the lysogenic cycle, the phage DNA becomes incorporated into the host cell's DNA and is replicated along with the host cell's genome.

▌ **Retroviruses** are RNA viruses that use the enzyme reverse transcriptase to transcribe DNA from an RNA template. The new DNA then permanently integrates into a chromosome in the nucleus of an animal cell. The host transcribes the viral DNA into RNA that may be used to synthesize viral proteins or may be released from the host cell to infect more cells. HIV is an example of a retrovirus.

Concept 18.2 Viruses, viroids, and prions are formidable pathogens in animals and plants

▌ **Viroids** are circular RNA molecules, only several hundred nucleotides long, that infect plants. They cause errors in regulatory systems that control plant growth.

▌ **Prions** are misfolded, infectious proteins that cause the misfolding of normal proteins with which they come in contact in various animal species.

Concept 18.3 Rapid reproduction, mutation, and genetic recombination
contribute to the genetic diversity of bacteria

▌ The main component of the genome in most bacteria is one double-stranded, circular DNA molecule that is associated with a small amount of protein.

▌ In addition to the chromosome, many bacteria also have plasmids, much smaller circles of DNA with a few to a dozen genes.

▌ Most bacteria in a colony are genetically identical to the parent cell because bacteria reproduce asexually through **binary fission.** Mutation, however, can cause some offspring to differ slightly in genetic makeup.

▌ **Transformation** is the alteration of a bacterial cell's genotype and phenotype by the uptake of naked, foreign DNA from the environment.

▌ In **transduction,** a phage carries bacterial genes from one host cell to another as a result of aberrations in the phage's reproductive cycle.

Concept 18.4 Individual bacteria respond to environmental change by
regulating their gene expression

▌ In bacteria, genes are often clustered into operons, with one promoter serving several adjacent genes. An operator site on the DNA switches the operon on or off. An **operon** consists of an operator, promoter, and the genes they control—the entire stretch of DNA required for enzyme production in a pathway.

▌ In a **repressible operon,** binding of a specific repressor protein to the operator shuts off transcription. The repressor is active when bound to a **corepressor.** In an **inducible operon,** binding of an inducer to an innately active repressor inactivates the repressor and turns on transcription.

Concept 19.1 Chromatin structure is based on successive levels of DNA packing

▌ In eukaryotic cells, DNA and proteins are packed together as **chromatin.** The first level of packing in chromosomes involves DNA and proteins called **histones,** which are folded together and resemble beads on a string. **Nucleosomes,** the complex of DNA and histones, are the basic unit of DNA packing.

▌ In interphase cells, most chromatin is in the highly extended form (euchromatin), but some remains highly condensed (heterochromatin). Heterochromatin is largely inaccessible to transcription enzymes and, thus, generally is not transcribed.

Concept 19.2 Gene expression can be regulated at any stage, but the key step is transcription

▌ The expression of genes can be turned off and on at any point along the pathway from gene to functional protein.

▌ Genes in heterochromatin (which is highly packed) usually are not transcribed; this is one form of gene control. **DNA methylation** (the addition of methyl groups) is another way in which the transcription of genes is controlled. Apparently, methylation of DNA is responsible for the long-term inactivation of genes.

▌ In **histone acetylation,** acetyl groups are added to amino acids of histone proteins; this makes the chromatin less tightly packed and encourages transcription.

- **Transcription initiation** is another important control point in gene expression. At this stage, DNA control elements that bind transcription factors (needed to initiate transcription) are involved in regulation.
- Gene control also occurs after transcription, and during RNA processing, in **alternative RNA splicing.**
- The control of gene expression also occurs both prior to translation and just after translation, when proteins are processed.

Concept 19.3 Cancer results from genetic changes that affect cell cycle control

- **Oncogenes** are cancer-causing genes; **proto-oncogenes** are genes that code for proteins that are responsible for normal cell growth. Proto-oncogenes become oncogenes when a mutation occurs that causes an increase in the product of the proto-oncogene—or an increase in the activity of the proto-oncogene itself.
- **Cancer** can also be caused by a mutation in a gene whose products normally inhibit cell division. These genes are called tumor-suppressor genes.
- The incidence of cancer increases with age because multiple somatic mutations are required to produce a cancerous cell.

Concept 19.4 Eukaryotic genomes can have many noncoding DNA sequences in addition to genes

- Genes make up only a small portion of the genomes of most eukaryotes; about 98.5% of human DNA does not code for RNA or proteins. These noncoding regions of DNA are made up of introns, repetitive sequences, and sequences whose function is not yet understood. **Repetitive DNA** is responsible for a number of genetic disorders.
- **Transposons** are sections of DNA that can move from one location to another location within a genome. **Retrotransposons** can move from place to place in a genome only with the help of an RNA intermediate.
- A group of identical or similar genes is called a **multigene family,** and it is likely that the members of the family evolved from a single ancestral gene.

Concept 20.1 DNA cloning permits production of multiple copies of a specific gene or other DNA segment

- **Genetic engineering** is the process of manipulating genes and genomes.
- **Biotechnology** is the process of manipulating organisms or their components for the purpose of making useful products.
- **Recombinant DNA** is DNA that has been artificially made, using DNA from different sources and often different species. An example is the introduction of a human gene into an *E. coli* bacterium.
- **Gene cloning** is the process by which scientists can produce significant samples of specific segments of DNA that they can then work with in the lab.
- **Restriction enzymes** are used to cut strands of DNA at specific locations (called **restriction sites**). These enzymes are what make genetic engineering possible.
- When a DNA molecule is cut by restriction enzymes, the result will always be a set of **restriction fragments,** which will have at least one single-stranded end, called a **sticky end.** Sticky ends can form hydrogen bonds with complementary single-stranded pieces of DNA. These unions can be sealed with **DNA ligase.**

- ▌ The cloning of genes generally occurs in five steps:

  1. First, the **cloning vector** and the gene must both be isolated. The vector is the plasmid (usually bacterial) that will carry the DNA sequence to be cloned.
  2. The DNA in question must be inserted into the plasmid.
  3. The plasmid must be inserted into the cell in order to be copied.
  4. The cells must be cloned.
  5. The cells carrying the clones must be identified and isolated.

- ▌ A **genomic library** is a set of thousands of recombinant plasmid clones, each of which has a piece of one original genome being studied. A **cDNA library** is made up of complementary DNA made from mRNA transcribed from a number of different genes at one particular time.
- ▌ **PCR** (polymerase chain reaction) is a method used to greatly amplify a particular piece of DNA without the use of cells.

Concept 20.2 *Restriction fragment analysis detects DNA differences that affect restriction sites*

- ▌ **Gel electrophoresis** is a lab technique that is used to separate macromolecules on the basis of their size and charge with the use of an electrical current.
- ▌ **Southern blotting** is a technique that is used to determine the presence of specific nucleotide sequences in DNA.

Concept 20.3 *Entire genomes can be mapped at the DNA level*

- ▌ The **Human Genome Project** began in 1990 as an effort to map the entire human genome. The effort was largely completed in 2003.
- ▌ The comparison of genomes of different organisms suggests strong evolutionary relationships between organisms that appear very different externally.

Concept 20.4 *Genome sequences provide clues to important biological questions*

- ▌ **Genomics** is the study of an organism's entire genome.
- ▌ In **proteomics,** the entire set of proteins that are encoded by genomes is studied.

Concept 20.5 *The practical applications of DNA technology affect our lives in many ways*

There are many different uses for DNA technology, some of which are:

1. **Diagnosis of disease**—If the sequence of a particular virus's DNA is known, PCR can be used to amplify patients' blood samples to detect even small traces of the virus.
2. **Gene therapy**—This is the alteration of an afflicted individual's genes and holds great potential for treating disorders traceable to a single defective gene.
3. The **production of pharmaceuticals**—Gene splicing and cloning can be used to produce large amounts of particular proteins in the lab.
4. **Forensic applications**—DNA samples taken from the blood, skin cells, or hair of alleged criminal suspects can be compared to DNA collected from the crime scene. DNA fingerprints (small sets of markers, or specific bands that are

unique to each individual) can be compared and used to identify persons at that crime scene.

5. **Paternity**—DNA fingerprinting can also be used to determine paternity.
6. **Environmental cleanup**—Scientists engineer metabolic capabilities into microorganisms, which are then used to treat environmental problems, such as removing heavy metals from toxic mining sites.
7. The creation of **transgenic organisms**—Scientists can create organisms that carry genes from other organisms in order to enhance certain characteristics that humans find useful.
8. **Genetic engineering** in plants—Certain genes that produce desirable traits have been inserted into crop plants to increase their productivity or efficiency.

For Additional Review

Consider the similarities and differences between prokaryotic cells and eukaryotic cells, including their structure, how they replicate their DNA, and how they live in the world.

Multiple-Choice Questions

1. A couple has 6 children, all daughters. If the woman has a seventh child, what is the probability that the seventh child will be a daughter?
   (A) $\frac{6}{7}$
   (B) $\frac{1}{7}$
   (C) $\frac{1}{36}$
   (D) $\frac{1}{49}$
   (E) $\frac{1}{2}$

2. If alleles R and S are linked, and the probability of gamete R segregating into a gamete is $\frac{1}{4}$, while the probability of allele S segregating into a gamete is $\frac{1}{2}$, what is the probability that both will segregate into the same gamete?
   (A) $\frac{1}{4} \times \frac{1}{2}$
   (B) $\frac{1}{4} \div \frac{1}{2}$
   (C) $\frac{1}{4} + \frac{1}{2}$
   (D) $\frac{1}{4} + \frac{1}{4}$
   (E) $\frac{1}{2}$

3. In llamas, coat color is controlled by a gene that exists in two allelic forms. If a homozygous yellow llama is crossed with a homozygous brown llama, the offspring have gray coats. If two of the gray-coated offspring were crossed, what percentage of their offspring would have brown coats?
   (A) 100%
   (B) 75%
   (C) 50%
   (D) 25%
   (E) 0%

4. Which of the following is NOT true of meiosis?
   (A) During metaphase, spindle microtubules come into contact with chromosomes.
   (B) The chromosome number in the newly formed cells is half that of the parent cell.
   (C) The homologous chromosomes line up along the metaphase plate, or equator of the cell.
   (D) The cytoplasm of the cell and all its organelles are divided approximately in half.
   (E) In anaphase, the sister chromatids travel to opposite ends of the cell.

5. In rabbits, the trait for short hair (*S*) is dominant, and the trait for long hair (*s*) is recessive. The trait for green eyes (*G*) is dominant, and the trait for blue eyes (*g*) is recessive. A cross between two rabbits produces a litter of 6 short-haired rabbits with green eyes, and 2 short-haired rabbits with blue eyes. What is the most likely genotype of the parent rabbits in this cross?
   (A) *ssgg* × *ssgg*
   (B) *SSGG* × *SSGG*
   (C) *SsGg* × *SsGg*
   (D) *SsGg* × *SSGg*
   (E) *ssGG* × *ssGG*

6. Which of the following is NOT a potential control mechanism for regulation of gene expression in eukaryotic organisms?
   (A) The degradation of RNA
   (B) The transport of mRNA from the nucleus
   (C) The lactose operon
   (D) Transcription
   (E) Gene amplification

7. In humans, hemophilia is a sex-linked recessive trait. If a man and a woman have a son who is affected with hemophilia, which of the following is definitely true?
   (A) The mother carries an allele for hemophilia.
   (B) The father carries an allele for hemophilia.
   (C) The father is afflicted with hemophilia.
   (D) Both parents carry an allele for hemophilia.
   (E) The boy's paternal grandfather has hemophilia.

8. Which of the following explains a significantly low rate of crossing over between two genes?
   (A) They are located far apart on the same chromosome.
   (B) They are located on separate but homologous chromosomes.

(C) The genes code for proteins that have similar functions.
(D) The genes code for proteins that have very different functions.
(E) The genes are located very close together on the same chromosome.

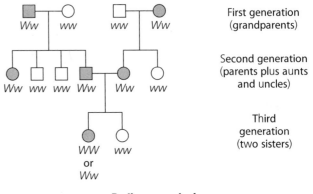

Pedigree analysis

9. In the pedigree above, circles represent females and squares represent males; those who express a particular trait are shaded, whereas those who do not are not shaded. Which pattern of inheritance best describes the pedigree for this trait?
   (A) Sex-linked recessive
   (B) Sex-linked dominant
   (C) Autosomal recessive
   (D) Autosomal dominant
   (E) Codominant

Questions 10–11 refer to an individual with blood type O, whose mother has blood type A.

10. The father must have which of the following blood types?
    (A) A, B, or O
    (B) AB or A
    (C) AB or B
    (D) AB only
    (E) O only

11. If the type O individual were to mate with a person with type AB blood, which of the following is the best calculation of the ratio of the offspring?
    (A) $3\ I^A i$:$1\ I^B i$
    (B) $2\ I^A i$:$1\ I^B i$
    (C) $I^A i$:$I^B i$
    (D) $1\ I^A i$:$2\ I^A I^B$:$1 I^B i$
    (E) $9\ I^A I^B$:$3\ I^A i$:$3\ I^B i$:1 O

12. Two yellow mice with the genotype *Yy* are mated. Two-thirds of their offspring are yellow, and ⅓ of their offspring are not yellow (a 2:1 ratio). Mendelian genetics dictates that this cross should produce offspring that were ¼ *YY* (yellow), ½ *Yy* (yellow) and ¼ *yy* (not yellow). What is the most likely conclusion from this experiment?
    (A) The mice did not bear enough offspring for the ratio calculation to be specific.
    (B) *Y* is a lethal allele and caused death early in development.
    (C) Nondisjunction occurred.
    (D) A mutation masked the effects of the *Y* allele.
    (E) A mutation masked the effects of the *y* allele.

13. In organisms that undergo alternation of generations, the diploid stage is called the
    (A) gametophyte.
    (B) ovum.
    (C) sporophyte.
    (D) hybrid.
    (E) dicot.

14. All of the following contribute to genetic recombination EXCEPT
    (A) random fertilization.
    (B) independent assortment.
    (C) crossing over.
    (D) gene linkage.
    (E) random gene mutation.

15. In cucumbers, warty (*W*) is dominant over dull (*w*), and green (*G*) is dominant over orange (*g*). A cucumber plant that is homozygous for warty and green is crossed with one that is homozygous for dull and orange. The F_1 generation is then crossed. If a total of 144 offspring are produced in the F_2 generation, which of the following is the closest to the number of dull green cucumbers expected?
    (A) 3
    (B) 10
    (C) 28
    (D) 80
    (E) 111

16. Which of the following exists as DNA surrounded by a protein coat?
    (A) a retrovirus
    (B) a virus
    (C) a eukaryote
    (D) a prokaryote
    (E) ampicillin

17. A goat can produce milk containing the same polymers present in the silk produced by spiders when particular genes from a spider are inserted into the goat's genome. Which of the following reasons describes why this is possible?
    (A) Goats and spiders share a common ancestor and, thus, produce similar protein excretions.
    (B) The opposite is true, too—when genes from a goat are inserted into a spider's genome, the spider produces goats' milk instead of silk.
    (C) The proteins in goats' milk and spiders' silk have the same amino acid sequence.
    (D) The processes of transcription and translation in the cells of spiders and goats are fundamentally similar.
    (E) The processes of transcription and translation in the cells of spiders and goats produce exactly the same proteins anyway.

18. Restriction enzymes are generally used in the laboratory for which of the following reasons?
    (A) Restricting the replication of DNA
    (B) Restricting the transcription of DNA
    (C) Restricting the translation of mRNA
    (D) Cutting DNA molecules at specific locations
    (E) Cutting DNA into manageable sizes for manipulation

Directions: The group of questions below consists of five lettered choices followed by a list of numbered phrases or sentences. For each numbered phrase or sentence, select the one choice that is most closely related to it. Each choice may be used once, more than once, or not at all.

Questions 19–23
    (A) Transcription
    (B) Translation
    (C) Transposon
    (D) DNA methylation
    (E) Histone acetylation

19. A mobile segment of DNA that travels from one location on a chromosome to another, one element of genetic change

20. The addition of groups to certain bases of DNA after DNA synthesis, this is thought to be an important control mechanism for gene expression

21. The synthesis of polypeptides from the genetic information coded in mRNA

22. The synthesis of RNA from a DNA template

23. The attachment of groups to particular amino acids of specific proteins, this is thought to be an important control mechanism for gene expression

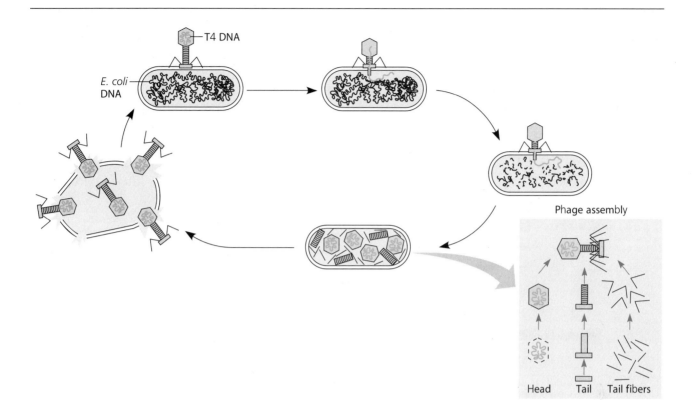

T4 DNA

E. coli DNA

Phage assembly

Head   Tail   Tail fibers

24. The above figure shows which of the following processes?
    (A) the lytic cycle of a phage
    (B) the lysogenic cycle of a phage
    (C) transcription
    (D) translation
    (E) DNA replication

25. The actions of which of the following enzymes are responsible for ensuring that chromosomes do not decrease in length with every round of replication?
    (A) telomerase
    (B) DNA ligase
    (C) DNA polymerase
    (D) helicase
    (E) primase

26. PCR (polymerase chain reaction) makes gene cloning possible because it enables lab technicians to do which of the following very quickly?
    (A) isolate gene-source DNA
    (B) insert DNA into an appropriate vector
    (C) introduce the cloning vector into a host cell
    (D) amplify DNA samples
    (E) identify clones carrying the gene of interest

Questions 27–30 refer to an experiment that was performed to separate DNA fragments from 3 samples radioactively labeled with ^{32}P. The fragments were then separated using gel electrophoresis. The visualized bands are depicted below:

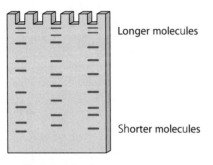

Longer molecules

Shorter molecules

Completed gel

Gel electrophoresis: completed gel

27. When the electric field was applied, the fragments of DNA in each of the 3 samples migrated to different locations along the gel because
    (A) the fragments differed in their levels of radioactivity.
    (B) the fragments differed in their charges— some were positively charged, while others were negatively charged.
    (C) the fragments differed in size.
    (D) the fragments differed in polarity.
    (E) the fragments differed in solubility.

28. How many sites on DNA were cut by the particular restriction enzyme used in Sample 1 (the leftmost sample)?
    (A) 5
    (B) 6
    (C) 7
    (D) 8
    (E) 9

29. The DNA in this experiment was labeled with ^{32}P because
    (A) without ^{32}P, the DNA would not migrate through the gel.
    (B) without ^{32}P, we would not be able to visualize the DNA fragments.
    (C) ^{32}P is required in order to allow the restriction enzymes to make their cuts.
    (D) radioactivity limits the interference of scrap fragments of DNA.
    (E) radioactivity enables the DNA fragments to clump together and produce bands.

30. Gel electrophoresis can also be used for which of the following purposes?
    (A) to group molecules based on their polarity
    (B) to measure the acidity of certain large molecules
    (C) to measure the polarity of certain large molecules
    (D) to separate out the proteins in a mixture
    (E) to measure the amount of protein in a mixture of substances

31. In genetic engineering, DNA ligase is used for which of the following purposes?
    (A) to act as a probe for locating cloned genes
    (B) to create breaks in DNA in order to allow foreign DNA fragments to be inserted
    (C) to seal up nicks created in newly created recombinant DNA
    (D) to ensure that "sticky ends" of like DNA fragments do not re-anneal
    (E) in Southern blotting

Directions: The group of questions below consists of five lettered choices followed by a list of numbered phrases or sentences. For each numbered phrase or sentence, select the one choice that is most closely related to it. Each choice may be used once, more than once, or not at all.

Questions 32–36
(A) tRNA
(B) mRNA
(C) poly-A tail
(D) RNA polymerase
(E) rRNA

32. An example of a post-transcriptional modification

33. Binds to the promoter on DNA to initiate transcription

34. Along with proteins, comprises ribosomes

35. Loosely binds to free amino acids in the cytoplasm

36. Travels out of the nucleus and into the cytoplasm to participate in translation

37. All of the following nitrogenous bases are included in DNA EXCEPT
(A) adenine.
(B) cytosine.
(C) guanine.
(D) thymine.
(E) uracil.

38. The expression of genes can be controlled at all the following stages of protein synthesis EXCEPT
(A) initiation of transcription.
(B) RNA processing.
(C) DNA unpacking.
(D) degradation of protein.
(E) protein folding.

39. After eukaryotic transcription takes place, mRNA undergoes several modifications before leaving the nucleus to take part in translation. One of these is the cutting out of nonessential sections of mRNA, and the subsequent splicing together of stretches of mRNA necessary for the final functional molecule. Which of the following mRNA sections are spliced together into the finished mRNA molecule?
(A) introns
(B) exons
(C) genes
(D) coding sequences
(E) ribozymes

40. In the process of eukaryotic translation, the term *wobble* refers to
(A) the tendency of the two ribosome subunits to come closer to one another and to separate at different points in translation.
(B) the tendency of the amino acid loosely attached to the tRNA to move back and forth before finally attaching to the polypeptide chain.
(C) the fact that the genetic code is redundant.
(D) the fact that the anticodon and codon bind very loosely.
(E) the fact that the third nucleotide of a tRNA can form hydrogen bonds with more than one kind of base in the third position of a codon.

41. Which of the following is an example of a missense mutation?
    (A) A nucleotide and its partner are replaced with an "incorrect" pair of nucleotides, which destroys the function of the final protein.
    (B) A nucleotide pair is added into a gene, destroying the reading frame of the genetic message.
    (C) A nucleotide pair is lost from the gene, destroying the reading frame of the genetic message.
    (D) A frameshift mutation occurs, ultimately causing the production of nonfunctional proteins.
    (E) A nucleotide pair substitution occurs, which causes the codon to code for an amino acid that may not be the "correct" one, although translation continues.

42. Which of the following is an example of a nonsense mutation?
    (A) A chemical change occurs in just one base pair of a gene, and it has no effect on the final protein.
    (B) Part of the gene breaks off and travels to a distant location on the chromosome, inserting itself there.
    (C) A substitution occurs, which changes a regular amino acid codon into a stop codon, causing translation to cease.
    (D) A substitution occurs, which changes a regular amino acid codon into a start codon, and translation begins again, creating two unfinished polypeptides.
    (E) A nucleotide pair substitution occurs, which causes the codon to code for an amino acid that may not be the "correct" one, although translation continues.

43. At the end of DNA replication, each of the daughter molecules has one old strand, derived from the parent strand of DNA, and one strand that is newly synthesized. This explains why DNA replication is described as
    (A) conservative.
    (B) largely conservative.
    (C) nonconservative.
    (D) semiconservative.
    (E) unconservative.

Free-Response Question

1. Genes are located on chromosomes and are the basic unit of heredity that is passed on from parent to child, through generations.

    (a) Explain how a chromosome mutation could occur and why mutations are detrimental to the organism in which they take place.

    (b) Explain why it is that—although there are very few genes located on the Y chromosome—human males may suffer from having just one copy of the X chromosome, while females have two.

ANSWERS AND EXPLANATIONS

Multiple-Choice Questions

1. (E) is correct. The probability that the woman will have a seventh child who is a daughter is ½. Since the probability that a sperm carrying an X chromosome and the probability that a sperm carrying a Y chromosome will fertilize an egg is equal—both 50%—fertilization is considered an independent event. The outcome of independent events is unaffected by what events occurred before or will occur after. Therefore, the probability that this woman's next child will be a girl is ½. Likewise, the probability that she will have a child that is a boy is also ½.

2. (A) is correct. If the probability of allele *R* segregating into a gamete is ¼, and that of *S* segregating is ½, you can calculate the probability of two independent events occurring in a specific combination, order, or sequence by multiplying their probabilities. So in this case, you need to multiply ¼ by ½.

3. (D) is correct. Let's say that the yellow coat parent is $C^Y C^Y$, and the homozygous brown coat parent is $C^B C^B$. Because the yellow coat parent can only produce gametes C^Y, and the brown coat parent can only produce gametes C^B, the F_1 generation will all have genotype $C^Y C^B$. Crossing two members of this generation would give you a ratio of 1 yellow coat:2 gray coats:1 brown coat. This means that 25% of the offspring would have brown coats, 25% would have yellow coats, and 50% would have gray coats.

4. (A) is correct. All of the statements about meiosis are true except A. The spindle fibers attach during prophase, not metaphase.

5. (D) is correct. To find the answer to this problem, first look at the ratio of the offspring. It's 6:2, which can be reduced to 3:1. Next, you can quickly work through the crosses listed. You can immediately rule out answers *A* and *B*, because *A* would give you only offspring that exhibited the dominant traits, short hair and green eyes, and *B* would give you all offspring that had the recessive traits—long hair and blue eyes. If you look carefully at the remaining answers, you will want to choose the one that will give you all short-haired offspring, so you will need the dominant allele to be present in both parents. This rules out answer *E*. If you still cannot choose between *C* and *D*, write out what gametes the parents could produce, and then use a Punnett square to determine their offspring. By doing this, you can see that *D* is correct: the ratio of offspring is 12:4, or 3:1, which matches the ratio in the original question.

■ **6. (C) is correct.** Operons are gene expression mechanisms of bacteria. They are not found in eukaryotic cells.

■ **7. (A) is correct.** If the boy is afflicted with hemophilia, then he must have inherited the recessive hemophilia gene from his mother. Sex-linked genes are usually located on the X chromosome. In order for the child to be a boy, he must have inherited a Y chromosome from his father. Because the gene causing hemophilia is located on the X chromosome, you can rule out answers *B* and *C* (it would not matter if the father possessed the allele for hemophilia, because he can't pass on his X to a son). Therefore, you need to look for an answer choice that shows that the source of his X chromosome was a carrier of the allele—afflicted or not. This is answer *A*.

■ **8. (E) is correct.** While genes that are on the same chromosome tend to be inherited together, the process of crossing over enables "linked" genes to sort independently. Those that are linked but located farther apart on the chromosome will undergo crossing over more frequently than those located very close together on a chromosome, simply because there are more sites between the two genes at which crossing over can take place.

■ **9. (D) is correct.** Autosomal dominant traits appear with equal frequency in both sexes, and they do not skip generations. These qualities are all exhibited by the trait that is illustrated in the pedigree. All three generations are affected with the trait; the sexes are affected roughly equally (4 women and 2 men are affected).

■ **10. (A) is correct.** The father either has type A, B, or O blood. The mother, who has the phenotype blood type A, has the genotype $I^A i$. In order to produce a son with genotype *ii* (the genotype of people with blood type O), she would need to reproduce with a man who had genotype $I^A i$, genotype $I^B I$, or genotype *ii*. Try writing out the Punnett square if you aren't confident of this.

■ **11. (C) is correct.** If the type O individual were to mate with an individual who was type AB, since I^A and I^B are both dominant over *i*, the genotype would be $1\ I^A{:}1\ I^B$, and the phenotype would be a ratio of 1:1 offspring with type A or type B blood.

■ **12. (B) is correct.** The most likely reason for this 2:1 ratio in the offspring is that *Y* is lethal in homozygous form, and this caused the death of all of the *YY* individuals in the litter. The expected ratio of this cross would be 1 *YY*:2 *Yy*:1 *yy*. If you remove the *YY*, you get a ratio of 2 *Yy* (yellow mice, since the gene for yellow, *Y*, is dominant) to 1 *yy* (nonyellow mouse).

■ **13. (C) is correct.** Organisms that undergo alternation of generations, such as plants and some algae, have both a haploid and diploid stage in their life cycle. The diploid stage is the sporophyte, and meiosis in the diploid phase creates haploid spores, which divide mitotically to produce a gametophyte. The gametophyte produces haploid gametes through mitosis, and the fertilization occurs to produce a diploid zygote that may develop into a sporophyte.

■ **14. (D) is correct.** The only process listed that does not lead directly to genetic recombination, or the recombining (scrambling) of genes in the offspring, is gene linkage. If genes are linked, they are located on the same chromosome and are more likely to segregate together into the same cell.

15. (C) is correct. Recall that a dihybrid cross between two heterozygotes produces a 9:3:3:1 offspring ratio. The question is asking for one of the heterozygotes (which would be one of the 3s in the above ratio). To come up with the answer you could complete a Punnett square and see that the ratio of offspring produced is 9 warty green, 3 warty orange, 3 dull green, and 1 dull orange. The total number of offspring produced is 144; thus, you can deduce that that's 9 times 16 (the sum of 9 + 3 + 3 + 1). So the number of dull green cucumbers must be equal to $9 \times 3 = 27$. The closest answer choice to 27 is 28.

16. (B) is correct. Viruses are made up of nucleic acid surrounded by a protein coat. The answer cannot be *A* because retroviruses consist of RNA. They reproduce by injecting their genetic material into a host cell and using the cell's replicative machinery to replicate their DNA and proteins. The new viruses leave the cell to infect more cells, sometimes killing the host cell in the process.

17. (D) is correct. The process of genetic engineering is possible because the processes of transcription and translation are so similar in all eukaryotic cells. Once the spider gene or genes that were responsible for coding for the silk proteins were isolated and then inserted into a bacterial plasmid (which would serve as the vector), the cloning vector would be taken up by the goat's cells, and the goat's cells' transcription/translation machinery would begin the process of producing the spider protein, along with its own proteins.

18. (D) is correct. Restriction enzymes can be used to cut DNA at specific locations, and this enables researchers to perform recombinant DNA techniques. When specific restriction enzymes are added to the DNA, they produce cuts in the sugar-phosphate backbone and create "sticky ends," which can bind to DNA fragments from a different source to produce recombinant DNA. DNA ligase is then added to seal the strands together permanently.

19. (C) is correct. Transposons are also called transposable genetic elements, and they are pieces of DNA that can move from location to location in a chromosome—or a genome. Transposons are also called "jumping genes," and most of them are capable of moving to many different target sites in the genome.

20. (D) is correct. One of the two important ways that the cell has of controlling gene expression is through DNA methylation. In DNA methylation, methyl groups are attached to certain DNA bases after DNA is synthesized. This appears to be responsible for the long-term inactivation of genes.

21. (B) is correct. The process by which genetic information flows from mRNA to protein is called translation. Translation occurs in the cytoplasm of the cell, at ribosomes. A molecule of mRNA is moved through the ribosome, and codons are translated into amino acids one at a time. Transfer RNAs add their associated amino acids onto a growing polypeptide as its anticodon pairs with a codon on the mRNA and then departs from the ribosome to bind more free amino acids.

22. (A) is correct. In transcription, RNA is synthesized using the genetic information encoded by DNA. Transcription occurs in the nucleus of the cell. The double-stranded DNA helix unwinds, allowing enzymes and proteins to synthesize a new complementary single-stranded mRNA molecule from the template strand of DNA.

23. (E) is correct. In histone acetylation, acetyl groups are attached to certain amino acids of histones. Deacetylation is the process by which they are removed. Acetylation makes the histones change shape so they are less tightly bound to DNA, and this allows the proteins involved in transcription to move in and begin the process. Therefore acetylation is one way for the cell to initiate transcription and to control the expression of its genes.

24. (A) is correct. This art portrays the lytic cycle of phage reproduction. In the lytic cycle, the phage first attaches to the cell surface and injects its DNA into the cell. It then hydrolyzes the host cell's DNA and uses the cell's machinery to produce phage proteins and to replicate its genome. The phage proteins are then assembled in the cell until the host cell lyses (breaks open), and the new phages are released to infect other cells. In the lysogenic cycle, the phage genome becomes incorporated into the host cell's DNA without destroying the host cell.

25. (A) is correct. The enzyme responsible for adding nucleotides to the replicating DNA strand, DNA polymerase can only add nucleotides to the 3′ end of a molecule. This means that it would have no way to complete the 5′ end of the molecule; thus, the linear chromosomes of eukaryotes use an enzyme called telomerase, which catalyzes the ends of the molecules (called telomeres).

26. (D) is correct. PCR, the polymerase chain reaction, is a technique by which any piece of DNA can be copied many times without the use of cells. The DNA is heated to separate its strands then cooled to allow primers to attach to the single strands. DNA polymerase is added, which begins to add nucleotides to the 3′ end of each primer on the two strands. With each turn of the cycle, the amount of DNA is multiplied by two.

27. (C) is correct. The fragments of DNA separated out from one another along the gel once the electric field was applied because they differ in size. For DNA in gel electrophoresis, how far a molecule travels through a gel (while the current is applied) is inversely proportional to its size. The larger a fragment is, the more slowly it will migrate.

28. (D) is correct. The restriction enzyme used to cut the DNA that was placed into the first well of the gel must have cut the DNA at 8 sites, because it produced 9 DNA fragments. The number of fragments produced is always one more than the number of restriction sites cut.

29. (B) is correct. Radioactivity is conferred to the DNA fragments so we can visualize them once they have ceased migrating through the gel. This can be done by applying a piece of film to the gel—the radioactivity exposes the film to form an image that corresponds to the bands of DNA shown.

30. (D) is correct. Gel electrophoresis is a method used to separate macromolecules (DNA, protein, most types of macromolecule) based on their rate of movement through a gel once an electric field has been applied. The rate of their movement will be inversely proportional to their size.

31. (C) is correct. In genetic engineering (the manipulation of genes for practical purposes), DNA ligase is an enzyme that is used to seal the strands of newly recombinant DNA (DNA that is spliced together from two different sources) by catalyzing the formation of phosphodiester bonds.

32. (C) is correct. The addition of a poly-A tail after transcription is one example of post-transcriptional modifications that the mRNA undergoes. This poly-A tail inhibits the degradation of the newly synthesized mRNA strand and is thought also to help ribosomes attach to it. Another important modification that mRNA undergoes is the addition of a 5′ cap. The 5′ cap helps protect mRNA from degradation and also acts as the point of attachment for the ribosomes, just prior to translation.

33. (D) is correct. RNA polymerase is the most prominent enzyme involved in the transcription of DNA to make mRNA. It is responsible for binding to the promoter sequence on the template DNA, prying the two DNA strands apart, and hooking the RNA nucleotides together as they base-pair along the DNA template. RNA polymerases add nucleotides to the 3′ end of the growing chain until a terminator sequence is reached—it transcribes entire transcription units.

34. (E) is correct. Ribosomal RNA (rRNA), together with proteins, makes up ribosomes. Ribosomes, the sites of protein synthesis, are composed of two subunits, the large and the small subunit. The large subunit of the ribosome contains the A, P, and E sites, which shuttle through the tRNA and mRNA during translation.

35. (A) is correct. tRNA, or transfer RNA, interprets the genetic message coded in mRNA. It transfers amino acids taken from the cytoplasmic pool to a ribosome, which adds the specific amino acid brought to it by tRNA to the end of a growing polypeptide chain. Each type of tRNA binds loosely to a specific amino acid at one end; its other end contains an anticodon, which base-pairs with a complementary codon on the mRNA strand.

36. (B) is correct. mRNA, also known as messenger RNA, is a type of RNA that is synthesized from DNA and attaches to ribosomes in the cytoplasm to specify the primary structure of a protein. Since mRNA is the product of transcription, which occurs in the nucleus, it must travel out of the nucleus and into the cytoplasm in order to participate in translation.

37. (E) is correct. The base uracil is found in RNA but not in DNA. The bases in DNA are cytosine, guanine, thymine, and adenine, whereas the bases found in RNA are cytosine, guanine, adenine, and uracil. In DNA, cytosine is capable of forming three hydrogen bonds with guanine, and thymine and adenine form two hydrogen bonds between them—the bases form the "rungs" of the double helix ladder, and sugar-phosphate groups form the rails of the ladder.

38. (E) is correct. Protein folding is the mechanism by which the polypeptide assumes its functional conformation. It is the only answer listed that does not describe a stage in the pathway from gene to protein that is involved in controlling gene expression. At almost all of the stages in this pathway, the cell has some mechanism for controlling the expression of its genes or the amount of gene product produced.

39. (B) is correct. In the modification of mRNA that occurs after transcription, a process called RNA splicing occurs. In this process, noncoding regions of nucleic acid that are situated between coding regions are cut out. These noncoding regions are called introns. The remaining regions are called exons, and these are spliced together to form the final mRNA product. When you think of exons, think expressed—because they are actually translated into proteins, whereas introns are not.

40. (E) is correct. In eukaryotic translation, the term wobble refers to the fact that more than one tRNA exists for every mRNA codon that specifies for an amino acid. Some tRNAs have codons that can recognize two or more different codons because of wobble—wherein the base-pairing rules are relaxed, and the third nucleotide of a tRNA can form hydrogen bonds with more than one kind of base in the third position of a codon.

41. (E) is correct. A missense mutation is a base-pair substitution (the replacement of a nucleotide and its partner in the cDNA strand with a different pair of nucleotides) that still enables the codon to code for an amino acid. The amino acid may or may not ultimately contribute to a functional protein, but a missense mutation is one where an amino acid is still chosen to be added to the polypeptide chain, and translation will continue.

42. (C) is correct. In a nonsense mutation, a base-pair substitution takes place—one base-pair is replaced by another—and the point mutation changes the codon for a regular amino acid into a stop codon. This makes translation end prematurely, and this results in a shortened and usually nonfunctional protein.

43. (D) is correct. DNA replication is semiconservative. Each new daughter molecule contains one newly synthesized strand, and one strand that used to belong to the parent double helix DNA.

Free-Response Question

(a) The reason that it is detrimental to an organism to have an abnormal chromosome number is that genes, which are located on chromosomes, code for proteins, which have specific functions in the cell. If an organism has two copies of a particular gene, then this gene will be transcribed twice, creating twice the usual gene product. This alters the relative amounts, or doses, of interacting products in the cell, and this can cause serious developmental problems. Likewise, if a gene is missing from a chromosome, it will not be transcribed, and its corresponding protein will not be produced. If that protein has an important cellular function, the organism will be seriously affected.

There are many ways by which chromosomes can be altered to cause problems for the cell. Among these is nondisjunction—when during mitosis or meiosis the chromosomes fail to separate properly, and one cell ends up with two copies of a chromosome while the other gets no copies. This results in a condition called aneuploidy. Smaller chromosomal mutations are deletions (in which part of the chromosome breaks off and is lost), inversions (in which a chromosome segment is reversed within a chromosome), duplications (in which a chromosome segment is repeated in a chromosome), and translocation (in which part of a chromosome is moved from one chromosome to another).

(b) When fertilization occurs and a sperm carrying a Y chromosome penetrates the egg first, a male zygote with one X and one Y chromosome is produced. If a sperm carrying an X chromosome penetrates the egg first, a female zygote with XX is produced. Although it seems as though the female zygote would have the advantage of having twice the cell product as the male, due to its double dose of genes located on the large X versus the small Y, this is not the case. The reason for this is that, in every cell of the female human body, one of the X chromosomes is inactivated. The mechanisms for this are not understood, but the X chromosome that is inactivated condenses into a structure called a Barr body, which then associates with the nuclear envelope. As a Barr body, most of the X chromosome's genes are not expressed—although some of them do remain active. As a result of this, females are a mosaic consisting of cells with the X chromosome from their mother activated and cells with the X chromosome from their father activated in about a 50-50 ratio. This is also the reason sex-linked disorders are usually not expressed in females. Though one of the X chromosomes may be incapable of producing a crucial gene product, this mosaic effect ensures that the other half of the somatic cells produce sufficient amounts of the protein in question.

This response demonstrates knowledge of the following terms and processes:

chromosome	*inversion*
gene	*duplication*
gene product	*translocation*
doses	*X and Y chromosome*
transcription	*zygote*
nondisjunction	*X chromosome inactivation*
aneuploidy	*Barr body*
deletion	*somatic cell*

Moreover, the response describes the following processes in a clear, concise, and organized way:

> *—the function of genes and why their loss or duplication affects the cell*
> *—the many types of chromosome mutations that can occur*
> *—the difference between X and Y chromosomes*
> *—the process and result of X chromosome inactivation*

CHAPTER 4

Mechanisms of Evolution

Concept 22.1 The Darwinian revolution challenged traditional views of a young Earth inhabited by unchanging species

▌ Darwin's view of life as expressed in *The Origin of Species* (1859) contrasted sharply with traditional beliefs of an Earth only a few thousand years old, populated by forms of life that had been created at the beginning and remained unchanged ever since.

▌ The concept of **natural selection** states that a population can change over generations if individuals with certain heritable traits produce more viable offspring than other individuals. The result of natural selection is **evolutionary adaptation,** which is an accumulation of inherited characteristics that enhance organisms' ability to survive and reproduce in specific environments.

▌ **Taxonomy** is the branch of biology dedicated to the naming and classification of all forms of life. Carolus Linnaeus developed **binomial nomenclature,** a two-part naming system that includes the organism's genus and species.

▌ **Fossils,** which are found in sedimentary rock, are remains or traces of organisms from the past. Fossils provide evidence for the theory of evolution. **Paleontology** is the study of fossils.

▌ **Gradualism** is a geologic theory that states that profound changes in Earth's features over the course of geologic time are the result of slow, continuous processes. **Uniformitarianism** is the idea that the geologic processes that have shaped the planet have not changed over the course of Earth's history.

▌ **Jean-Baptiste de Lamarck** developed an early theory of evolution, which in part stated that characteristics acquired during an organism's lifetime could be passed on to the next generation. Our modern understanding of genetics provides no evidence that this is possible.

Concept 22.2 In The Origin of Species, Darwin proposed that species change through natural selection

▌ **Charles Darwin's** voyage on the HMS *Beagle* in 1831 was the impetus for the development of his theory of evolution.

▌ The phrase **descent with modification** refers to Darwin's idea that all living organisms are related by descent (i.e., they evolved) from a remote common ancestor.

▌ Darwin's theory of natural selection can be summarized by the following three statements:

   1. Natural selection is the differential success in reproduction (the unequal ability of individuals to survive and reproduce) that results

from the interaction between individuals that vary in heritable traits and their environment.

2. Natural selection can produce an increase over time in the adaptation of organisms to their environment.

3. If an environment changes over time, or if individuals of a particular species move to a new environment, natural selection may result in adaptation to these new conditions, sometimes giving rise to new species in the process.

▌ **Artificial selection** is the process by which species are modified by humans. Plants and animals are specifically chosen to breed with the desired goal of producing offspring with specific characteristics.

▌ A **population** is defined as a group of interbreeding individuals who live in a certain geographic area—it is the smallest unit that can evolve. Individuals cannot evolve.

▌ Natural selection can work only on **heritable traits** (traits that are passed from organisms to their offspring), not on traits that cannot be inherited.

Concept 22.3 Darwin's theory explains a wide range of observations

▌ Darwin's theory of evolution by natural selection explains observations in living populations of organisms, and observation of homology, vestigial organs, molecular homologies, biogeography, and the fossil record.

▌ Natural selection explains changes in living populations—for example, the ongoing evolution of drug-resistant bacteria and viruses.

▌ Because animals are related evolutionarily, species that share common ancestry should have similarities. This phenomenon, in which related species share characteristics resulting from common ancestry, is known as **homology.**

▌ **Homologous structures** are variations on a structural theme and are anatomical signs of evolution. One example of this is the forelimbs of mammals that are now used for a variety of purposes, such as flying in bats or swimming in whales, but were present and used in a common ancestor for walking. The comparison of early stages of animal development reveals many anatomical homologies in embryos that are not visible in adult organisms.

▌ **Vestigial organs** are structures of marginal, if any, importance to the organism. They are remnants of structures that served important functions in the organisms' ancestors. For example, the pelvis and the leg bones found in some snakes are vestigial structures.

▌ **Molecular homologies** are shared characteristics on the molecular level, such as the use of the same genetic code written in DNA or other molecular similarities. Because the genetic code is shared by all organisms, it is likely that all species descended from a common ancestor.

▌ **Biogeography** refers to the geographic distribution of species. Species that live closer to one another tend to be more closely related than those that do not. Species that are **endemic** to a certain geographic location are found at that location and nowhere else.

▌Darwin's theory of evolution through natural selection explains the succession of forms in the fossil record. Transitional fossils have been found that link ancient organisms to modern species, just as Darwin's theory predicts.

Concept 23.1 Population genetics provides a foundation for studying evolution

▌Individual organisms do not evolve; populations evolve.

▌Today we define evolutionary change on it smallest scale as **microevolution.** Microevolution is change in the genetic makeup of a population from generation to generation.

▌In the mid-20th century, population genetics gave rise to the **modern synthesis,** a comprehensive theory of evolution that integrates ideas from many fields, including genetics, statistics, biogeography, and paleontology.

▌**Population genetics** is the study of how populations change genetically over time.

▌Populations of the same species may be geographically isolated and exchange genetic material only rarely.

▌The **gene pool** is the total aggregate of genes in a population at any one time. It is made up of all the alleles at all loci in all the members of a population. Remember that in diploid species, each individual has two alleles for a particular gene, and the individual may be either heterozygous or homozygous.

▌If all members of a population are homozygous for the same allele, the allele is said to be **fixed.** Only one allele exists at that particular locus in the population.

▌The **Hardy-Weinberg theorem** is used to describe a population that is not evolving. It states that the frequencies of alleles and genes in a population's gene pool will remain constant over the course of generations unless they are acted upon by forces *other* than Mendelian segregation and the recombination of alleles. The situation in which the allele frequencies within a population are not changing is termed **Hardy-Weinberg equilibrium.**

▌Consider a gene locus that exists in two allelic forms in a population, one having a frequency of p and one having a frequency of q. If we know the frequency of one of the alleles, we can calculate the frequency of the other allele:

$$p + q = 1, \text{ so}$$
$$p = 1 - q$$
$$q = 1 - p$$

And the two are related by the equation for Hardy-Weinberg equilibrium:

$$p^2 + 2pq + q^2 = 1$$

Where p^2 is equal to the frequency of the homozygous dominant in the population, $2pq$ is equal to the frequency of all the heterozygotes in the population, and q^2 is equal to the frequency of the homozygous recessive in the population.

- The Hardy-Weinberg equation can be used to determine or predict the allelic frequencies that exist in populations. In order for a population to be in Hardy-Weinberg equilibrium, it must meet these five conditions:

  1. The population size must be extremely large. The smaller the population, the greater the role of chance fluctuations in allelic frequencies from one generation to the next, known as **genetic drift.**
  2. There must be no migration in a population. Gene flow, which is the transfer of alleles between populations, cannot occur, because that would alter gene frequencies.
  3. There can be no mutations. By introducing or removing genes from chromosomes or by changing one allele into another, mutations modify the gene pool.
  4. Mating must occur randomly. If individuals mate only with other individuals of a certain genotype, this does not meet the criteria of a random mixing of genes.
  5. Natural selection cannot be taking place. This would alter gene frequencies and cause a deviation from Hardy-Weinberg equilibrium.

Concept 23.2 Mutation and sexual recombination produce the variation that makes evolution possible

- New genes and new alleles originate only by **mutations,** which are changes in the nucleotide sequence of DNA. Because mutations in somatic cells disappear when the individual dies, only mutations in cell lines that produce gametes can be passed to offspring.
- **Point mutations,** changes in one base in a gene, can have significant impact on phenotype, as in sickle-cell disease. But most point mutations neither harm nor improve the genome.
- **Chromosomal mutations** that delete, disrupt, duplicate, or rearrange many loci at once are almost certain to be harmful. Only on rare occasions are rearrangements beneficial.
- Most of the genetic differences that exist in a population are due to the sexual recombination of alleles that already exist in a population. Sexual reproduction rearranges alleles into new combinations in every generation.

Concept 23.3 Natural selection, genetic drift, and gene flow can alter a population's genetic composition

- Natural selection, genetic drift, and gene flow are the three major factors that alter allelic frequencies and bring about most evolutionary change.
- Individuals with variations that are better suited to their environment tend to produce more offspring than those with variations that are less suited. Therefore, **natural selection** results in alleles being passed to the next generation in proportions different from their relative frequencies in the present generation.
- **Genetic drift** is the unpredictable fluctuation in allelic frequencies from one generation to the next. The smaller the population, the greater the chance is for genetic drift.

- One example of genetic drift is the **bottleneck effect** in which a sudden change in the environment (for example, an earthquake, flood, or fire) drastically reduces the size of a population. The few survivors that pass through the restrictive bottleneck may have a gene pool that no longer reflects the original population's gene pool.
- Another example of genetic drift is the **founder effect,** which occurs when a few individuals become isolated from a larger population and establish a new population whose gene pool is not reflective of the source population.
- A population may gain or lose alleles by **gene flow,** genetic additions to and/or subtractions from a population resulting from the movement of fertile individuals or gametes.

Concept 23.4 *Natural selection is the primary mechanism of adaptive evolution*

- **Genetic variation** exists naturally in populations. Quantitative characters, such as height in humans, vary in a continuum in a population.
- A population is said to be **polymorphic** for a character if this character exists in two or more discrete forms in the population—for example, if a plant species produces flowers of different colors. **Geographic variation** refers to differences in gene pools, among populations or parts of populations. A **cline** is a graded change in a trait along a geographic axis.
- Factors that contribute to the preservation of genetic variation in a population are **diploidy** and **balanced polymorphism.** Because most eukaryotes are diploid, they are capable of hiding genetic variation (recessive alleles) from selection. Balanced polymorphism refers to the ability of natural selection to keep stable the frequencies of two or more phenotypes in a population.
- Individuals with **heterozygote advantage** are heterozygous at a certain locus, which gives them an advantage for survival. An example of this is seen in the case of sickle-cell disease. Heterozygotes benefit from protection from malaria, but due to their dominant allele, they do not suffer from full-blown sickle-cell disease.
- An organism's **fitness** refers to the contribution an organism makes to the gene pool of the next generation relative to the contributions of other members.
- The three modes of selection are **directional, disruptive,** and **stabilizing.**
- The following are four reasons natural selection cannot produce perfection:

  1. Evolution is limited by historical constraints.
  2. Adaptations are often compromises.
  3. Chance and natural selection interact.
  4. Selection can only edit existing variations.

Concept 24.1 *The biological species concept emphasizes reproductive isolation*

- **Speciation** is the process by which new species arise.
- **Microevolution** is change in the genetic makeup of a population from generation to generation. It refers to adaptations that are confined to a single gene pool.

- **Macroevolution** refers to evolutionary change above the species level, such as the appearance of feathers and other such novelties, used to define higher taxa.
- The **biological species concept** defines a species as a population or group of populations whose members have the potential to interbreed in nature and produce viable, fertile offspring, but are unable to produce viable, fertile offspring with members of other populations. Other definitions of species include the morphological species concept, the paleontological species concept, ecological species concept, and the phylogenetic species concept.
- **Reproductive isolation** is defined as the existence of biological barriers that impede members of two species from producing viable, fertile hybrids. A population may gain or lose alleles by **gene flow,** genetic additions to and subtractions from a population resulting from the movement of fertile individuals or gametes.
- **Prezygotic** and **postzygotic** are two types of barriers that prevent members of different species from producing offspring that can also successfully reproduce. Examples of prezygotic barriers, those that prevent mating or hinder fertilization, include:

  1. **Habitat isolation**—Two species can live in the same geographic area but not in the same habitat; this will prevent them from mating.
  2. **Behavioral isolation**—Some species use certain signals or types of behavior to attract mates, and these signals are unique to their species. Members of other species do not respond to the signals, and thus mating does not occur.
  3. **Temporal isolation**—Species may breed at different times of day, different seasons, or different years, and this can prevent them from mating.
  4. **Mechanical isolation**—Species may be anatomically incompatible.
  5. **Gametic isolation**—Even if the gametes of two species do meet, they might be unable to fuse to form a zygote.

Examples of postzygotic barriers, those that prevent a fertilized egg from developing into a fertile adult, include:

  1. **Reduced hybrid viability**—When a zygote *is* formed, genetic incompatibility may cause development to cease.
  2. **Reduced hybrid fertility**—Even if the two species produce a viable offspring, reproductive isolation is still occurring if the offspring is sterile and can't reproduce.
  3. **Hybrid breakdown**—Sometimes two species mate and produce viable, fertile hybrids; however, when the hybrids mate, their offspring are weak or sterile.

Concept 24.2 Speciation can take place with or without geographic separation

- The two main types of speciation are **allopatric speciation,** in which a population forms a new species because it is geographically isolated from the parent population, and **sympatric speciation,** in which a small part of a population becomes a new population without being geographically separated from the parent population.

▌ Some **geologic events or processes** that can fragment a population include the emergence of a mountain range, the formation of a land bridge, or evaporation in a large lake that produces several small lakes.

▌ Small, newly isolated populations undergo **allopatric speciation** more frequently because they are more likely to have their gene pools significantly altered. Allopatric speciation is confirmed when individuals from the new population are unable to mate successfully with individuals from the parent population.

▌ One mechanism that can lead to **sympatric speciation** in plants is the formation of **autopolyploid** plants through nondisjunction in meiosis. For example, these plants may have a $4n$ chromosome number, instead of the normal $2n$ number. They cannot breed with diploid members and produce fertile offspring.

▌ **Polyploid speciation** occurs in animals, but it is not common. Instead, in animals, sympatric speciation can result from part of the population switching to a new habitat, food source, or other resource.

▌ **Adaptive radiation** occurs when many new species arise from a single common ancestor. Adaptive radiation typically occurs when a few organisms make their way to new, distant areas or when environmental changes cause numerous extinctions, opening up ecological niches for the survivors.

▌ **Punctuated equilibrium** is a term used to describe periods of apparent stasis punctuated by sudden change observed in the fossil record.

Concept 24.3 Macroevolutionary changes can accumulate through many speciation events

▌ Evolutionary novelty can arise when structures that originally played one role gradually acquire a different one. Structures that evolve in one context but become co-opted for another function are sometimes called **exaptations.** For example, it is possible that feathers of modern birds were co-opted for flight after functioning in some other capacity, such as thermoregulation.

▌ **"Evo-devo"** is a field of study where evolutionary biology and developmental biology converge. This field is illuminating how slight genetic divergences can be magnified into major morphological differences between species.

▌ **Allometric growth** refers to the different growth rates of various parts of an organism's body during development. Changing relative rates of growth even slightly can change the adult form of organisms substantially, thus contributing to the potential for evolutionary change.

▌ **Homeotic genes** determine the location and organization of body parts. *Hox* genes are one class of homeotic genes. Changes in *Hox* genes and in the genes that regulate them can have a profound effect on morphology, thus contributing to the potential for evolutionary change.

Concept 25.1 Phylogenies are based on common ancestries inferred from fossil, morphological, and molecular evidence

▍ **Phylogeny** is the evolutionary history of a species or a group of related species. To construct phylogenies, biologists use the fossil record and **systematics,** an analytical approach to understanding the diversity and relationships of organisms. Traditional systematics has used morphological and biochemical resemblance among organisms as a basis for inferring evolutionary relationships. Molecular systematics is a newer tool that uses comparisons of DNA, RNA, and other molecules to infer evolutionary relationships.

▍ The **fossil record** is the sequence in which fossils appear in the layers of sedimentary rock that constitute Earth's surface. **Paleontologists** study the fossil record. Fossils, which may be remnants of dead organisms or impressions they left behind, are most often found in sedimentary rock formed from layers of minerals settling out of water. The fossil record is incomplete because it favors organisms that existed for a long time, were relatively abundant and widespread, and had shells or hard bony skeletons.

▍ **Convergent evolution** has taken place when two organisms developed similarities as they adapted to similar environmental challenges—not because they evolved from a common ancestor. The likenesses that result from convergent evolution are considered **analogous** rather than homologous. For example, the four-chambered heart of birds and mammals is analogous. The most recent common ancestor of birds and mammals had a three-chambered heart.

▍ The comparison of different genes and proteins (**molecular systematics**) of organisms allows us to determine evolutionary relationships on a molecular level. The more alike the DNA sequences of two organisms are, the more closely related they are evolutionarily.

▍ The rate of evolution of DNA sequences varies from one part of the genome to another; therefore, comparing these different sequences helps us to investigate relationships between groups of organisms that diverged a long time ago.

Concept 25.2 Phylogenetic systematics connects classification with evolutionary history

▍ **Taxonomy** is an ordered division of organisms into categories based on a set of characteristics used to assess similarities and differences.

▍ **Binomial nomenclature** is used to describe species. It consists of the **genus** to which the species belongs, as well as the organisms' **species** within the genus. Organisms also have common names, such as cat or dog.

▍ The hierarchical classification of organisms consists of the following levels (in order of increasing broadness): **species, genus, family, order, class, phylum, kingdom,** and **domain.** Each categorization at any level is called a **taxon.**

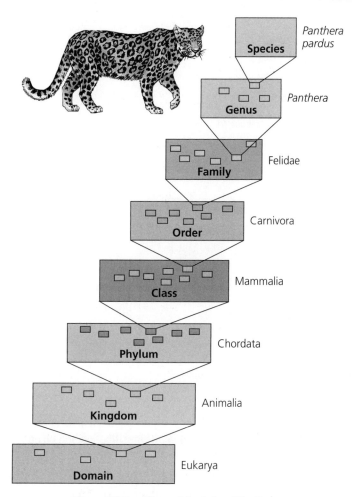

Figure 25.8   Hierarchical classification

▌ Systematists use branching diagrams called **phylogenetic trees** to depict hypotheses about evolutionary relationships. The branches of such trees reflect the hierarchical classifications of groups nested within more inclusive groups. (See the next page for an example.)

Concept 25.3 *Phylogenetic systematics informs the construction of phylogenetic trees based on shared characters*

▌ Patterns of shared characteristics among taxa can be depicted in a diagram called a **cladogram.** If the shared characteristics are explained by common ancestry, then the cladogram forms the basis of a **phylogenetic tree.** A **clade,** within a tree, is defined as a group of species that includes an ancestral species and all its descendants. The analysis of how species may be grouped into clades is called cladistics.

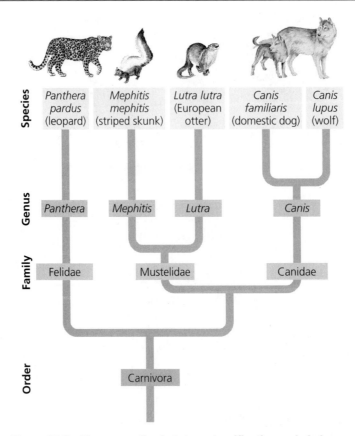

Figure 25.9   The connection between classification and phylogeny

▌ The principle of **maximum parsimony** dictates that a theory with the simplest explanation that is consistent with the facts should be investigated first. This way of thinking is used to create phylogenies.

▌ Parsimony can be applied to the evaluation of hypotheses in the form of phylogenetic trees. The most efficient way to study the various phylogenetic hypotheses is to begin by first considering which is the most parsimonious—that is, which hypothesis requires the fewest total evolutionary events.

Concept 25.5   Molecular clocks help track evolutionary time

▌ **Molecular clocks** are methods used to measure the absolute time of evolutionary change based on the observation that some genes and other regions of the genome appear to evolve at constant rates.

For Additional Review

Analyze the underlying causes of evolution on a molecular scale. Consider how changes in gene structure could cause alterations in the appearance of an organism and eventually lead to speciation.

Multiple-Choice Questions

1. The condition in which there are barriers to inbreeding between individuals of the same species separated by a portion of a mountain range is referred to as
   - (A) minute variations.
   - (B) geographic isolation.
   - (C) infertility.
   - (D) reproductive isolation.
   - (E) differential breeding capacity.

2. Which of the following statements best expresses the concept of gradualism?
   - (A) Minute changes in the genome of individuals eventually lead to the evolution of a population.
   - (B) The five conditions of Hardy-Weinberg equilibrium will prevent populations from evolving quickly.
   - (C) Evolution occurs in rapid bursts of change alternating with long periods in which species remain relatively unchanged.
   - (D) Profound change over the course of geologic history is the result of an accumulation of slow, continuous processes.
   - (E) When two species compete for a single resource in the same environment, one of them will gradually become extinct.

3. A number of different phylogenies have been proposed by scientists over the decades. These are useful because they
   - (A) predict which species will evolve the most quickly in the future.
   - (B) give us information about which species evolved most quickly in the past.
   - (C) allow us to determine when two populations that are similar evolved into separate species.
   - (D) show that molecular resemblances among closely related organisms are rare.
   - (E) allow us to study evolutionary relationships and evaluate the relatedness of living organisms.

4. All of the following statements are part of Darwin's theory of evolution EXCEPT:
   - (A) The most prominent contribution to evolution is made by the process of genetic mutation.
   - (B) Natural selection is the force behind evolution.
   - (C) Natural selection occurs as a result of the differing reproductive success of individuals in a population.
   - (D) The driving force of evolution is the adaptation of a population of organisms to their environment.
   - (E) More individuals are born in a population than will survive to reproduce.

5. In a certain group of rabbits, the presence of yellow fur is the result of a homozygous recessive condition in the biochemical pathway producing hair pigment. If the frequency of the allele for this condition is 0.10, which of the following is closest to the frequency of the dominant allele in this population? (Assume that the population is in Hardy-Weinberg equilibrium.)
   - (A) 0.01
   - (B) 0.20
   - (C) 0.40
   - (D) 0.90
   - (E) 1.0

Directions: The group of questions below consists of five lettered choices followed by a list of numbered phrases or sentences. For each numbered phrase or sentence, select the one choice that is most closely related to it. Each choice may be used once, more than once, or not at all.

Questions 6–10
   (A) Artificial selection
   (B) Homology
   (C) Gene pool
   (D) The founder effect
   (E) The bottleneck effect

6. Leads to new species with certain traits desired by humans

7. Can result in a new island population with a limited gene pool

8. One result of evolution from a common ancestor

9. A result of drastic reduction in population size due to a sudden change in the environment

10. Constitutes all of the alleles in a population

11. All of the following are examples of prezygotic barriers EXCEPT:
   (A) habitat isolation
   (B) behavioral isolation
   (C) temporal isolation
   (D) mechanical isolation
   (E) hybrid breakdown

12. Species that are found only in one particular geographic location are said to be
   (A) behaviorally evolved.
   (B) endemic.
   (C) speciated.
   (D) undergoing behavioral isolation.
   (E) undergoing mechanical isolation.

13. The allele that causes sickle-cell disease is found with greater frequency in Africa, where malaria is more of a threat, than in the United States. Which genetic phenomena most likely contributes to the difference in frequency?
   (A) heterozygote advantage
   (B) heterozygote protection theory
   (C) balanced polymorphism
   (D) frequency-dependent selection
   (E) neutral variations

14. In a population of squirrels, the allele that causes bushy tail (B) is dominant, while the allele that causes bald tail is recessive (b). If we know the frequency with which the bushy tail (B) allele occurs, we can calculate the frequency of the bald tail (b) allele with which of the following equations?
   (A) $b - B = 1$
   (B) $2b = B$
   (C) $b = 1 - B$
   (D) $b^2 - 1 = B$
   (E) $b + 1 = B$

15. The categories in which systematists place species, in order of increasing specificity, are
   (A) species, genus, family, order, class, phylum, kingdom, domain
   (B) domain, kingdom, phylum, class, order, family, genus, species
   (C) class, domain, family, genus, kingdom, order, phylum, species
   (D) family, genus, order, phylum, species, kingdom, domain, class
   (E) phylum, genus, order, species, class, domain, kingdom

16. A marsupial living in Australia has evolved to eat tree leaves, be diurnal, and raise its young until they are of reproductive age. A grazing placental mammal has also evolved to eat tree leaves, be diurnal, and raise its young until they are of reproductive age. This is an example of which of the following types of evolution?
    (A) divergent evolution
    (B) species-specific evolution
    (C) convergent evolution
    (D) neutral evolution
    (E) sibling evolution

17. Which of the following can lead to sympatric speciation?
    (A) migration of a small number of individuals
    (B) natural disaster that cuts off contact between members of a population
    (C) a newly formed river separates segments of a population
    (D) autopolyploidy
    (E) bottleneck effect

18. Which of the following is the basis upon which biologists construct cladograms?
    (A) patterns of shared characteristics
    (B) analogies among related organisms
    (C) molecular similarities, but not structural similarities
    (D) paraphyletic groupings
    (E) similarities within populations

19. In a phylogeny of the animal kingdom, the wings of butterflies and the wings of birds would best be described as
    (A) shared derived characters.
    (B) shared primitive characters.
    (C) homologous structures.
    (D) analogous structures.
    (E) clades.

20. Which of the following constitutes the smallest unit capable of evolution?
    (A) an individual
    (B) a group
    (C) a population
    (D) a clade
    (E) a community

Free-Response Question

1. *Microevolution is the change in the gene pool from one generation to the next.*

    (a) **Describe** three ways in which microevolution can take place.
    (b) **Describe** the difference between microevolution and macroevolution.

ANSWERS AND EXPLANATIONS

Multiple-Choice Questions

▌ **1. (B) is correct.** When two members of the same species are prevented from breeding by a geographic barrier such as a mountain range or river, the fact that they live in different ponds, or any other physical obstruction, the two individuals are said to be geographically isolated.

▌ **2. (D) is correct.** The concept of gradualism was put forth by James Hutton in 1795. He stated that it was possible to understand the modern landforms by looking at the mechanisms currently at work in the world. This concept was meant to apply not to living creatures necessarily, but rather to Earth's geologic features. However, the concept influenced Darwin's thinking and may have contributed to the development of his theory of natural selection.

3. (E) is correct. Phylogenies are hypothetical evolutionary trees showing the history of a species or group of related species. Systematists name and classify organisms, and create phylogenies based on the fossil record and accumulated physical and molecular data. Phylogenetic trees reflect the hierarchical classification of groups of species and of singular species, and they demonstrate hypotheses of how species and groups of species are related to one another.

4. (A) is correct. All the answers are parts of Darwin's theory of evolution except A—genetic mutation is not the most important factor contributing to the process of evolution. In fact, when Darwin was developing his ideas, no one knew about genes. Darwin's theory centered on his observation of changing populations rather than molecular evidence.

5. (D) is correct. If the frequency of the recessive allele is 0.10, then we know that the frequency of the other allele is 1 - 0.10, which is equal to 0.90. The Hardy-Weinberg equation states that, if a population contains just two alleles for a given trait, and we know the frequency of one of the alleles, we can calculate the frequency of the other using the equation $p + q = 1$. If we designate the frequency of the occurrence of the recessive allele as q, and use a value of 0.1, we can rearrange the equation to read $p + 0.10 = 1$. Then, $1 - 0.10 = 0.9$, which is equal to p, or the frequency of the other allele—in this case the dominant one.

6. (A) is correct. Artificial selection is the selective breeding of domesticated plants and animals in order to modify them to better suit the needs of humans. Humans have been practicing artificial selection for thousands of generations, and many of the common foods we eat are a result of this process.

7. (D) is correct. The founder effect occurs when a few individuals from a population colonize a new, isolated habitat. The smaller the number of individuals who start this new population, the more limited will be the starting gene pool for the population—and the less the new gene pool will resemble that of the parent population.

8. (B) is correct. Homology is the result of descent from a common ancestor. It can be described as the underlying structural or molecular similarities (even in structures that are no longer used for the same function) that exist in organisms as a result of common ancestry.

9. (E) is correct. Bottleneck effects are often the result of a natural disaster such as a flood, drought, fire, or anything that destroys most members of a population. The gene pool of the surviving members of the population may not resemble the gene pool of that of the parent population—some genes will be overrepresented, and some will be underrepresented. Bottlenecking reduces the genetic variability in a population because of the loss of alleles.

10. (C) is correct. The gene pool is the collection of all the alleles that exist in a population—a population is defined as a group of individuals living in a certain geographic location that are capable of interbreeding.

11. (E) is correct. Prezygotic barriers are those that prevent or hinder the mating of two species, or they prevent fertilization even if two species mate. All the answers are examples of prezygotic barriers except the last one. Hybrid breakdown is an example of a postzygotic barrier (postzygotic barriers are those that prevent hybrid zygotes from developing into viable adults) in which the second generation of offspring from two species is either weak or sterile.

12. (B) is correct. Species that are found in only one geographic location are said to be endemic. Some examples of endemic species are kangaroos (endemic to Australia) and blue-footed boobies (endemic to the Galápagos Islands).

13. (A) is correct. The allele that causes sickle-cell disease also prevents severe malarial infections. Individuals who have two copies of the sickle-cell allele will come down with the disease and most likely die. Those who are heterozygous, however have an advantage. Because they have one normal allele, they will not contract full-blown sickle-cell disease, however they will have an increased protection against malaria. Individuals with two normal alleles will not have this same protection and are more likely to die from malaria.

14. (C) is correct. We can calculate the frequency of the recessive allele for bald tail in squirrels using the equation $b = 1 - B$, where B is the frequency of the allele that causes bushy tail in squirrels. This is just a rearrangement of the Hardy-Weinberg equation, which in this case would read $B + b = 1$. If there are only two alleles for a given trait in a population, the sum of their gene frequencies will always be 1.

15. (B) is correct. The categories in which systematists place organisms—in order of increasing specificity-is domain, kingdom, phylum, class, order, family, genus, and species. This means that the broadest category is the domain. According to the existing school of thought, there are three domains— Archaea, Bacteria, and Eukarya. The second-largest and most inclusive group under domain is kingdom, and so on.

16. (C) is correct. In convergent evolution, species from different evolutionary branches appear alike as a result of undergoing evolution in very similar ecological roles and environments. Similarity between species that have undergone convergent evolution is known as analogy, and structures they share are analogous (not homologous) structures. Homologous structures are those that are shared in two species as a result of those species' having a common ancestor.

17. (D) is correct. One mechanism that can lead to sympatric speciation, which is the formation of a small new population within the parent population in plants, is the formation of autopolyploids through nondisjunction in meiosis. These plants have $4n$ chromosomes, instead of the normal $2n$ number, and they are unable to breed with members of the parent population—though they are still able to breed with other tetraploids.

18. (A) is correct. Patterns of shared characteristics can be depicted in a diagram called a cladogram. If the shared characteristics are due to common ancestry (that is, they are homologous), then the cladogram forms the basis of a phylogenetic tree. In constructing cladograms, biologists can use a variety of types of characters, including those that are morphological (structural) and molecular. Within a cladogram, valid clades are those that are monophyletic— that is, ones that consist of the ancestor species and all its descendants.

19. (D) is correct. Analogous structures are similar structures that arise due to convergent evolution rather than shared ancestry. Convergent evolution occurs when similar environmental pressures and natural selection produce similar (analogous) adaptations in organisms from different evolutionary lineages. Butterflies (invertebrates) and birds (vertebrates) are in different evolutionary lineages, and therefore, their wing structures evolved independently. Analogous structures are sometimes called homoplasies. In constructing phylogenies, it is important for biologists to sort analogous structures from homologous structures (ones that do arise from shared ancestry).

20. (C) is correct. The smallest unit capable of evolution is the population. Individuals cannot undergo evolution because they exist for only one generation, and evolution is the changing and refinement of a group's gene pool to best fit the group's environment.

Free-Response Question

(a) Microevolution is the change in the gene pool of a population that occurs from one generation to the next, and three factors that contribute to microevolution are genetic drift (including both the bottleneck effect and the founder effect), natural selection, and gene flow.

The term genetic drift refers to any change in a population's allele frequencies due to chance. Two examples of what this "chance" can consist of are the bottleneck effect and the founder effect. The bottleneck effect occurs after a natural disaster such as a violent storm or fire causes a drastic reduction in the size of the population. Such an event leaves only a few individuals to continue to produce offspring, so bottlenecking usually reduces the genetic variability in a population because some alleles are lost from the gene pool and others are overrepresented. Similarly, the founder effect occurs when a few members of a population colonize an isolated location that isn't accessed by members of the parent population. The smaller the number of founders, the more limited the variability of the genes in the new population.

Natural selection is another route by which microevolution can take place. This term refers to the differing reproductive success of all the individuals in a population. Those who are best suited to their environment will survive to pass on their alleles to the next generation.

Gene flow refers to genetic exchange due to the migration of individuals or gametes between populations. This can take place in the course of one generation to the next, so this is another valid contributor to microevolution.

(b) Macroevolution is the process of the evolution of new taxonomic groups (meaning, new species, families, or kingdoms) through evolution. It differs from microevolution in that microevolution refers only to changes that occur in populations from generation to generation—no new species or other taxonomic groups need arise in the course of microevolution. Microevolution occurs on a small scale, whereas macroevolution concerns the "bigger picture."

This is a good free-response answer because it shows knowledge of the following key terms that you will be expected to know for the exam:

microevolution	*founder effect*
gene pool	*natural selection*
population	*gene flow*
genetic drift	*macroevolution*
bottleneck effect	*taxonomic groups*

It also shows that the student understands the following processes: microevolution, genetic drift, including the bottleneck effect and the founder effect, natural selection, gene flow, and macroevolution.

CHAPTER 5

The Evolutionary History of Biological Diversity

Concept 26.1 Conditions on early Earth made the origin of life possible

▎ Most scientists agree that life on Earth began after **nonliving materials** became organized into **molecular aggregates** that eventually became capable of reproducing themselves and metabolizing molecules. In the past, many people thought that life arose from nonliving matter by **spontaneous generation.**

▎ **Biogenesis** is the theory that life can arise only from the reproduction of pre-existing life.

▎ Current theory about how life arose consists of four main stages:

    1. Small organic molecules were synthesized.
    2. These small molecules joined into polymers, such as proteins and nucleic acids.
    3. Self-replicating molecules emerged that made inheritance possible.
    4. All these molecules were packaged into membrane-containing droplets, whose internal chemistry differed from that of the external environment.

▎ Hypothetical early conditions of Earth have been simulated in laboratories, and organic polymers have been produced.

▎ It is hypothesized that RNA (not DNA) was the **first genetic material.**

▎ Before cells, **protobionts** may have existed. Protobionts would have been aggregates of molecules that were produced abiotically with consistent internal environments and some other properties associated with life.

Concept 26.2 The fossil record chronicles life on Earth

▎ Life on Earth started about **3.8 to 3.9 billion years ago,** but for the first three-quarters of Earth's history, all of its living organisms were microscopic and primarily unicellular.

▎ The earliest living organisms were **prokaryotes.**

▎ About 2.7 billion years ago, **oxygen** began to accumulate in Earth's atmosphere.

▎ **Eukaryotes** appeared about 2.1 billion years ago, and **multicellular eukaryotes** evolved about 1.2 billion years ago.

▎ About 500 million years ago, **plants, fungi, and animals** began to appear on Earth.

Table 26.1 The Geologic Record

Relative Duration of Eons	Era	Period	Epoch	Age (Millions of Years Ago)	Some Important Events in the History of Life
Phanerozoic	Cenozoic	Neogene	Holocene		Historical time
				0.01	
			Pleistocene		Ice ages; humans appear
				1.8	
			Pliocene		Origin of genus *Homo*
				5.3	
			Miocene		Continued radiation of mammals and angiosperms; apelike ancestors of humans appear
				23	
		Paleogene	Oligocene		Origins of many primate groups, including apes
				33.9	
			Eocene		Angiosperm dominance increases; continued radiation of most modern mammalian orders
				55.8	
			Paleocene		Major radiation of mammals, birds, and pollinating insects
				65.5	
Proterozoic	Mesozoic	Cretaceous			Flowering plants (angiosperms) appear; many groups of organisms, including dinosaurs, become extinct at end of period (Cretaceous extinctions)
				145.5	
		Jurassic			Gymnosperms continue as dominant plants; dinosaurs abundant and diverse
				199.6	
		Triassic			Cone-bearing plants (gymnosperms) dominate landscape; radiation of dinosaurs; origin of mammal-like reptiles
				251	
	Paleozoic	Permian			Radiation of reptiles; origin of most present-day orders of insects; extinction of many marine and terrestrial organisms at end of period
				299	
		Carboniferous			Extensive forests of vascular plants; first seed plants; origin of reptiles; amphibians dominant
				359.2	
		Devonian			Diversification of bony fishes; first tetrapods and insects
				416	
		Silurian			Diversification of early vascular plants
				443.7	
		Ordovician			Marine algae abundant; colonization of land by plants and arthropods
				488.3	
		Cambrian			Sudden increase in diversity of many animal phyla (Cambrian explosion)
				542	
Archaean				600	Diverse algae and soft-bodied invertebrate animals
				2,200	Oldest fossils of eukaryotic cells
				2,500	
				2,700	Concentration of atmospheric oxygen begins to increase
				3,500	Oldest fossils of cells (prokaryotes)
				3,800	Oldest known rocks on Earth's surface
				Approx. 4,600	Origin of Earth

Concept 26.6 New information has revised our understanding of the tree of life

▌ Introduced in the late 1960s, the **five-kingdom system** of classification includes the Monera, Protista, Plantae, Fungi, and Animalia kingdoms.

▌ Relatively recently, the **three-domain system,** which consists of the domains Bacteria, Archaea, and Eukarya, was proposed. This system arose from the finding that there are two distinct lineages of prokaryotes. The domains Bacteria and Archaea contain prokaryotic organisms and Eukarya contains eukaryotic organisms divided into four kingdoms—Plantae, Animalia, Fungi, and Protista.

▌ **Taxonomy** is a work in progress—the kingdom Protista is now being studied more closely, too, because many of its members are so different they should be placed in different kingdoms.

Concept 27.1 Structural, functional, and genetic adaptations contribute to prokaryotic success

▌ Life is divided into three domains: **Archaea, Bacteria, and Eukarya.** Both domain Bacteria and domain Archaea are made up of prokaryotes.

▌ The most common shapes of prokaryotes are spheres, rods, and helices; most are about 1–5 μm in size.

▌ Outside their cell membranes, most prokaryotes possess a cell wall that contains **peptidoglycans. Gram-positive** bacteria have simpler walls with more peptidoglycan, whereas **gram-negative** cells have walls that are structurally more complex.

▌ Prokaryotes use appendages called **pili** to adhere to each other or to surrounding surfaces. About half of the prokaryotes are **motile,** because they possess whiplike **flagella.** Prokaryotes do not have true nuclei or internal compartmentalization. Relative to eukaryotes, prokaryotes have simple, small genomes. The DNA is concentrated in a nucleoid region and has little associated protein.

▌ In addition to their one major chromosome, prokaryotic cells may also possess smaller, circular, independent pieces of DNA called **plasmids.**

▌ Prokaryotes reproduce through an asexual process called **binary fission,** and they continually synthesize DNA.

▌ Three mechanisms by which bacteria can transfer genetic material between each other are:

1. **transformation,** in which a prokaryote takes up genes from its environment
2. **conjugation,** in which genes are directly transferred from one prokaryote to another
3. **transduction,** in which viruses transfer genes between prokaryotes.

▌ The major source of genetic variation in prokaryotes is **mutation.**

Concept 27.2 A great diversity of nutritional and metabolic adaptations have evolved in prokaryotes

▌ Prokaryotes can be placed in four groups according to how they take in carbon and how they obtain energy.

- **Photoautotrophs** are photosynthetic, and they use the power of sunlight to convert carbon dioxide into organic compounds.
- **Chemoautotrophs** also use carbon dioxide as their source of carbon, but they get energy from oxidizing inorganic substances.
- **Photoheterotrophs** use light to make ATP but must obtain their carbon from an outside source already fixed in organic compounds.
- **Chemoheterotrophs** get both carbon and energy from organic compounds.

▌ Most prokaryotes are chemoheterotrophs. There are two types of chemo-heterotrophs: **saprobes** (decomposers that absorb nutrients from dead organic matter) and **parasites** (which absorb nutrients from the body fluids of living hosts).

▌ Some prokaryotes can use atmospheric nitrogen as a direct source of nitrogen in a process called **nitrogen fixation.** They convert N_2 to NH_4^+.

▌ **Obligate aerobes** cannot grow without oxygen. They need oxygen for cellular respiration. **Obligate anaerobes** are poisoned by oxygen. Some use fermentation, while others extract chemical energy by anaerobic respiration. **Facultative anaerobes** use oxygen if it is available; when oxygen is not available, they undergo fermentation.

Concept 27.3 Molecular systematics is illuminating prokaryotic phylogeny

▌ Most known prokaryotes are bacteria.

▌ The first prokaryotes that were classified in the domain Archaea are known as **extremophiles** and live in extreme environments such as geysers.

▌ There are three types of extremophiles. **Methanogens** use carbon dioxide to oxidize H_2 and produce methane as a waste product; **extreme halophiles** live in saline environments (highly concentrated with salt); and **extreme thermophiles** live in very hot environments.

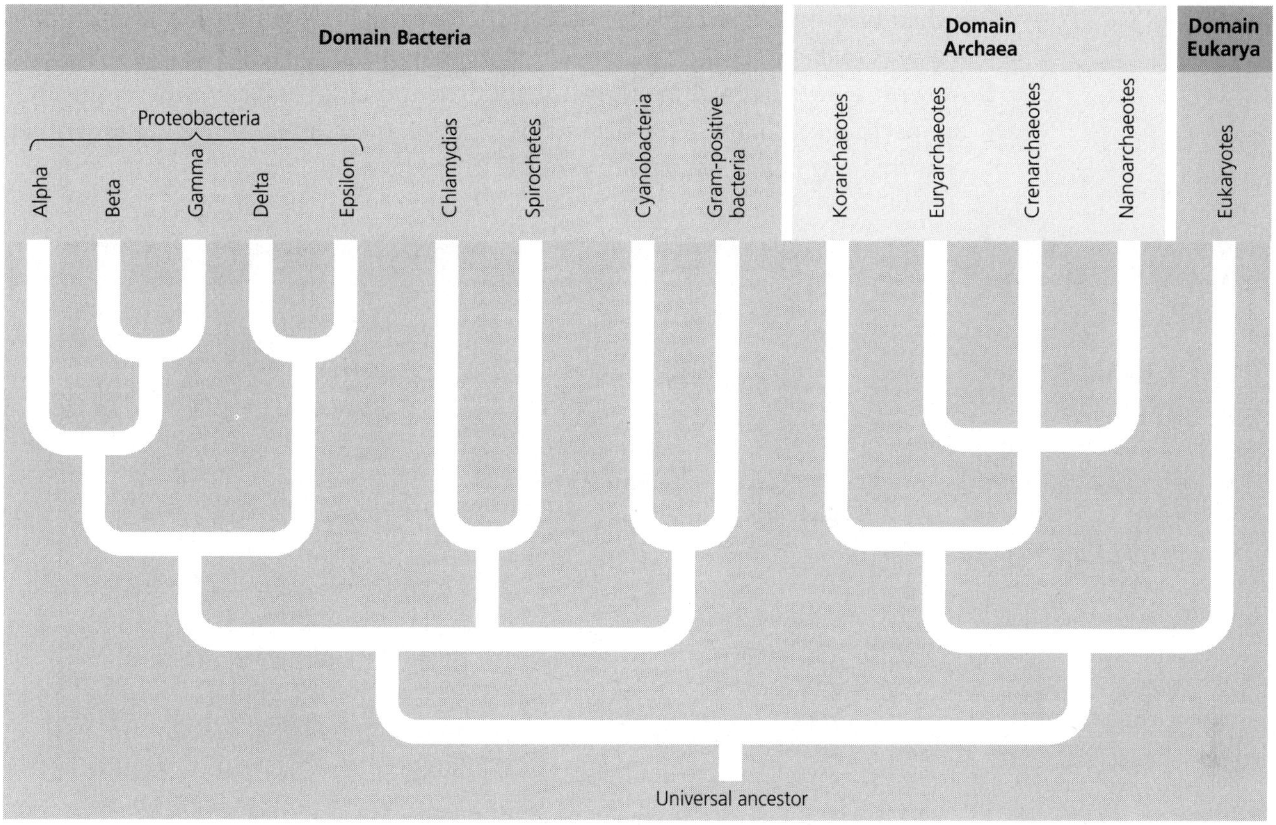

Figure 27.12   A simplified phylogeny of prokaryotes

Concept 27.4 *Prokaryotes play crucial roles in the biosphere*

▌ Prokaryotes are responsible for the **decomposition of living matter,** the first step in the cycling of essential elements through the environment.

▌ Many prokaryotes are **symbiotic,** meaning that they form relationships with other species. In symbiotic relationships where one organism is significantly larger than the other, the larger one is called the **host.** The three types of symbiosis are:

   1. **mutualism**—in which both symbiotic organisms benefit.
   2. **commensalism**—in which one organism benefits while the other is neither helped nor harmed.
   3. **parasitism**—in which one organism benefits at the expense of the other.

Concept 28.1 *Protists are an extremely diverse assortment of eukaryotes*

▌ **Protists** are the simplest but most diverse of all eukaryotes. They vary in structure and function more than any other group of eukaryotes, although most are unicellular. Most protists use aerobic metabolism and have mitochondria.

▌ Protists can be divided into three categories: photosynthetic (plant-like) algae; ingestive (animal-like) protozoans; and absorptive (fungus-like) organisms.

▌ Protists are a paraphyletic group. Some are more closely related to plants, fungi, or animals than to other protists.

▌ Most protists are aquatic and are important constituents of plankton. Many other protists live as symbionts in other organisms.

- Eukaryotes have internal membranes and compartmentalization, and these features make them much more complex than prokaryotes.
- According to current theory, mitochondria and chloroplasts evolved through endosymbiosis. They were originally unicellular organisms engulfed by other cells that ultimately became organelles in the host cell.

Table 28.1 A Sample of Protist Diversity

Major Clade	Key Characteristics	Examples
Diplomonadida (diplomonads)	Two equal-sized nuclei; modified mitochondria	*Giardia*
Parabasala (parabasalids)	Undulating membrane; modified mitochondria	*Trichomonas*
Euglenozoa (euglenozoans)	Spiral or crystalline rod inside flagella	
Kinetoplastida (kinetoplastids)	Kinetoplast (DNA in mitochondrion)	*Trypanosoma*
Euglenophyta (euglenids)	Paramylon as storage molecule	*Euglena*
Alveolata (alveolates)	Alveoli beneath plasma membrane	
Dinoflagellata (dinoflagellates)	Armor of cellulose plates	*Ceratium, Pfiesteria*
Apicomplexa (apicomplexans)	Apical complex of organelles	*Plasmodium*
Ciliophora (ciliates)	Cilia used in movement and feeding; macro- and micronuclei	*Paramecium, Stentor*
Stramenopila (stramenopiles)	Hairy and smooth flagella	
Oomycota (oomycetes)	Hyphae that absorb nutrients	Water molds, white rusts, downy mildews
Bacillariophyta (diatoms)	Glassy, two-part wall	
Chrysophyta (golden algae)	Flagella attached near one end of cell	*Dinobryon*
Phaeophyta (brown algae)	All multicellular, some with alternation of generations	*Laminaria, Macrocystis, Postelsia*
Cercozoa (cercozoans) and Radiolaria (radiolarians)	Amoebas with threadlike pseudopodia	
Foraminfera (forams)	Porous shell	*Globigerina*
Radiolaria (radiolarians)	Pseudopodia radiating from central body	
Amoebozoa (amoebozoans)	Amoebas with lobe-shaped pseudopodia	
Gymnamoeba (gymnamoebas)	Soil-dwelling, freshwater, or marine	*Amoeba*
Entamoeba (entamoebas)	Parasites	*Entamoeba*
Myxogastrida (plasmodial slime molds)	Multinucleate plasmodium; fruiting bodies that function in sexual reproduction	*Physarum*
Dictyostelida (cellular slime molds)	Multicellular aggregate that forms asexual fruiting bodies	*Dictyostelium*
Rhodophyta (red algae)	Phycoerythrin (accessory pigment); no flagellated stages	*Bonnemaisonia, Delesseria, Palmaria*
Chlorophyta (one group of green algae)	Plant-type chloroplasts	*Caulerpa, Chlamydomonas, Spirogyra, Ulva, Volvox*

Concept 29.1 Land plants evolved from green algae

- Land plants evolved from green algae more than 500 million years ago. Evidence for this event includes the similar (homologous) chloroplasts, walls with cellulose, peroxisomes, and sperm of these organisms.

Concept 29.2 *Land plants possess a set of derived terrestrial adaptations*

▌ Plants are multicellular, eukaryotic, photosynthetic autotrophs.

▌ There are four main groups of land plants: **bryophytes, pteridophytes, gymnosperms,** and **angiosperms.**

▌ Bryophytes live on land and have several adaptations for land-living that distinguish them from algae. They lack vascular tissues, which are found in pteridophytes, gymnosperms, and angiosperms.

▌ Pteridophytes have vascular tissue but lack seeds, which are found in both gymnosperms and angiosperms.

▌ All land plants have a life cycle that consists of two multicellular stages, called **alternation of generations.** The two stages are the **gametophyte** stage (in which the plant cells are haploid) and the **sporophyte** stage (in which the plant cells are diploid).

▌ In the gametophyte stage, the gametes are produced. During fertilization, egg and sperm fuse to form a diploid zygote—the sporophyte—which divides mitotically.

▌ A **spore** is a cell produced by a plant that can develop into a new plant without fusing with another cell.

▌ Following are a few examples of unique plant adaptations that make life on land possible.

1. Adaptations for the conservation of water include the cuticle on the epidermis. The **cuticle** is a waxy layer made up of polymers that prevents water loss from above-ground organs. Another adaptation is the **stomata.** These openings on the undersurface of the leaf open and close to control the passage of CO_2, O_2, and H_2O.
2. An adaptation for the transport of water through the plant is **xylem.** Xylem tissue is made up of dead cells through which water is conducted from the roots to the stem.
3. The adaptation for the transport of photosynthesized food (glucose) is the **phloem** tubules. They conduct glucose from the leaves down the stem to the roots.
4. Walled spores are very tough and resistant to harsh environments.

Concept 29.3 *The life cycles of mosses and other bryophytes are dominated by the gametophyte stage*

▌ Bryophytes currently are represented by three phyla—**mosses, liverworts,** and **hornworts.**

▌ The dominant generation in bryophytes is the gametophyte, and bryophytes disperse spores in great amounts.

▌ Bryophytes have the smallest, simplest sporophytes of all plant groups. Even though the sporophytes are photosynthetic when young, they must absorb water, sugars, and other nutrients from parental gametophytes.

Concept 29.4 *Ferns and other seedless vascular plants formed the first forests*

▌ The seedless vascular plant life cycle is dominated by the **sporophyte** stage.

▌ **Ferns, horsetails,** and **lycophytes** are prominent examples of pteridophytes.

▌ Seedless vascular plants formed forests of great heights in the Carboniferous period, eventually forming deposits of coal that we use for fuel today.

Concept 30.1 The reduced gametophytes of seed plants are protected in ovules and pollen grains

- **Gymnosperms** and **angiosperms** are the two types of seed plants.
- **Seed plants** are defined as vascular plants that produce seeds.
- **Seeds** are plant embryos packaged with a food supply in a protective coat.
- The three most crucial adaptations of plants that led to the evolution of seed plants are

  1. reduction of the gametophyte stage
  2. evolution of the seed
  3. evolution of **pollen.**

- The microspores of seed plants develop into pollen grains, which are dispersed by wind or animals, so the process of **pollination** can take place.

Concept 30.2 Gymnosperms bear "naked" seeds, typically on cones

- The prominent gymnosperms are the **conifers,** which are cone-bearing plants such as pine trees.
- Pine trees bear both pollen cones and ovulate cones.

Concept 30.3 The reproductive adaptations of angiosperms include flowers and fruits

- **Angiosperms** are flowering plants classified in the phylum **Anthophyta.**
- The **monocots** are generally described as having veins that run parallel on the surface of a leaf, whereas **eudicots** have netlike vein patterns on their leaves. There are other distinctions between monocots and eudicots, but this trait is the easiest to spot.

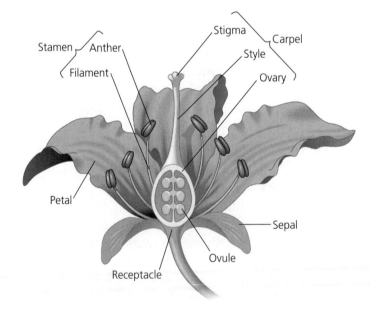

Figure 30.7   The structure of an idealized flower

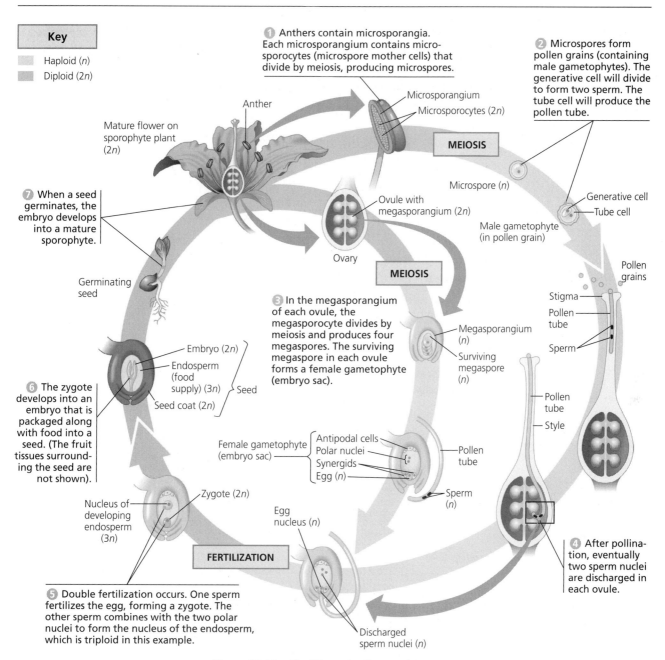

Key

Haploid (*n*)
Diploid (2*n*)

1 Anthers contain microsporangia. Each microsporangium contains microsporocytes (microspore mother cells) that divide by meiosis, producing microspores.

Microsporangium
Microsporocytes (2*n*)

2 Microspores form pollen grains (containing male gametophytes). The generative cell will divide to form two sperm. The tube cell will produce the pollen tube.

MEIOSIS

Anther

Mature flower on sporophyte plant (2*n*)

Microspore (*n*)

Generative cell
Tube cell

7 When a seed germinates, the embryo develops into a mature sporophyte.

Ovule with megasporangium (2*n*)

Male gametophyte (in pollen grain)

Pollen grains

Ovary

MEIOSIS

Stigma
Pollen tube
Sperm

Germinating seed

3 In the megasporangium of each ovule, the megasporocyte divides by meiosis and produces four megaspores. The surviving megaspore in each ovule forms a female gametophyte (embryo sac).

Megasporangium (*n*)
Surviving megaspore (*n*)

Embryo (2*n*)
Endosperm (food supply) (3*n*)
Seed coat (2*n*)
Seed

Pollen tube
Style

6 The zygote develops into an embryo that is packaged along with food into a seed. (The fruit tissues surrounding the seed are not shown).

Female gametophyte (embryo sac)
Antipodal cells
Polar nuclei
Synergids
Egg (*n*)

Pollen tube

Nucleus of developing endosperm (3*n*)
Zygote (2*n*)

Egg nucleus (*n*)

Sperm (*n*)

4 After pollination, eventually two sperm nuclei are discharged in each ovule.

FERTILIZATION

5 Double fertilization occurs. One sperm fertilizes the egg, forming a zygote. The other sperm combines with the two polar nuclei to form the nucleus of the endosperm, which is triploid in this example.

Discharged sperm nuclei (*n*)

Figure 30.10   The life cycle of an angiosperm

▌ The major reproductive adaptation of the angiosperm is the **flower.**
▌ **Fruits** are mature ovaries of the plant. They help disperse the seeds of angiosperms.
▌ The life cycle of the angiosperm is a refined version of the alternation of generations that all plants undergo.
▌ The angiosperm life cycle consists of the following steps (see the diagram above): (1) The anthers of the flower produce microspores. The microspores form (2) male gametophytes, also known as pollen. (3) Meanwhile, the ovules produce megaspores that form female gametophytes (embryo sacs). (4) Pollination

brings the gametophytes together in the ovary. (5) Double fertilization takes place, and (6) the zygote develops into an embryo that is packaged along with food (endosperm) into seeds.

▌ Animals have influenced the evolution of plants, and vice versa. Plant-pollinator relationships have likely increased angiosperm and animal diversity.

Concept 31.1 Fungi are heterotrophs that feed by absorption

▌ All fungi are eukaryotes, most are multicellular. They are different from other eukaryotes in their nutrition, structure, growth, and reproduction.

▌ Fungi are **heterotrophs** that obtain nutrients by **absorption.** Fungi secrete hydrolytic enzymes, digest food outside their bodies, and absorb the small molecules.

▌ The bodies of fungi are composed of filaments called **hyphae** that are entwined to form a **mycelium** (the body).

▌ Most fungi are multicellular with hyphae divided into cells by cross walls called **septa.** Septa have pores large enough to allow organelles generally to pass through.

▌ Coenocytic fungi lack septa and consist of a continuous cytoplasmic mass containing hundreds of nuclei.

▌ The cell walls of fungi are made of chitin.

▌ Fungi produce spores either sexually or asexually, and they disperse these spores in order to reproduce. The spores of most fungal species are haploid.

Concept 31.4 Fungi have radiated into a diverse set of lineages

▌ There are **five phyla of fungi:** Chytridiomycota, Zygomycota, Glomeromycota, Ascomycota, and Basidiomycota.

1. **Chytridiomycota** (chytrids) are aquatic saprobes or parasites; they are thought to be the most primitive fungi.
2. **Zygomycota** (zygote fungi) are terrestrial, and include fast-growing molds, parasites, and commensal symbionts. A common zygomycete is bread mold, *Rhizopus.*
3. **Glomeromycota** form a distinct type of mycorrhizae with plant roots in which the tips of hyphae push into plant root cells. The plant receives minerals and other nutrients through the mycorrhizae.
4. **Ascomycota** (sac fungi) live in a variety of habitats and produce sexual spores in saclike structures called asci; ascomycetes include some of the most devastating plant pathogens.
5. **Basidiomycota** (club fungi) include mushrooms and shelf fungi and are important decomposers of organic material.

Concept 31.5 Fungi have a powerful impact on ecosystems and human welfare

▌ Fungi are important decomposers that release inorganic nutrients, enabling them to cycle through the environment.

▌ **Lichens** are symbiotic associations of photosynthetic microorganisms (algae) embedded in a network of fungal hyphae. They are very hardy organisms that are pioneers on rock and soil surfaces.

■ Thirty percent of known species of fungi are parasites. Many are plant pathogens (e.g., Dutch elm disease, wheat rust, and ergot). Some infect animals (e.g., ringworm, athlete's foot, and *Candida*).

Concept 32.1 Animals are multicellular, heterotrophic eukaryotes with tissues that develop from embryonic layers

Concept 32.2 The history of animals may span more than a billion years

■ The evolutionary episode that led to most of the animal phyla occurred during the late **Neoproterozoic** and **early Cambrian eras.**

■ During the "Cambrian explosion," the first animals that possessed **hard, mineralized skeletons** appeared in the fossil record. Paleontologists have found the oldest fossils of about half of all extant phyla in the strata from this time period.

Concept 32.3 Animals can be characterized by "body plans"

■ **Radial symmetry** occurs in jellies and other organisms, in which any cut through the central axis of the organism would produce mirror images.

■ **Bilateral symmetry** occurs in lobsters, humans, and many other organisms. These animals have a right side and a left side, and a single cut would divide the animal into two mirror image halves.

■ **Cephalization** is the concentration of sensory equipment at one end (usually the anterior, or head end) of the organism.

■ **Coelomates** possess a **body cavity** filled with fluid, and this space separates an animal's digestive tract from the outer body wall. A true coelom forms from tissue derived from mesoderm.

■ **Pseudocoelomates** are triploblastic animals with a cavity formed from the blastocoel, rather than the mesoderm.

■ **Acoelomates,** such as flatworms, have no cavities between their alimentary canal and the outer wall of their bodies.

Chapter 33 Overview: Life Without a Backbone

Invertebrates are animals that lack backbones. An outline of animal diversity and classification follows.

1. Subkingdom Parazoa: Phylum Porifera

■ **Parazoa** (sponges) are thought to be the oldest animals. They are sessile but very sedate and have no nerves or muscles. The body of a sponge looks like a sac with holes in it. Water is drawn through the pores into the **spongocoel** and flows out through the **osculum.**

■ Most sponges are **filter-feeders** that collect particles from water that passes through them.

■ Most sponges are **hermaphrodites.** That is, they function as both male and female and produce both sperm and eggs.

■ Sponges are capable of **regeneration** of lost parts.

2. Subkingdom Eumetazoa

■ **A. Radially symmetrical animals**

All animals except the Parazoa belong to the clade Eumetazoa; they are animals with true tissues. There are two phyla that have radial symmetry—cnidaria and ctenophora.

1. Members of **phylum Cnidaria** exist in polyp and medusa form, and they have radial symmetry, a central digestive compartment known as a gastrovascular cavity, and cnidocytes (cells that function in defense and the capture of prey). Examples of cnidarians are hydras, jellies, and corals.

2. **Phylum Ctenophora,** also known as comb jellies, look like medusal cnidarians. Most are spherical and possess rows of plates formed from fused cilia, which they use for locomotion.

■ **B. Bilaterally symmetrical animals**

1. **Acoelomates (animals without a body cavity)**
   • Members of **phylum Platyhelminthes (flatworms)** live in water or damp terrestrial habitats. They exist in parasitic and free-living form, are flat with dorsal and ventral surfaces, lack organs that are specialized for gas exchange/circulation, and reproduce asexually through regeneration. Platyhelminthes are divided into four classes—Turbellaria, Monogenea, Trematoda, and Cestoda. Some examples are flukes and tapeworms.
   • Members of **phylum Nemertea,** also called ribbon worms or proboscis worms, have excretory, sensory, and nervous systems similar to flatworms. They have a complete alimentary canal with a closed circulatory system but no heart.

2. **Pseudocoelomates**
   • Members of **phylum Nematoda,** or roundworms, are found in most aquatic habitats. Their bodies are not segmented but are cylindrical. Roundworms have an exoskeleton called a cuticle, a complete alimentary canal (but no circulatory system), and a pseudocoelom. They reproduce sexually, and sexes are separate in most species. Some examples are pinworms and hookworms.
   • **Phylum Rotifera** members inhabit fresh water. They have specialized organ systems, including a complete alimentary canal, jaws that grind food, and cilia that draw water into the mouth. Some species participate in **parthenogenesis** (females produce unfertilized eggs, from which more females hatch).

3. **Coelomates**
   • Phylums Ectoprocta (which look like mosses), Phoronida (marine worms), and Brachiopoda (lamp shells that look like clams) are traditionally called lophophorates. They contain a lophophore—a cir-

cular fold of the body wall with ciliated tentacles surrounding the mouth.

- **Phylum Mollusca** members are soft-bodied animals protected with a hard shell (except for slugs, squids, and octopuses). They possess a muscular foot for movement, a visceral mass made up of the organs, and a mantle, which drapes over the visceral mass and secretes a shell. Most have separate sexes (though many snails are hermaphrodites), and most are marine. Some examples are Polyplacophora (chitons), Gastropoda (snails and slugs), Bivalvia (clams and oysters, etc.), and Cephalopoda (squids and octopuses, etc.).

- **Phylum Annelida** contains worms (such as the earthworm) that are segmented both externally and internally. They live in the sea, in fresh water, or in damp habitats. They have a coelom, a closed digestive system with specialized regions (the crop, gizzard, esophagus, and intestine), a brainlike central ganglia, and a hydrostatic skeleton that enables them to move. They can be hermaphrodites. Some examples are Oligochaeta (earthworms and their relatives), Polychaeta (mostly marine segmented worms), and Hirudinea (leeches).

- **Phylum Arthropoda** members are segmented animals with a hard exoskeleton and jointed appendages. In order to grow, arthropods must occasionally shed their exoskeleton and secrete a new one—this process is known as **molting.** They have well-developed sensory organs, an open circulatory system, organs specialized for gas exchange, and a hemocoel (body sinuses functioning in transport of fluid through the body). Some examples are Crustacea (lobsters and shrimp), Cheliceriformes (spiders and scorpions), Hexapoda (insects), Trilobites (extinct), and Myriapoda (millipedes and centipedes).

4. **Deuterostomia**

The clade Deuterostomia contains a diverse array of organisms, from sea stars to chordates. All have radial cleavage and share common developmental processes. There are two main phyla.

- Members of **phylum Echinodermata,** or echinoderms, are slow-moving and radiate from the center. They have a thin skin covering an exoskeleton, as well as a water vascular system (a network of internal canals that branch into tube feet used for moving, feeding, and gas exchange). They reproduce sexually and can be divided into six classes. Some examples are sea stars, brittle stars, sea urchins, sand dollars, sea lilies, and sea cucumbers.

- **Phylum Chordata** includes two invertebrate subphyla as well as all vertebrates.

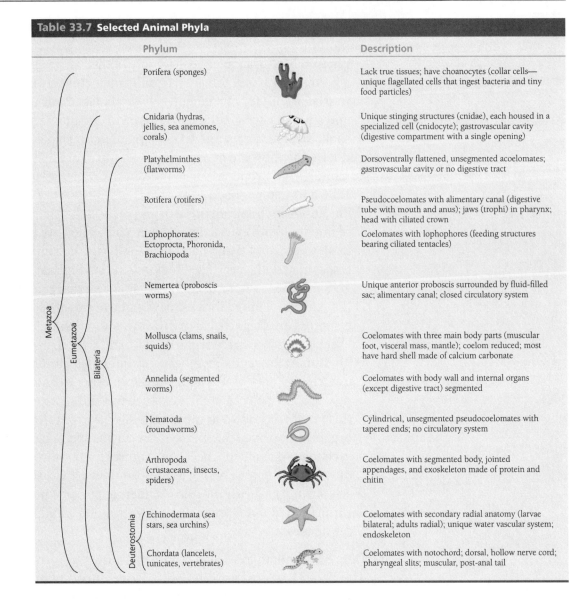

Table 33.7 Selected Animal Phyla		
Phylum		**Description**
Porifera (sponges)		Lack true tissues; have choanocytes (collar cells—unique flagellated cells that ingest bacteria and tiny food particles)
Cnidaria (hydras, jellies, sea anemones, corals)		Unique stinging structures (cnidae), each housed in a specialized cell (cnidocyte); gastrovascular cavity (digestive compartment with a single opening)
Platyhelminthes (flatworms)		Dorsoventrally flattened, unsegmented acoelomates; gastrovascular cavity or no digestive tract
Rotifera (rotifers)		Pseudocoelomates with alimentary canal (digestive tube with mouth and anus); jaws (trophi) in pharynx; head with ciliated crown
Lophophorates: Ectoprocta, Phoronida, Brachiopoda		Coelomates with lophophores (feeding structures bearing ciliated tentacles)
Nemertea (proboscis worms)		Unique anterior proboscis surrounded by fluid-filled sac; alimentary canal; closed circulatory system
Mollusca (clams, snails, squids)		Coelomates with three main body parts (muscular foot, visceral mass, mantle); coelom reduced; most have hard shell made of calcium carbonate
Annelida (segmented worms)		Coelomates with body wall and internal organs (except digestive tract) segmented
Nematoda (roundworms)		Cylindrical, unsegmented pseudocoelomates with tapered ends; no circulatory system
Arthropoda (crustaceans, insects, spiders)		Coelomates with segmented body, jointed appendages, and exoskeleton made of protein and chitin
Echinodermata (sea stars, sea urchins)		Coelomates with secondary radial anatomy (larvae bilateral; adults radial); unique water vascular system; endoskeleton
Chordata (lancelets, tunicates, vertebrates)		Coelomates with notochord; dorsal, hollow nerve cord; pharyngeal slits; muscular, post-anal tail

Concept 34.1 Chordates have a notochord and a dorsal, hollow nerve cord

▌ Many of the four anatomical features that characterize chordates appear only during embryonic development.

1. A **notochord**—a long, flexible rod that appears during embryonic development between the digestive tube and the dorsal nerve cord
2. A **dorsal, hollow nerve cord**—formed from a plate of ectoderm that rolls into a hollow tube
3. **Pharyngeal clefts**—grooves that separate a series of pouches along the sides of the pharynx. In most chordates (not tetrapods) the clefts develop into slits that allow water to enter and exit the mouth without going through the digestive tract.
4. A muscular **tail** posterior to the anus

▌ There are two subphyla of invertebrate chordates—**Urochordata** (tunicates) and **Cephalochordata** (lancelets). They are simpler versions of vertebrates.

Concept 34.2 *Craniates are chordates that have a head*

The oldest extant craniates are hagfishes (**class Myxini**). Hagfishes are marine dwellers and bottom-dwelling scavengers. They possess no vertebrae, but have a skull made of cartilage.

Concept 34.3 *Vertebrates are craniates that have a backbone*

Innovations of vertebrate evolution include the presence of a more extensive skull and a backbone composed of vertebrae. In the majority of vertebrates, vertebrae enclose the spinal cord and have assumed the roles of the notochord.

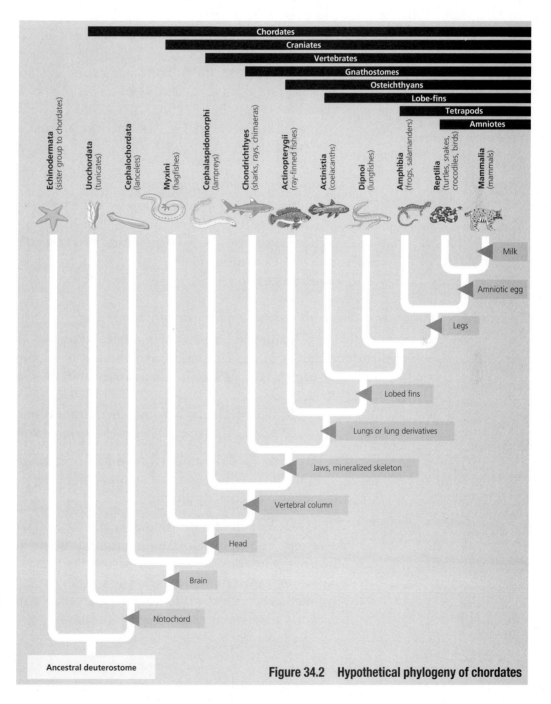

Figure 34.2   Hypothetical phylogeny of chordates

The oldest lineage of vertebrates is the lampreys (**class Cephalaspidomorphi**), which live in marine and fresh water. A cartilaginous pipe surrounds the notochord; lampreys lack skeleton-supported jaws. Their rasping mouths bore holes in the side of a fish. They live on the blood and tissue of a host.

Concept 34.4 *Gnathostomes are vertebrates that have jaws*

The jaws of vertebrates evolved from the modification of skeletal parts that had once supported the pharyngeal (gill) slits.

1. **Class Chondrichthyes** have flexible endoskeletons composed of cartilage, possess streamlined bodies, are denser than water, and will sink if they stop swimming. Some examples are sharks and rays (such as stingrays).
2. **Class Osteichthyes** are the bony fishes; these are the most numerous of all vertebrate groups. The two main classes of bony fishes are the ray-finned fishes and the lobe-fins. They have an ossified endoskeleton, are covered in scales, and possess a swim bladder. Some examples are common fish.

Concept 34.5 *Tetrapods are gnathostomes that have limbs and feet*

Class Amphibia members maintain close ties with water and rely on their skin for gas exchange with the environment. Not all amphibians have legs. Some, such as frogs, have a larval stage with a dual (aquatic and terrestrial) life. Their eggs lack a shell, and fertilization is external. They can exhibit complex social behavior.

Concept 34.6 *Amniotes are tetrapods that have a terrestrially adapted egg*

- The clade of **Amniotes** consists of mammals and reptiles (including birds).
- The **amniotic egg** was an important evolutionary development for life on land. Amniotic eggs have a shell that retains water and, thus, can be laid in a dry environment.
- Amniotic eggs have **extraembryonic membranes** that function in gas exchange, waste storage, and the transport of nutrients to the embryo.

1. **Reptiles** have **scales,** containing keratin, which are an adaptation for terrestrial living. They obtain oxygen through their lungs, not their skin. They lay eggs on land, and undergo internal fertilization.

   - Extinct reptiles included **dinosaurs** (which lived on land), **pterosaurs** (flying reptiles), and **plesiosaurs** (marine reptiles).
   - Modern reptiles consist of the turtles, tuataras, lizards and snakes, and alligators and crocodiles.
   - Most reptiles are ectothermic. They regulate body temperature through behavioral adaptations rather than by metabolism.

2. **Birds** lay **amniotic eggs** and have keratin-containing **scales** on their legs—both of which are reptilian characteristics.

   - Most birds' bodies are constructed for flight, with light, hollow bones; relatively few organs; wings; and feathers.
   - Birds are **endotherms** and maintain a warm, consistent body temperature. **Feathers** and, in some cases, a layer of fat insulate birds and help them maintain internal temperature.
   - Birds have a **four-chambered heart** and a high rate of **metabolism,** and they have larger brains (compared proportionally) than amphibians and nonbird reptiles do.

Concept 34.7 *Mammals are amniotes that have hair and produce milk*

- Most or all mammals share certain characteristics. For instance, all possess **mammary glands** that produce milk; all possess **hair**; all are **endothermic** and have an active metabolism; most are **born** rather than hatched; all use internal fertilization; all have **proportionally larger brains** than other vertebrates; and all have **teeth** of differing size and shape.
- Mammals can be placed into three groups.

  1. **Monotremes** are egg-laying mammals that have hair and produce milk. Some examples are platypuses and spiny anteaters.
  2. **Marsupials** are born early in development and complete embryonic development in a marsupium (pouch) while nursing. Examples include wombats, Tasmanian devils, and kangaroos.
  3. **Placental mammals (eutherians)** have a longer period of pregnancy; they complete their development in the uterus. Examples include deer mice, moles, flying squirrels, and wolverines.

- Some characteristics common to all **primates** include hands and feet that grasp, large brains and short jaws, forward-looking eyes, flat nails, well-developed parental care, and complex social behavior.
- The three subgroups of primates are lemurs, lorises, and pottos; tarsiers; and **anthropoids** (monkeys, apes, and humans).
- Some features of **human evolution** are increased brain volume, shortening of the jaw, bipedal posture, reduced size-difference between the sexes, and certain important changes in family structure.

For Additional Review

Compare the land adaptations of plants and animals, including how each manages the uptake of nutrients and water as well as the excretion of wastes.

Multiple-Choice Questions

1. Which group thrives in extreme heat and acidic environments?
   (A) Bryophytes
   (B) Protists
   (C) Archaea
   (D) Fungi
   (E) Deuterostomia

2. Which of the following groups is best characterized as being heterotrophic and eukaryotic with a plasma membrane?
   (A) Plantae
   (B) Animalia
   (C) Fungi
   (D) Viruses
   (E) Monera

3. A biologist captures an aquatic organism from a freshwater pond. It has a segmented body and a brainlike pair of central ganglia. It is also a bottom dweller that burrows into the pond floor. Most likely this organism is
   (A) a protist.
   (B) an annelid.
   (C) an arachnid.
   (D) a eurypterid.
   (E) a reptile.

4. In which of the following pairs are the organisms most closely related taxonomically?
   (A) squid; snails
   (B) mushrooms; tulips
   (C) clams; lobsters
   (D) sponges; hydras
   (E) lancelets; roundworms

Directions: The group of questions below consists of five lettered choices followed by a list of numbered phrases or sentences. For each numbered phrase or sentence, select the one choice that is most closely related to it. Each choice may be used once, more than once, or not at all.

Questions 5–9
   (A) Chordata
   (B) Arthropoda
   (C) Annelida
   (D) Platyhelminthes
   (E) Porifera

5. Parasitic, lack a body cavity, acoelomates, freshwater and damp terrestrial habitats

6. Bodies segmented internally and externally, freshwater habitat, respiration occurs through the skin

7. Possess a notochord; a dorsal, hollow nerve cord; pharyngeal clefts; and a post-anal tail at some point during development

8. Segmented coelomates that have exoskeletons and jointed appendages

9. Sessile, possessing no nerves or muscles, have a central cavity, are filter feeders

10. Systematists categorize all living creatures into what three domains?
    (A) Bacteria, Euglena, Eukarya
    (B) Bacteria, Archaea, Eukarya
    (C) Archaea, Plantae, Eukarya
    (D) Protista, Plantae, Eukarya
    (E) Prokaryota, Eukarya, Plantae

11. The cell walls of bacteria contain which of the following materials?
    (A) peptidoglycans
    (B) polynucleotides
    (C) pyrimidines
    (D) disaccharides
    (E) ribose

12. The most common method of locomotion in prokaryotes occurs via the movement of
    (A) claws.
    (B) contractions of the vascular cavity.
    (C) flagella.
    (D) tentacles.
    (E) repeated alteration of cell shape.

13. Heterotrophic cells are unable to synthesize which of the following compounds?
    (A) cholesterol
    (B) glycerol
    (C) polypeptides
    (D) ribonucleic acids
    (E) glucose

14. Which of the following is a symbiotic relationship in which both organisms benefit?
    (A) parasitism
    (B) commensalism
    (C) mutualism
    (D) obligate
    (E) heterotrophic

15. One example of a commensal symbiotic relationship is
    (A) the legume plant, which houses prokaryotes that fix nitrogen.
    (B) the intestine of a pig, which houses roundworms.
    (C) the vagina of a human, which hosts fermenting bacteria that produce acids.
    (D) cowbirds feeding on insects flushed out by grazing cattle.
    (E) animal cells hosting a virus.

16. Which of the following constitutes the kingdom containing the widest array of organisms?
    (A) Animalia
    (B) Plantae
    (C) Fungi
    (D) Protista
    (E) Bacteria

17. From an evolution perspective, certain organelles contained in animal cells are the result of what process?
    (A) endosymbiosis
    (B) conjugation
    (C) transformation
    (D) ectosymbiosis
    (E) compartmentalization

18. Slime molds are contained in which of the following kingdoms?
    (A) Plantae
    (B) Archaea
    (C) Eukarya
    (D) Protista
    (E) Euglena

Directions: The group of questions below consists of five lettered choices followed by a list of numbered phrases or sentences. For each numbered phrase or sentence, select the one choice that is most closely related to it. Each choice may be used once, more than once, or not at all.

Questions 19–22
    (A) Bryophytes
    (B) Pteridophytes
    (C) Gymnosperms
    (D) Angiosperms
    (E) Fungi

19. Contain the mosses, lack vascular tissue

20. Contain the flowering plants, possess vascular tissue

21. Contain the ferns, are the seedless plants, and have vascular tissue

22. Contain the conifers, have seeds and vascular tissue

23. In alternation of generations in land plants, which of the following represents the haploid stage?
(A) zygote
(B) gametophytes
(C) sporophyte
(D) spore
(E) sporangies

24. All of the following are adaptations of land plants EXCEPT
(A) stomata.
(B) cuticle.
(C) xylem.
(D) phloem.
(E) photosynthesis.

25. Which of the following is one of the three types of bryophytes?
(A) anthophytes
(B) brown algae
(C) green algae
(D) liverworts
(E) lycophytes

26. Which of the following is the dominant stage of the life cycle for seedless vascular plants?
(A) gametophyte
(B) sporophyte
(C) zygote
(D) heterosporous
(E) homosporous

27. A student is collecting samples of plants from a field in Connecticut. He picks one from the ground to study it more closely. In the process, he notices that the leaves show veins that run parallel from end to end. This plant is mostly likely a
(A) eudicot.
(B) conifer.
(C) monocot.
(D) dicot.
(E) tracheid.

28. The tiny filaments that comprise the body of fungi are known as
(A) hyphae.
(B) mycelium.
(C) chitin.
(D) mycorrhizae.
(E) basidium.

Directions: The group of questions below consists of five lettered choices followed by a list of numbered phrases or sentences. For each numbered phrase or sentence, select the one choice that is most closely related to it. Each choice may be used once, more than once, or not at all.

Questions 29–33
(A) Mold
(B) Yeast
(C) Lichen
(D) Mycorrhizae
(E) Deuteromycetes

29. Mutualistic associations of plant roots and fungi

30. Unicellular fungi that live in damp environments

31. Symbiotic associations of photosynthetic microorganisms in a network of fungal hyphae

32. Phylum for fungi with unknown sexual stages

33. Term applied to rapidly growing, asexually reproducing fungi

34. All of the following terms reflect characteristics of almost all animals EXCEPT
(A) multicellularity.
(B) heterotrophic nutrition.
(C) presence of tissues.
(D) eukaryotic.
(E) diurnal.

35. The body plans of sea anemones exhibit
    (A) bilateral symmetry.
    (B) radial symmetry.
    (C) dorsal and ventral symmetry.
    (D) anterior and posterior symmetry.
    (E) no symmetry.

36. Most of the animal phyla originated in what geologic time span?
    (A) Paleozoic
    (B) Jurassic
    (C) Proterozoic
    (D) Cambrian
    (E) Mesozoic

37. Evolution of which feature enabled vertebrates to reproduce successfully on land?
    (A) the amniotic egg
    (B) quadruped locomotion
    (C) body hair
    (D) opposable thumbs
    (E) cloaca

38. Which of the following animals is characterized by a relatively short period of pregnancy followed by a period of nursing as its offspring completes development?
    (A) placental mammals
    (B) marsupial mammals
    (C) monotremes
    (D) therapsids
    (E) carnites

39. A body cavity that is not completely lined by tissue derived from the mesoderm is called a(n)
    (A) coelom.
    (B) subcoelom.
    (C) pseudocoelom.
    (D) anticoelom.
    (E) transcoelom.

40. The above photograph represents which of the following cnidarian forms?
    (A) medusa
    (B) polyp
    (C) hermaphrodite
    (D) radula
    (E) mantle

Free-Response Question

1. *Systematists are scientists who study evolutionary relationships between organisms; they use scientific evidence to construct hypothetical phylogenies that show these relationships. Systematists have replaced the five-kingdom system with a more accurate, three-domain system, containing the Archaea, the Bacteria, and the Eukarya.*

   (a) **Describe** how this scheme for classification differs from the old five-kingdom one.
   (b) **Describe** three types of evidence that scientists used to develop this three-domain system.

ANSWERS AND EXPLANATIONS

Multiple-Choice Questions

1. (C) is correct. The prokaryotes are split into two domains, Archaea and Bacteria. Many Archaea are known as extremophiles; they are often found in extreme (i.e., salty or very hot) environments, such as the geysers of Yellowstone National Park.

2. (B) is correct. Animals are heterotrophic—they are not capable of fixing carbon and must obtain it from phototropic organisms. They belong to the kingdom Eukarya, and they possess plasma membranes made up of phospholipids and proteins that control the movement of substances into and out of the cell.

3. (B) is correct. Annelids are characterized by internally and externally segmented bodies; they are 1 mm to 3 m in length and live in freshwater habitats, the soil, and the sea. Earthworms are a common annelid.

4. (A) is correct. The two organisms most closely related are the squids and snails. These two are members of the phylum Mollusca. The other choices do not include members of the same phylum.

5. (D) is correct. Platyhelminthes are flatworms—acoelomates that have gastrovascular cavities.

6. (C) is correct. Phylum Annelida contains organisms with segmented body plans that inhabit freshwater or damp terrestrial habitats. They have closed circulatory systems, and respiration occurs through the skin.

7. (A) is correct. The chordates are mostly vertebrates, although there are two groups of invertebrate chordates. The chordates are grouped according to the presence of a notochord; a dorsal, hollow nerve cord; pharyngeal clefts; and a post-anal tail. Many of these features exist only during embryonic development.

8. (B) is correct. Including the lobsters, spiders, and other related organisms, the arthropods are characterized by having an exoskeleton (which is sometimes shed in a process called molting), jointed appendages, and segmentation.

9. (E) is correct. Porifera are the simplest invertebrates. They are sessile and have no muscles or nerve cells. They resemble a sac with holes in it, and they draw water into their central cavity (spongocoel), filtering out food particles.

10. (B) is correct. The three domains into which all the living organisms are placed by systematists are Bacteria, Archaea, and Eukarya. Domains are one taxonomic level above kingdoms. Prokaryotes make up Archaea and Bacteria, whereas eukaryotes make up Eukarya.

11. (A) is correct. Peptidoglycans are polymers of modified sugars that are linked by short polypeptides that differ from species to species.

12. (C) is correct. The flagella account for most movements in prokaryotes. Prokaryotic flagella are much smaller than eukaryotic flagella and operate under different mechanisms.

13. (E) is correct. Heterotrophs need at least one organic compound in order to make others. Chemotrophs get their energy from chemicals in the environment. Autotrophs can make organic compounds from CO_2.

14. (C) is correct. In mutualistic symbiosis, both organisms benefit from the association; in commensalistic symbiosis, one organism benefits, while the other is neither helped nor harmed; and in parasitic symbiosis, one organism benefits, while the other is harmed.

15. **(D) is correct.** Commensal association sometimes involves one species (the cowbirds) inadvertently helped out by another (the grazing cattle). Because the birds increase their feeding rate when following the cattle, they clearly benefit.

16. **(D) is correct.** Protista is by far the most varied kingdom. Most of the protists are unicellular, but there are multicellular protists, too. Protists can be divided into protozoa (animal-like protists), algae (plant-like protists), and fungus-like protists.

17. **(A) is correct.** Endosymbiosis—the theory of serial endosymbiosis—proposes that mitochondria and chloroplasts evolved from small prokaryotes that were engulfed by larger host cells. Eventually they became permanent functional parts of the cell.

18. **(D) is correct.** Slime molds are decomposers and are part of the kingdom Protista. They have structures called pseudopodia that are used for moving and feeding.

19. **(A) is correct.** Bryophytes are one of the four main types of land plants. The most common bryophytes are the mosses, which do not have vascular tissue and are relatively simple.

20. **(D) is correct.** The angiosperms are the flowering plants. They have vascular tissue, and the flower is their reproductive structure. They also have seeds enclosed within their fruits.

21. **(B) is correct.** Pteridophytes are seedless plants with vascular tissue. One prominent member of this group is the ferns.

22. **(C) is correct.** Gymnosperms are seed plants that have "naked" seeds. These seeds are not enclosed in any specialized chambers. But these plants do possess vascular tissue. Pine trees are a common example of gymnosperms.

23. **(B) is correct.** The cells of the gametophyte are haploid (n) and have a single set of chromosomes. The fusion of sperm and egg cells during fertilization produces the zygote, which is diploid. The zygote divides mitotically to produce the sporophyte.

24. **(E) is correct.** Photosynthesis in plants does not necessarily contribute to their ability to conserve water or to store water in their structure. The other plant structures listed are all evolutionary adaptations for terrestrial plants.

25. **(D) is correct.** There are three phyla of bryophytes—mosses, liverworts, and hornworts. In bryophytes, the gametophyte is the dominant generation, whereas sporophytes typically are present only briefly.

26. **(B) is correct.** The sporophyte stage is the dominant one in the life cycle of the seedless vascular plant. The sporophyte is the diploid stage, whereas gametophytes are tiny and exist only briefly.

27. **(C) is correct.** This plant is probably a monocot. Monocots have veins that run parallel, whereas eudicot leaves have a netlike vein arrangement. Grasses are good examples of monocots.

■ **28. (A) is correct.** Hyphae are filaments made up of tube-like walls that surround cytoplasm and plasma membranes. They group together to form a woven mat called a mycelium.

■ **29. (D) is correct.** Mycorrhizae are mutual associations of fungi and plant roots. They exchange minerals extracted from the soil and nutrients produced by the plants.

■ **30. (B) is correct.** Yeasts are unicellular fungi that live in moist environments or liquids. They reproduce by cell division or budding.

■ **31. (C) is correct.** Lichens are symbiotic associations of millions of photosynthetic organisms in a network of fungal hyphae. They are very hardy and frequently colonize newly broken rock faces.

■ **32. (E) is correct.** Whenever a sexual stage of a so-called deuteromycete is discovered, the species is classified in the appropriate phylum.

■ **33. (A) is correct.** Molds are rapidly growing fungi that reproduce asexually. They grow on a variety of mediums and go through a series of different reproductive stages.

■ **34. (E) is correct.** The first four answer choices represent characteristics common to almost all animals; the last one does not. The characteristic of being diurnal (the opposite of nocturnal—being active during the day) is not a requirement for belonging to the kingdom Animalia.

■ **35. (B) is correct.** Sea anemones can best be described as having radial symmetry. Radial animals have a top and bottom but no head or rear end, or left and right side.

■ **36. (D) is correct.** The Cambrian explosion led to the relatively quick appearance of most of the major animal phyla. Many fossils dating from that era have been discovered.

■ **37. (A) is correct.** The amniotic egg is composed of extraembryonic membranes that function in gas exchange, waste storage, and the delivery of nutrients to the embryo.

■ **38. (B) is correct.** Marsupials are predominantly located in Australia, where they have radiated to fill niches occupied by placental mammals elsewhere. Marsupials have a short period of pregnancy, and the embryo completes its development nursing within the pouch of the mother.

■ **39. (C) is correct.** Animals that have no cavity between their alimentary canal and their body wall are acoelomates. Those that have a cavity not derived from the mesoderm are pseudocoelomates, and those that have a true coelom derived from the mesoderm are coelomates.

■ **40. (A) is correct.** This represents the medusa form of the cnidarian. Despite the fact that they can move, polyps (like hydras and sea anemones) adhere to a substrate with their mouth side up. Medusas (jellies) are free swimming and "upside down" compared to polyps—that is, their tentacle side faces downward. Cnidarians are characterized by having radial symmetry, a gastrovascular cavity, and cnidocytes—cells that function in defense and capture of prey.

Free-Response Question

(a) The old five-kingdom system contained the kingdoms Monera, Protista, Plantae, Fungi, and Animalia. However, scientists have determined that the Monera kingdom should be further separated into two groups. Thus, they split Monera into Archaea and Bacteria. They realized that the Archaea and Bacteria are as different from each other as they are different from us, the Eukarya. The new system is a three-domain system, with the domains Archaea, Bacteria, and Eukarya. Archaea and Bacteria are composed of prokaryotes, and Eukarya is made up of eukaryotes. From the old five-kingdom system, the Protista, Plantae, Fungi, and Animalia are all placed in the domain Eukarya.

(b) Three methods or types of evidence that scientists use to classify organisms and study their degree of evolutionary relatedness are fossil evidence, the structure and development of organisms, and molecular evidence.

Systematists can also study patterns of homologous structures to determine evolutionary relationships. Species that were derived from the same ancestor should have similarities, called homologies. Here, scientists would look for homologous structures—structures that are similar in different species—and use these to tie organisms together.

The third way that systematists can study evolutionary relationships is on a molecular level. Because DNA is heritable, related species should share common genes, and the more recently the species branched off from a common ancestor, the more similar their DNA should be. Studying the DNA of organisms makes it possible for systematists to determine the degree of evolutionary difference between two species that are nearly identical in appearance, and it also allows systematists to judge the relatedness of two species that they might not guess would be related at all, based on external appearance. It is a much more precise and quantitative method for appraising evolutionary relatedness.

This response uses the following key terms in context, showing the writer's knowledge of their meanings and relatedness:

Monera	*Bacteria*
Protista	*Eukarya*
Plantae	*systematists*
Fungi	*homologous structures*
Animalia	*DNA*
Archaea	

This response also accurately describes the rationale behind the process of the reorganizing of the five-kingdom system into the three-domain system. It clearly describes three methods for studying the evolutionary relatedness of species, thus answering the question in a complete and organized way. Always check your final response to make sure it addresses the original question.

CHAPTER 6

Plant Form and Function

Concept 35.1 The plant body has a hierarchy of organs, tissues, and cells

- Plants have a **root system** beneath the ground and a **shoot system** above the ground.
- **Fibrous roots** are made up of a mat of thin roots that are spread just below the soil's surface. **Taproots** are made up of one thick, vertical root with many lateral roots that come out from it.
- Stems are made up of **nodes** (points at which leaves are attached) and **internodes** (the parts of the stem between the nodes).
- **Axillary buds** are located in the V formed between the node and the stem, and these have the potential to form a branch (or lateral shoot).
- The **terminal bud** is located at the top end of the stem and is where growth usually occurs. In apical dominance, the terminal bud prohibits the growth of the axillary buds.
- Leaves are the main sites of photosynthesis in plants. Leaves consist of a **blade,** which is flat, and the **petiole,** which joins the leaf to a node of the stem.
- Plant organs—leaf, stem, and root—are composed of three tissue types.

  1. **Dermal tissue** is a single layer of closely packed cells that covers the entire plant and protects it.
  2. **Vascular tissue** is continuous through the plant and transports materials between the roots and shoots. Vascular tissue is made up of:
     (a) **xylem,** which transports water and minerals up from the roots. Components of xylem—tracheids and vessel elements—are dead cells that form a conduit through which water passes.
     (b) **phloem,** which transports food from the leaves to the other parts of the plant. In seedless vascular plants and gymnosperms organic nutrients are transferred through long, narrow cells called sieve cells. In angiosperms these nutrients are transported through sieve tubes, which consists of chains of cells called sieve-tube members.
  3. **Ground tissue** is anything that isn't dermal tissue or vascular tissue. Any ground tissue internal to the vascular tissue is **pith;** any ground tissue external to the vascular tissue is **cortex.**
- Plants have three cell types.

  1. **Parenchyma cells** are the most abundant cell type and are present throughout the plant. These cells perform most of the metabolism (including photosynthesis) in the plant.

2. **Collenchyma cells** are grouped in cylinders and help support growing parts of the plant.
3. **Sclerenchyma cells** exist in parts of the cell that are no longer growing, and they have tough cell walls. Two types of these are specialized just for support—**fibers** and **sclereids.**

Concept 35.2 Meristems generate cells for new organs

▌ Based on their life cycle, flowering plants can be classified as **annuals** (life cycle completed in one year), **biennials** (life cycle completed in two years), or **perennials** (life cycle continues for many years).

▌ **Meristems** are perpetually embryonic tissues that are responsible for indeterminate growth.

▌ **Apical meristems** are located at the tips of roots and in buds of shoots, and these are the sites of cell division, allowing the plant to grow in length.

▌ **Primary growth** occurs when the plant grows at the apical meristems (length), while secondary growth (which occurs in woody plants) is when the shoots and roots of a plant thicken. **Secondary growth** is the product of **lateral meristems.**

Concept 35.3 Primary growth lengthens roots and shoots

▌ The **root cap** protects the delicate meristem of the root tip as it pushes through the soil. It also secretes a polysaccharide lubricant. The **root tip** contains three zones of cells in various stages of growth.

1. The **zone of cell division** includes root apical meristem and its derivatives. New root cells are produced in this region, including the cells of the root cap.
2. Above the zone of cell division is the **zone of elongation,** in which cells elongate significantly.
3. In the **zone of maturation,** the three systems in primary growth complete their differentiation and become functionally mature.

▌ At a shoot, the apical meristem is a dome of dividing cells at the tip of a terminal bud.

▌ The epidermis of the underside of the leaf is interrupted by **stomata,** which are small pores flanked by guard cells, which open and close the stomata.

▌ In leaves, the ground tissue is sandwiched between the upper and lower epidermis, in the mesophyll. It is made up of parenchyma cells, the sites of photosynthesis.

Concept 35.4 Secondary growth adds girth to stems and roots in woody plants

▌ Two lateral meristems take part in plant growth. The **vascular cambium** produces secondary xylem (wood). The **cork cambium** produces a tough covering that replaces epidermis early in secondary growth. Cork cambium produces cork cells. The cork and cork cambium make up the **periderm.**

■ The periderm contains small, raised areas called **lenticels** that form spaces between the cork cells. This allows for gas exchange between cells in the woody stem and the outside.

■ **Bark** is all the tissues outside the vascular cambium.

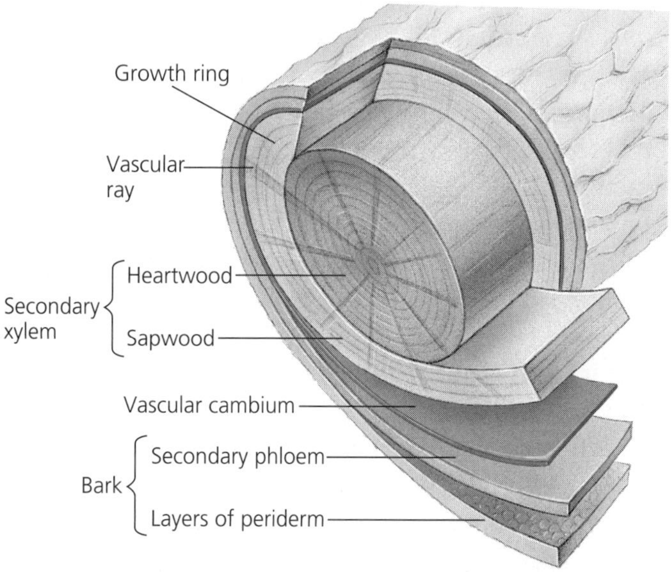

Figure 35.20   Anatomy of a tree trunk

Concept 35.5 *Growth, morphogenesis, and differentiation produce the plant body*

■ By increasing cell number, division in meristems increases the potential for growth. However, it is cell expansion that accounts for the actual increase in plant mass.

■ **Morphogenesis**—development of body form and organization—must occur in order for cells to be organized into multicellular arrangements such as tissues. The development of specific structures in specific locations is called **pattern formation.** Many developmental biologists postulate that pattern formation is determined by **positional information** in the form of signals that continuously indicate to each cell its location within a developing structure.

■ One type of positional information is associated with **polarity,** the condition of having structural differences at opposite ends of an organism. Plants typically have an axis, with a root end and a shoot end.

Concept 36.1 *Physical processes drive the transport of materials in plants over a range of distances*

■ Three kinds of transport occurs in plants:

1. Uptake of water and solutes by individual cells, such as a root hair.
2. Short-distance from cell to cell at the level of tissues and organs.
3. Long-distance in xylem and phloem at the level of the whole plant.

■ The uptake of water across cell membranes occurs through osmosis, the passive transport of water across a membrane.

- The water potential ψ is defined as the combined effects of solute concentration and the pressure that the cell wall contributes. The water potential equation is $\psi = \psi_s + \psi_p$
- **Turgor pressure** is produced by the plasma membrane exerting force against the cell wall. A walled cell that has a greater solute concentration (greater water potential) than its surroundings is turgid. Loss of turgor results in wilting, as cells become flaccid.
- **Aquaporins** are the transport proteins (channels) in the plant cell plasma membrane specifically designed for the passage of water.
- Plant cells have a membrane called a **tonoplast** surrounding their central vacuole; the tonoplast regulates molecules going into and out of the vacuole.
- The cytosol of neighboring cells are connected through plasmodesmata. This allows for the exchange of materials between cells. The cytoplasmic continuum is known as the **symplast.**
- The **apoplast** is the continuum of cell walls and extracellular spaces.
- Water moves from a higher to lower water potential through both the apoplast and the symplast.
- **Bulk flow** is the movement of water through the plant by pressure.

Concept 36.2 Roots absorb water and minerals from the soil

- Most water absorption occurs near the root tips through the root hairs.
- Water and minerals from the soil enter the plant through the root epidermis, cross the cortex, pass into the vascular cylinder and then flow up tracheids and vessels to the shoot system.
- The roots of many types of plants have symbiotic relationships with fungi. This type of relationship is called **mycorrhizae,** and leads to the absorption and transport of water and certain minerals deep into the plant.
- The endodermis, the innermost most layer of cells in the root cortex, surrounds the vascular cylinder (stele) and functions as a last checkpoint for the selective passage of minerals from the cortex into the vascular tissue. These cells have a waterproof Casparian strip, which forces water to enter the stele through the symplast.

Concept 36.3 Water and minerals ascend from roots to shoots through the xylem

- **Transpiration** is the loss of water vapor from the leaves and other parts of the plant that are in contact with air.
- There are two mechanisms that influence how water is pulled up through the plant.

  1. **Root pressure** occurs when water diffusing in from the root cortex generates a positive pressure that forces fluid up through the xylem.
  2. In the **transpiration-cohesion-tension mechanism,** water is lost through transpiration from the leaves of the plant due to the lower water potential of the air. The cohesion of water due to hydrogen bonding plus the adhesion of water to the plant cell walls enables the water to form a column, which is drawn up through the xylem as water evaporates from the leaves.

Concept 36.4 Stomata help regulate the rate of transpiration

▌ Turgor changes in **guard cells** control the size of the openings in the stomata. When the stomata are open, the exchange of carbon dioxide and oxygen takes place. Water also exits through the open stomata due to transpiration.

▌ Guard cells control the size of the stomata opening by changing shape, widening or closing the gap between them. Taking up water causes the guard cells to swell and buckle, increasing the size of the pore between them. When the guard cells lose water, the cells become less bowed and the pore closes.

▌ In addition to light, three factors influence the opening and closing of stomata: the reversible uptake of potassium ions, the level of CO_2 in leaf air spaces, and the internal clock of the guard cells.

Concept 36.5 Organic nutrients are translocated through the phloem

▌ **Phloem** transports organic products of photosynthesis from the leaves throughout the plant.

▌ Sieve tubes always carry sugars from a sugar source to a sugar sink. A **sugar source** is an organ that is a net producer of sugar. A **sugar sink** is an organ that is a net consumer or storer of sugar.

▌ Flow through the phloem occurs mainly as a result of bulk flow driven by positive pressure; loading of sugar into cells creates a high solute concentration at the source end of the sieve tube, and this lowers the water potential and causes the water to flow in the tube.

Concept 37.1 Plants require certain chemical elements to complete their life cycle

▌ Mineral nutrients are those required by plants that are chemical elements absorbed from the soil as inorganic ions.

▌ Plants need nine macronutrients in great amounts: carbon, oxygen, hydrogen, nitrogen, sulfur, phosphorus, potassium, calcium, and magnesium. They need at least eight micronutrients in small amounts: chlorine, iron, boron, manganese, zinc, copper, molybdenum, and nickel. Essential nutrients are those that the plant needs to complete the life cycle.

Concept 37.2 Soil quality is a major determinant of plant distribution and growth

▌ **Topsoil** is defined as a mixture of particles from rock, living organisms, and **humus** (partially decayed organic material).

▌ Humus builds a crumbly soil that retains water. It is also a reservoir of mineral nutrients.

▌ To be available to roots, minerals must be released from the soil particles into the soil solution. Anions are not bound tightly to soil particles and are easily released. Cations are involved in **cation exchange**—roots add H^+ to soil, which displaces cation minerals from soil particles into the soil solution.

Concept 37.3 Nitrogen is often the mineral that has the greatest impact on plant growth

▌ In order for plants to absorb nitrogen, it must first be converted to NH_4^+ or NO_3^-.

▌ The main source of nitrogen for plants is the decomposition of humus by microbes.

▌ **Nitrogen-fixing bacteria** convert N_2 to NH_3, in the process of nitrogen fixation. Ammonifying bacteria convert NH_3 (ammonia) to NH_4^+ (ammonium). Although plants absorb some ammonium from the soil, they absorb mainly nitrate (NO_3^-) produced from ammonium by nitrifying bacteria.

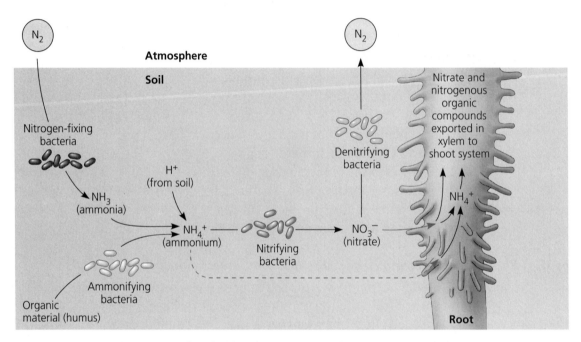

Figure 37.9   The role of soil bacteria in the nitrogen nutrition of plants

Concept 37.4 Plant nutritional adaptations often involve relationships with other organisms

▌ Plant roots, specifically legume roots, have swellings called **nodules** that are composed of plant cells that contain nitrogen-fixing bacteria. This is a mutualistic symbiotic association.

▌ In mycorrhizae, the fungus benefits from a steady supply of sugar donated by the host plant. In return, the fungus increases the surface area for water uptake, selectively absorbs minerals that are taken up by the plant, and secretes substances that stimulate root growth and antibiotics that protect the plant from invading bacteria.

▌ Mistletoe is a parasitic plant. Some parasitic plants are not photosynthetic and rely on other plants for their nutrients.

▌ **Epiphytes** are not parasitic, they just grow on the surfaces of other plants instead of the soil.

▌ **Carnivorous plants** are photosynthetic, but they get some nitrogen and other minerals by digesting small animals.

Concept 38.1 *Pollination enables gametes to come together within a flower*

▪ Angiosperms and other plants undergo an alternation of generations in their life cycle, in which the diploid plant, or sporophyte, produces haploid spores by meiosis. The spores develop into male and female gametophytes. The gametophytes develop and produce gametes (by mitosis), which may undergo fertilization and form new sporophytes.

▪ In angiosperms, the sporophyte is called the dominant generation, because that is the form of the plant we see. The gametophyte is the pollen and embryo sac of the flower.

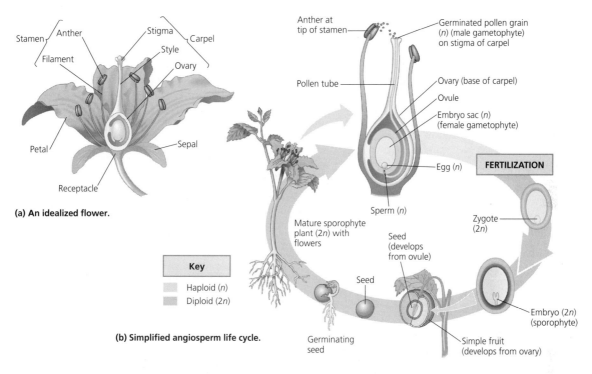

(a) An idealized flower.

(b) Simplified angiosperm life cycle.

Figure 38.2   An overview of angiosperm reproduction

▪ Flowers contain the gametophyte(s) and are the reproductive organs of angiosperms. Some important flower structures are:

  ▪ **sepals**—which protect the floral bud before it opens.
  ▪ **petals**—which attract insects and other pollinators to the plant with their color and fragrance.
  ▪ **stamens**—male reproductive organs (consist of anthers and filaments).
  ▪ **carpels**—female reproductive organs (consist of an ovary, stigma, and style).

▪ Complete flowers have all four basic organs. Incomplete flowers lack one or more of these organs.

▪ **Staminate** (male) and **carpellate** (female) flowers are incomplete because they contain *either* functional stamens or functional carpels. **Monoecious** species have staminate and carpellate flowers located on the same plant. **Dioecious** species have staminate flowers and carpellate flowers on different plants.

- In the **sporangia** of an anther, there are many diploid cells called **microsporocytes.** Each microsporocyte undergoes meiosis to produce four haploid microspores, which can eventually become haploid male gametophytes.
- In the ovary, ovules form—each of them containing a single sporangium. Within the sporangium, a single cell called the **megasporocyte** grows and undergoes meiosis to produce four haploid megaspores. In many angiosperms, only one megaspore survives, and a series of steps produces an embryo sac.

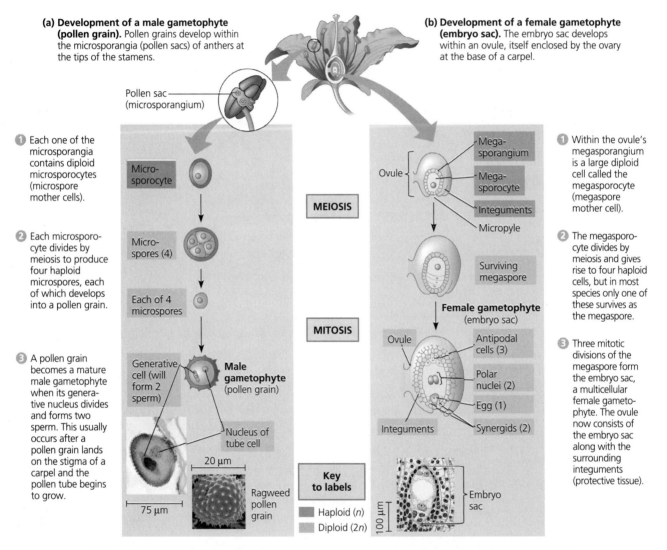

Figure 38.4   The development of angiosperm gametophytes (pollen grains and embryo sacs)

- While some flowers self-fertilize, others have methods to prevent self-fertilization and maximize genetic variation. One of these is self-incompatibility, in which a plant rejects its own pollen or that of a closely related plant.

Concept 38.2 *After fertilization, ovules develop into seeds and ovaries into fruits*

▌ When a pollen grain lands on a stigma, it germinates and produces a pollen tube that extends toward the ovary. Then one sperm fertilizes the egg to form the *2n* embryo. The other combines with the two polar nuclei to form a triploid nucleus (*3n*), which will eventually give rise to the endosperm. The **endosperm** nourishes the plant embryo. This process of forming an embryo and endosperm is called **double fertilization.**

▌ After double fertilization, the ovule develops into a seed, and the ovary develops into a fruit, which encloses the seed.

▌ The **seed coat** protects the embryo and its food supply. A **radicle** is the embryonic root. The portion of the embryonic axis above where the **cotyledons** are attached is the **epicotyl** (from the Greek *epi*—on or over). It consists of the shoot tip with a pair of miniature leaves.

▌ As the seed matures, it enters dormancy, in which it has a low metabolic rate and its growth and development are suspended.

▌ The seed resumes growth when there are suitable environmental conditions.

Concept 38.3 *Many flowering plants clone themselves by asexual reproduction*

▌ Asexual reproduction, or **vegetative reproduction,** produces clones. In this process, **fragmentation** occurs, in which pieces of the parent plant break off to form new individuals who are exact genetic replicas of the parent.

▌ Agriculture uses several techniques of artificial vegetative reproduction such as grafting, growing clones from cuttings, and test-tube cloning.

Concept 38.4 *Plant biotechnology is transforming agriculture*

▌ Humans have intervened in the reproduction and genetic makeup of plants for thousands of years through **artificial selection.**

▌ **Genetically modified organisms** are engineered to express a gene from another species. Examples are Golden Rice, engineered to include large amounts of vitamin A; and *Bt* corn, engineered to contain a toxin that kills specific crop pests. There is some debate over the creation of these crops due to fear of human allergies and possible effects on nontarget organisms, among other concerns.

Concept 39.2 *Plant hormones help coordinate growth, development, and responses to stimuli*

▌ **Hormones** are defined as chemical messengers that coordinate the different parts of a multicellular organism. They are produced by one part of the body and transported to another.

▌ A **tropism** is a plant growth response that results in the plant growing either toward or away from a stimulus.

▌ **Phototropism** is the growth of a shoot in a certain direction in response to light. **Positive phototropism** is the growth of a plant toward light; **negative phototropism** is growth of a plant away from light.

Table 39.1 An Overview of Plant Hormones

Hormone	Where Produced or Found in Plant	Major Functions
Auxin (IAA)	Embryo of seed, meristems of apical buds, young leaves	Stimulates stem elongation (low concentration only), root growth, cell differentiation, and branching; regulates development of fruit; enhances apical dominance; functions in phototropism and gravitropism; promotes xylem differentiation; retards leaf abscission
Cytokinins	Synthesized in roots and transported to other organs	Affect root growth and differentiation; stimulate cell division and growth; stimulate germination; delay senescence
Gibberellins	Meristems of apical buds and roots, young leaves, embryo	Promote seed and bud germination, stem elongation, and leaf growth; stimulate flowering and development of fruit; affect root growth and differentiation
Brassinosteroids	Seeds, fruit, shoots, leaves, and floral buds	Inhibit root growth; retard leaf abscission; promote xylem differentiation
Abscisic acid	Leaves, stems, roots, green fruit	Inhibits growth; closes stomata during water stress; promotes seed dormancy
Ethylene	Tissues of ripening fruit, nodes of stems, aging leaves and flowers	Promotes fruit ripening, opposes some auxin effects; promotes or inhibits growth and development of roots, leaves, and flowers, depending on species

Concept 39.3 Responses to light are critical for plant success

▍ **Photomorphogenesis** is the term used to describe the effects of light on plant morphology.

▍ Blue light has the greatest effect on plant growth and movement. Plants use three different pigments to detect blue light: **cryptochromes, phototropin, and zeaxanthin.**

▍ **Phytochromes** are pigments that are involved in many of a plant's responses to light.

▍ Many plant processes are in response to changes in light, temperature, and humidity.

▍ **Circadian rhythms** are physiological cycles that have a frequency of about 24 hours and that are not paced by a known environmental variable.

▍ A physiological response to a photoperiod (the relative lengths of night and day), such as flowering, is called **photoperiodism.**

▍ **Short-day plants** require a period of light shorter than a certain critical length in order to flower. **Long-day plants** flower in the late spring or early summer; they require the most daylight to flower. **Day-neutral plants** can flower in days of any length.

(*Note:* It is night length—not day length—that controls flowering and certain other responses to photoperiod.)

Concept 39.4 Plants respond to a wide variety of stimuli other than light

- **Gravitropism** is a plant's response to gravity. Roots show **positive gravitropism,** and grow toward the source of gravity, whereas shoots show **negative gravitropism** and grow away from gravity.
- **Thigmomorphogenesis** is the change in form of a plant that results from mechanical disturbance. Even repeatedly touching a plant with a ruler to measure its height can affect its growth pattern.
- **Thigmotropism** is directional growth in a plant as a response to a touch.
- Plants have various responses to stresses. In times of **drought,** the guard cells lose turgor. This causes the stomata to close; young leaves will stop growing, and they will roll into a shape that slows transpiration rates. Also, deep roots continue to grow, while those near the surface (where there isn't much water) do not grow very quickly.
- In times of **flooding,** certain cells in the root cortex die, which creates air tubes that bring in oxygen and enable the plant to continue cellular respiration.
- Plants respond to **salt stress** by producing organic compounds that keep the water potential of cells more negative than that of the soil solution. Most plants cannot survive salt stress for very long periods of time.
- In **heat stress** environments, plants produce **heat-shock proteins,** which are thought to prevent other proteins from denaturing.
- In **cold stress** situations, plants respond by altering the composition of their cell membranes.

Concept 39.5 Plants defend themselves against herbivores and pathogens

- Some physical defenses plants have against predators (herbivores) are thorns, chemicals such as distasteful or poisonous compounds, and airborne attractants that attract other animals to kill the herbivores.
- The first line of defense against viruses for a plant (as for humans) is the epidermal layer.
- Plants are capable of recognizing plant pathogens and dealing with them in complex biochemical ways.

For Additional Review

Describe the plant structures that make plants ideally suited for trapping and processing the sun's energy, and for the process of carbon fixation.

Multiple-Choice Questions

1. Which of the following is primarily responsible for fruit ripening in plants?
   (A) ethylene
   (B) auxin
   (C) gibberellins
   (D) abscisic acid
   (E) brassinosteroids

2. Which of the following processes is responsible for the bending of the stem of a plant toward a light source?
   (A) The amount of chlorophyll produced on the side facing the light increases.
   (B) The rate of cell division on the side facing the light increases.
   (C) The rate of cell division on the side away from the light increases.
   (D) The cells on the side of the stem facing the light elongate.
   (E) The cells on the side of the stem away from the light elongate.

3. The driving force for the movement of materials in the xylem of plants is
   (A) gravity.
   (B) root pressure.
   (C) transpiration.
   (D) the difference in osmotic pressure between the source and the sink.
   (E) osmosis.

4. The loss of leaves that some plants experience due to the onset of autumn is a result of which hormone?
   (A) auxin
   (B) gibberellic acid
   (C) cytokinin
   (D) ethylene
   (E) abscisic acid

5. Which statement below describing alternation of generations in angiosperms is true?
   (A) The gametophyte stage lasts longer than the sporophyte stage.
   (B) The sporophyte stage lasts longer than the gametophyte stage.
   (C) The sporophyte is the form of the plant that is independent and conspicuous.
   (D) The gametophyte is the form of the plant that is independent and conspicuous.
   (E) The sporophyte bears a reproductive structure.

6. In plants, translocation occurs as a result of
   (A) a difference in water potential between a sugar source and a sugar sink.
   (B) transpiration.
   (C) cohesion-adhesion.
   (D) active transport by sieve-tube members.
   (E) active transport by tracheid and vessel elements.

Directions: The group of questions below consists of five lettered choices followed by a list of numbered phrases or sentences. For each numbered phrase or sentence, select the one choice that is most closely related to it. Each choice may be used once, more than once, or not at all.

Questions 7–11
   (A) Abscisic acid
   (B) Auxin
   (C) Cytokinins
   (D) Ethylene
   (E) Gibberellins

7. Produced in the roots, affects root growth and differentiation

8. Produced in tissues of ripening fruits, affects leaf abscission

9. Produced in the meristems of buds and roots, promotes seed and bud germination

10. Produced in the leaves, stems, and roots; inhibits growth; closes stomata during drought

11. Produced in seed embryos and apical meristems, stimulates stem elongation and root growth

12. Which of the following is the correct name for a system of roots that grows as one large vertical root with smaller lateral offshoots?
    (A) tuberoot
    (B) taproot
    (C) toproot
    (D) stabroot
    (E) bladeroot

13. The three types of plant tissue, in order from the outside of the plant to the inside of the plant, are
    (A) vascular, ground, dermal.
    (B) vascular, dermal, ground.
    (C) ground, vascular, dermal.
    (D) ground, dermal, vascular.
    (E) dermal, ground, vascular.

14. A plant whose life span occurs over the course of two years is known as a(n)
    (A) annual.
    (B) diannual.
    (C) biennial.
    (D) perennial.
    (E) seasonal.

15. The region of the plant in which the parenchyma cells are located that are involved in photosynthesis is called
    (A) spongeophyll.
    (B) mesophyll.
    (C) epidermis.
    (D) xylem.
    (E) phloem.

16. In a mesophyll cell of a leaf, the synthesis of ATP takes place in the mitochondria and which of the following other cell organelles?
    (A) chloroplasts
    (B) Golgi apparatus
    (C) nucleus
    (D) ribosomes
    (E) lysosomes

17. All of the following enhance the uptake of water by a plant's roots EXCEPT
    (A) root hairs.
    (B) the large surface area of cortical cells.
    (C) mycorrhizae.
    (D) the attraction of water and dissolved minerals to root hairs.
    (E) gravitational force.

18. The barrier located in the epidermal wall, which prevents the passage of unwanted minerals into the vascular tissue, is called the
    (A) Narnian strip.
    (B) Octavian strip.
    (C) Casparian strip.
    (D) Gotham strip.
    (E) Tanzanian strip.

19. All of the following contribute to the closing of stomata during the day EXCEPT
    (A) water deficiency.
    (B) wilting.
    (C) high temperatures.
    (D) excessive rainfall.
    (E) excessive transpiration.

20. Which of the following constitute plant macronutrients?
    (A) Carbon, oxygen, nitrogen, and hydrogen
    (B) Carbon, boron, nitrogen, and chlorine
    (C) Phosphorus, oxygen, nitrogen, and iron
    (D) Potassium, oxygen, hydrogen, and zinc
    (E) Carbon, oxygen, nitrogen, and copper

21. Which term describes the symbiotic relation-
ship between the roots of legumes and fungi?
(A) bacterioids
(B) humus
(C) Casparian strip
(D) apoplast
(E) mycorrhizae

22. Which of the following terms describes a
species of plant that has male and female
flowers on the same individual plant?
(A) deciduous
(B) monoecious
(C) dioecious
(D) dihybrid
(E) monohybrid

23. The point of attachment of a plant leaf and
stem is called the
(A) carpel.
(B) petiole.
(C) blade.
(D) internode.
(E) axillary attachment.

24. Which vascular tissue in plants is responsible

for carrying sugars down from the leaves to
the rest of the plant?
(A) xylem
(B) phloem
(C) dermal tissue
(D) tracheids
(E) vessel elements

25. Which of the following colors of visible light
has the greatest effect on plants?
(A) red
(B) orange
(C) yellow
(D) green
(E) blue

Free-Response Question

1. *Describe the following processes in the plant life cycle and why they are
important for the plant to complete, listing all of the plant hormones involved
and describing their function:*

(a) elongation of the plant shoot.
(b) the process by which plants orient themselves with respect to the sun.
(c) photoperiodism.

ANSWERS AND EXPLANATIONS

Multiple-Choice Questions

▌ **1. (A) is correct.** Ethylene is a plant hormone that causes fruit to ripen. It also
causes apoptosis, or programmed cell death in plant cells; it changes patterns
of plant growth as a response to mechanical stress; and it causes the loss of
leaves in autumn.

2. (E) is correct. When the light source on either side of a plant is uneven, the plant will grow toward the light source. This is the result of auxin moving from the apex down to the cells that are less exposed to light, and causing them to elongate faster than the cells on the side that is illuminated.

3. (C) is correct. The driving force behind the movement of sap in xylem (in the direction from the roots to the leaves) is the transpiration of water through the stomata on the leaves. The mechanism responsible for movement up through the xylem is the transpiration-cohesion-tension mechanism, and it occurs through bulk flow, in which fluid moves because of a pressure difference at opposite ends of a tube. The pressure is created by transpiration from the leaves, and contributing to the movement of water and minerals up the plant are gradients of water potential from cell to cell within the plant.

4. (D) is correct. The loss of leaves that some plants experience in autumn is due to the plant hormone ethylene. The technical term for this loss of leaves is leaf abscission, and it occurs in order to prevent plants from dehydrating during the winter, when they can't take in water from the frozen ground. Auxin is also involved in this process, but it is the increase in ethylene that ultimately triggers abscission.

5. (C) is correct. In vascular plants that undergo alternation of generations, the dominant form of the plant is the sporophyte—it is the full-grown plant that we see growing in a field. It has a reproductive structure called a flower, which creates gametes. The fusion of gametes results in fertilization and the possible development of a sporophyte embryo, which may develop into a full-grown mature sporophyte.

6. (A) is correct. In plants, phloem is responsible for carrying sugar made in the leaves to other locations that are incapable of photosynthesis. This process is called translocation. In angiosperms phloem is made up of sieve-tube members that are arranged end to end in long sieve tubes. In phloem, sugar travels from a sugar source—any site in the plant involved in photosynthesis (though this is usually mature leaves)—to a sugar sink, which is any site in the plant not engaged in photosynthesis.

7. (C) is correct. Cytokinins are plant hormones that are involved in the control of cell division and differentiation, the control of apical dominance in plants, and have some anti-aging effects on plant tissues. Cytokinins often act in concert with auxin.

8. (D) is correct. Ethylene has the following effects on plants: It initiates a response to mechanical stress (such as when a plant must grow around an object in its regular path of growth); it is involved in apoptosis, which is programmed cell death; it is involved in leaf abscission; and it is responsible for the ripening of fruit.

9. (E) is correct. Gibberellins are plant hormones that are responsible for many different effects in plants, but three main ones are the elongation of the plant stem (they stimulate both cell division and cell elongation); fruit growth; and germination, which is the process by which a seed breaks dormancy and begins to grow.

10. (A) is correct. Abscisic acid is a plant hormone that prevents the seed from immediately germinating—it is responsible for seed dormancy. This hormone is also responsible for closing the stomata on plant leaves in times of drought; when plants start to wilt, abscisic acid causes changes in guard cells, closing the stomata and preventing further water loss through transpiration.

11. (B) is correct. Auxins appear to have many functions in all types of plants. They are involved in cell elongation, the formation of lateral and adventitious roots. They act as herbicides, and they are involved in phototropism. They are also involved in secondary growth, and this also promotes the growth of fruit.

12. (B) is correct. There are two main root systems in plants, the taproot system and the fibrous root system. Monocots, including grasses, usually have the fibrous root system, which firmly anchors them into the ground, while many eudicots have a taproot system, with one long, thick root extending down and smaller lateral branch roots shooting from it.

13. (E) is correct. The three types of tissue that make up plant organs, from the outermost layer to the innermost layer are dermal, ground, and vascular. The dermal layer is a single layer of very tightly packed cells that serves to protect the plant from harm. The vascular tissue consists of xylem and phloem, and it is responsible for transporting water, minerals, and food throughout the plant. The ground tissue has various functions, but it serves in neither transport nor protection.

14. (C) is correct. A plant whose life cycle spans two years is known as a biennial. One whose life cycle spans one year is known as an annual, and plants that live for many years are known as perennials.

15. (B) is correct. The name of the region of the plant leaf in which parenchyma cells are situated—and the site of photosynthesis in plants—is called mesophyll. The mesophyll lies between the upper and lower epidermis of the leaf, and consists mainly of parenchyma cells. Eudicots have two regions of mesophyll, spongy mesophyll and palisade mesophyll.

16. (A) is correct. The production of ATP in plant cells occurs in the mitochondria, as it does in the cells of animals, but it also occurs in the chloroplasts during photosynthesis. The light reactions of photosynthesis convert solar energy to the chemical energy of ATP and NADPH, and these light reactions take place in the chloroplasts, in the mesophyll cells of the plant leaf.

17. (E) is correct. All of the factors listed aid in the uptake of water and minerals by the roots of a plant except the last choice, gravity. Water and minerals flow from the soil into the epidermis of the plant, then through the root cortex, and then into the xylem of the plant, to be transported throughout the plant body.

18. (C) is correct. The Casparian strip is a belt made of a waxy material that runs through all of the endodermal cells, creating a ring that protects the vascular tissue from unwanted minerals. The water and mineral solution must pass from the cortex through the endodermis, and because of the Casparian strip, in order to pass through the endodermal wall, the solution must be screened through the plasma membrane of an endodermal cell.

19. (D) is correct. All of the answers listed, with the exception of excessive rainfall, are factors that would cause the stomata of a leaf to close during the day. All of the factors with the exception of answer *D* could lead to dehydration.

20. (A) is correct. The macronutrients (elements required in large amounts) in plants are carbon, oxygen, hydrogen, nitrogen, sulfur, phosphorus, potassium, calcium, and magnesium. The micronutrients (elements needed only in trace amounts) are chlorine, iron, boron, manganese, zinc, copper, molybdenum, and nickel.

21. (E) is correct. Mycorrhizae are mutualistic symbiotic associations of roots and fungi. The fungus benefits from having a "home" and a steady sugar supply from the plant, and the plant benefits because the fungus increases the surface area for water uptake and supplies the plant with certain minerals.

22. (B) is correct. Plants that have the staminate and carpellate flowers on the same individual plant are called monoecious. One example of a monoecious plant is the corn plant. Dioecious plants have the staminate flowers and carpellate flowers on different plants.

23. (B) is correct. The leaf is the main photosynthetic organ of the plant, and it varies quite a bit in form from plant to plant, but most plant leaves consist of a blade (which is the leaf part of the leaf) and a petiole, which joins the leaf to a node on the stem.

24. (B) is correct. The phloem transports the food made in mature leaves to the roots and other nonphotosynthetic parts of the plant, such as newly developing leaves and fruits. The xylem is responsible for carrying water and minerals up through the plant from the roots. Those are the two types of vascular tissue in plants.

25. (E) is correct. It has been shown that blue light is most effective in initiating germination in seeds, the opening of the stomata, and phototropism (when a plant bends toward or away from light).

Free-Response Question

(a) The elongation of the stem in plants is an important process in the plant life cycle because it enables the plant to reach its full size and complete development of the sporophyte stage. The sporophyte needs to complete development in order to produce reproductive structures.

    The apical meristems, which are located at the tips of roots and in the buds of shoots, provide additional cells that enable the plant to grow in length. The apical meristem produces internodes (which contribute to plant height through both cell elongation and cell division) and leaf-bearing nodes. Both auxins and gibberellins are hormones involved in stem elongation. Auxins stimulate growth when they are present in low concentrations; gibberellin concentration must be high.

(b) It is important for the plant to orient itself so that its roots reach into the soil and extract water and minerals, while its leaves point up to the sun so that they can trap light energy (to use in photosynthesis) and gas exchange can occur through transpiration. Gravitropism is the term used to describe plant growth in response to the force of gravity. Roots show positive gravitropism—they grow into the soil, toward the source of gravity—whereas shoots show negative gravitropism—that is, they grow away from the source of gravity, toward the sun. The major hormone involved in gravitropism is auxin. It has not yet been determined exactly how auxin influences the way roots and shoots grow, but it is theorized that certain dense molecules settle with gravity to one end of the plant root, and auxin accumulates as a result of this. The accumulation of auxin prevents cell elongation on that side of the root, and cells on the upper side elongate so that the root curves down, into the soil. (*Note: This would be a good place to illustrate your point with a sketch.*)

(c) Photoperiodism is defined as any physiological response to a photoperiod (meaning, a specific length of daylight or darkness). One example of a photoperiodism is flowering. It used to be thought that plant flowering depended on the length of the daylight, but then scientists concluded that it is actually night length that determines when a plant will flower. They realized this by interrupting the day with a dark period and observing that the plant still flowered. However, when they interrupted the night with a brief period of light, the plant did not flower. Auxins are involved in photoperiodism, but it is not clear yet exactly what their role is.

This response uses the following key terms in context, showing the writer's knowledge of their meanings and relatedness:

sporophyte	*leaf-bearing nodes*
flower	*auxins*
apical meristem	*gibberellins*
primary meristems	*gravitropism*
internodes	*photoperiodism*

It also shows an understanding of the following processes: plant growth via stem elongation, gravitropism, and photoperiodism.

CHAPTER 7

Animal Form and Function

Concept 40.1 Physical laws and the environment constrain animal size and shape

▌ **Anatomy** is defined as the study of the structure of an organism.

▌ **Physiology** is defined as the study of the functions of an organism.

▌ Physical laws limit the evolution of an organism's form. For example, the physics of flight prevents the possibility of an animal the size and shape of a mythical dragon from evolving through natural selection.

▌ **Convergent evolution** occurs because natural selection leads to similar adaptations when diverse organisms face a similar environmental challenge, such as traveling fast despite the resistance of water. Thus tuna, sharks, penguins, dolphins, and seals have the same general body shape, although they are not closely related.

▌ An animal's size and shape have a direct effect on how the animal exchanges energy and materials with its surroundings. For example, **surface-to-volume ratio** is one of the physical constraints on the size of single-celled organisms. In multicellular organisms, all of the cells of the animal must have access to a suitable aqueous environment. Extensively folded or branched internal surfaces facilitate this exchange with the environment.

Concept 40.2 Animal form and function are correlated at all levels of organization

▌ **Tissues** are groups of cells that have a common structure and function. The four types of tissue are listed below.

1. **Epithelial tissue** occurs in sheets of tightly packed cells, covers the body, lines the organs, and acts as a protective barrier. One side of an epithelial cell is always bound to an underlying supportive surface called the basement membrane. The outside surface is facing either air or a fluid environment.

2. **Connective tissue** mainly supports and binds other tissues. It consists of scattered cells within an extracellular matrix. Some connective tissues are cartilage, tendons, ligaments, bone, and blood.

3. The functional unit of **nervous tissue** is the nerve cell, or neuron. This tissue senses stimuli and transmits signals from one part of the body to other neurons, glands, muscles, and the brain.

4. **Muscle tissue** is composed of long cells called muscle fibers. Muscle fibers contract when they are stimulated by a nerve impulse. This is the most abundant tissue in most animals. There are three types of muscle—skeletal muscle, cardiac muscle, and smooth muscle.

▌ **Organs** are organized groups of tissue. **Organ systems** (for example the digestive, circulatory, and excretory systems) consist of several organs, and they carry out the major body functions.

Concept 40.3 Animals use the chemical energy in food to sustain form and function

▮ The **metabolic rate** of an animal is defined as the amount of energy it uses in a unit of time.

▮ **Endothermic** animals are warmed by the heat generated by their metabolism. **Ectothermic** animals do not produce enough heat by metabolism to influence their body temperature, and they gain their heat mostly from external sources.

▮ The **basal metabolic rate** of an animal is defined as its metabolic rate when it is at rest, is experiencing no stress, and has an empty stomach.

▮ An ectotherm (such as an amphibian or reptile) requires much less energy per kilogram than does an endotherm (a mammal or bird) of equivalent size.

▮ A small animal, such as a mouse, has a much greater energy demand per kilogram than does a large animal of the same taxonomic class, such as a human (both mammals).

Concept 40.4 Many animals regulate their internal environment within relatively narrow limits

▮ **Homeostasis** is the state of internal balance in the face of external changes. One of the main objectives in physiology is to study how animals maintain homeostasis.

▮ Homeostatic control systems have three components—a **receptor,** a **control center,** and an **effector.** The receptor detects a change; the control center processes information and directs the effector to make an appropriate response.

▮ In **negative feedback systems,** a change in the variable being monitored triggers a change in the control center that prevents further change in the variable or brings the variable back within desirable parameters. Human body temperature is kept within narrow limits by negative feedback systems.

▮ In **positive feedback systems,** a change in some variable triggers mechanisms that amplify rather than reverse the change. For example, during childbirth, pressure of the baby's head against receptors near the opening of the uterus stimulates greater uterine contractions, which cause greater pressure against the uterine opening, which heighten the contractions, and so forth. Positive feedback thus brings childbirth to completion.

Concept 40.5 Thermoregulation contributes to homeostasis and involves anatomy, physiology, and behavior

▮ **Thermoregulation** refers to how animals maintain their internal temperature.

▮ Endotherms (such as mammals and birds) can use their high metabolic rates to maintain a stable body temperature across a wide range of environmental temperatures. Ectotherms (such as most invertebrates, fishes, amphibians, and most nonbird reptiles) generate relatively little metabolic heat and conform to environmental temperatures.

▮ Fishes and aquatic invertebrates are conformers. They live in relatively stable environments and can accommodate some slight change in body temperature if the environment is altered.

- **Conduction** is the transfer of heat between molecules of objects that are in direct contact with one another—for example, when an animal sits in water that is cooler than its body temperature.
- **Convection** is the transfer of heat through the movement of air or a liquid past a surface—for example, when a breeze causes heat loss from the surface of an animal.
- **Radiation** is the emission of electromagnetic waves by all objects that are warmer than absolute zero.
- **Evaporation** is the removal of heat from the surface of a liquid, as molecules leave the surface as gas.
- Thermoregulation takes place through the following processes.

  1. The **adjustment of the rate of heat exchange** between the animal and its environment—through insulating hair, feathers, and fat—is accomplished through vasodilation (an increase in diameter of blood vessels at the skin, which cools the blood) or vasoconstriction (the opposite of vasodilation).
  2. **Evaporation** across the skin (through panting or sweating).
  3. **Behavioral responses** (changes in location or posture).
  4. **Alteration of the rate of metabolic heat production** (only in endotherms).

Concept 41.1 Homeostatic mechanisms manage an animal's energy budget

- There are four main feeding mechanisms of animals. **Suspension feeders,** such as humpback whales, are animals that sift small food particles from water. **Substrate feeders,** such as moth larvae, live in or on their food source, eating their way through the food. **Fluid feeders,** such as mosquitoes, pull nutrient-rich fluid from a living host. **Bulk feeders,** such as most animals—including humans, eat relatively large pieces of food.
- **Herbivores** eat mainly autotrophs.
- **Carnivores** eat other animals.
- **Omnivores** eat both plants and animals.
- Glucose regulation is an example of homeostasis. Animals store excess calories as glycogen in the liver and muscles and as fat in fat tissues. These energy stores can be tapped when an animal is in need of ATP. Blood glucose level is maintained within a relatively narrow range by a negative feedback mechanism.
- **Caloric imbalance** can result in undernourished animals that have diets deficient in calories, or overnourished (obese) animals that consume more calories than they need.

Concept 41.2 An animal's diet must supply carbon skeletons and essential nutrients

- The **essential nutrients** required by an animal are those that must be obtained in preassembled organic form because the animal cannot produce them.
- About half of the 20 amino acids required by animals are **essential amino acids** and must be obtained from food. There are also essential fatty acids that animals cannot make and must ingest.

- **Vitamins,** such as the B vitamins and vitamin E, are organic molecules that are required in the diet in small amounts.
- **Minerals,** such as calcium and phosphorus, are simple inorganic nutrients that are also required in the diet in small amounts.

Concept 41.3   *The main stages of food processing are ingestion, digestion, absorption, and elimination*

- **Ingestion** is the act of taking in food.
- **Digestion** is the breakdown of food into small molecules capable of being absorbed by the cells of the body. **Enzymatic hydrolysis** is the reaction by which macromolecules are broken up. It involves the addition of water.
- **Absorption** is the stage in food processing when the body's cells take up small molecules from the digestive tract.
- **Elimination** is the passing of undigested material from the digestive tract.
- **Intracellular digestion** occurs within a cell enclosed by a protective membrane. Sponges digest their food this way.
- **Extracellular digestion** is carried out by most animals; in this type of digestion, food is broken down outside of cells.
- In many simple animals digestion takes place in a **gastrovascular cavity.** These animals have a single opening through which food enters and waste is eliminated.
- More complex animals have **complete digestive tracts (alimentary canals),** which are one-way digestive tubes that begin at the mouth and terminate at the anus.

Concept 41.4   *Each organ of the mammalian digestive system has specialized food-processing functions*

- When food is in the mouth, or oral cavity, a nervous reflex occurs that causes **saliva** to be secreted into the mouth. Saliva lubricates the food to facilitate swallowing. It also contains the enzyme **salivary amylase,** which hydrolyzes starch and glycogen into smaller polysaccharides and the disaccharide maltose.
- During chewing, food is shaped into a ball called a **bolus.** After swallowing, the bolus enters the **pharynx**—a junction that opens to the esophagus and the trachea. During swallowing, the **epiglottis** (a flap made of cartilage) covers the trachea. This diverts the food down the esophagus.
- The **esophagus** moves food from the pharynx down to the stomach through **peristalsis**—rhythmic waves of contraction by smooth muscle in the walls of the esophagus.
- The stomach's functions include storing food and secreting gastric juice. **Gastric juice** contains hydrochloric acid, which is very acidic (pH of about 2). Gastric juice breaks down the extracellular matrix of meat and plant materials, and it also kills most of the bacteria ingested with food.
- **Pepsin** is an enzyme in gastric juice that begins to hydrolyze proteins into smaller polypeptides. Pepsin is secreted in an inactive form called pepsinogen, which is activated by hydrochloric acid in the stomach.
- The result of digestion in the stomach is a substance called **acid chyme.** The acid chyme is shunted from the stomach into the small intestine via the **pyloric sphincter.**

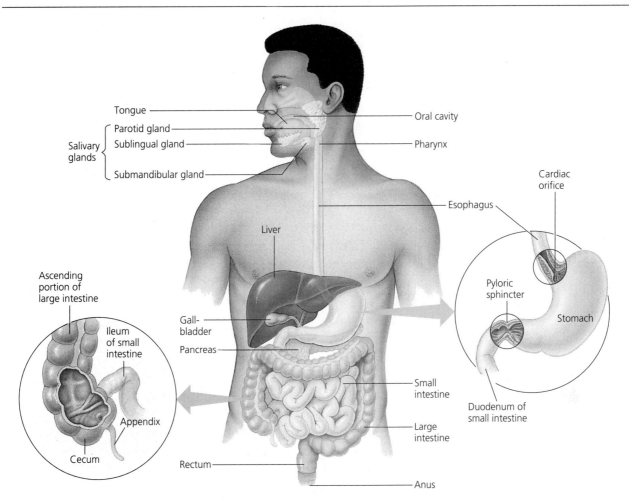

Figure 41.15   The human digestive system

▌ The first section of the **small intestine** is known as the **duodenum.** In the duodenum, the acid chyme mixes with secretions from the pancreas (**bicarbonate,** which acts as a buffer against acid chyme), the gallbladder (**bile,** which contains bile salts—detergents that aid in digestion), and the intestinal wall itself. The rest of the small intestine is responsible for the absorption of nutrients.

▌ Particular macromolecules are broken down in the small intestine by the following processes.

1. **Carbohydrates**—The breakdown of starch and glycogen begins with salivary amylase in the mouth. In the small intestine, **pancreatic amylases** break starch, glycogen, and small polysaccharides into disaccharides. The breakdown of these disaccharides occurs at the wall of the intestinal epithelium, and the monosaccharides are quickly absorbed.

2. **Proteins**—Pepsin begins the breakdown of proteins in the stomach, and in the small intestine, **trypsin** and **chymotrypsin** break polypeptides into smaller chains. **Dipeptidases, carboxypeptidase,** and **aminopeptidase** break apart proteins into amino acids.

3. **Nucleic acids**—The breakdown of nucleic acids is similar to that of proteins. In the small intestine, nucleases break them down into nucleosides, nitrogenous bases, sugars, and phosphate groups.
4. **Fats**—Digestion of fats starts in the small intestine. Bile salts coat the fat droplets and keep them from clumping (**emulsification**), and **lipase** hydrolyzes them.

▌ The epithelial lining of the small intestine has folds called **villi,** which in turn bear projections called **microvilli**—both of which radically increase the surface area available for absorption.

▌ In each villus is a set of tiny blood vessels called capillaries and a lymph vessel called a **lacteal,** which absorbs small fatty acids.

▌ Monosaccharides, such as glucose, cross the lining via passive diffusion, whereas amino acids and dipeptides are pumped across in active transport.

▌ The capillaries and veins that drain the nutrients away from the villi all join the **hepatic portal vessel,** which brings them to the **liver.** The liver metabolizes the organic molecules in various ways.

▌ Some other hormones involved in digestion are **gastrin,** which stimulates the secretion of gastric juice; **enterogastrone,** which slows digestion; and **secretin** and **cholecystokinin (CCK),** which are secreted by the walls of the duodenum and that prompt the digestion of various macromolecules.

▌ The **large intestine,** also called the **colon,** is connected to the small intestine by a sphincter. The point of the connection is the site of the **cecum,** a small pouch with an extension called the **appendix.**

▌ The main function of the large intestine is to compact waste and recover water. The wastes become more solid as they travel along and form feces.

▌ At the end of the colon is the **rectum,** where feces are stored until they are eliminated.

Concept 41.5 *Evolutionary adaptations of vertebrate digestive systems are often associated with diet*

▌ A mammal's **dentition** is generally correlated with its diet. In particular, mammals have specialized dentition that best enables them to ingest their usual diet.

▌ Herbivores generally have longer alimentary canals than carnivores, reflecting the longer time needed to digest vegetation.

Concept 42.1 *Circulatory systems reflect phylogeny*

▌ Some animals with simple body plans, such as cnidarians, hydras, planarians, and other flatworms possess a gastrovascular cavity rather than a true circulatory system. A **gastrovascular cavity** serves both in digestion and distribution of substances throughout the body.

▌ Both **open and closed circulatory systems** have **blood** (a circulatory fluid), **vessels** (tubes through which blood moves), and a **heart** (a structure that pumps the blood).

- In open circulatory systems, blood bathes the organs directly. The blood and lymph combined are called **hemolymph,** and a heart pumps hemolymph into cavities called sinuses.
- In closed circulatory systems, blood is contained within vessels and pumped around the body; the blood is separate from the interstitial fluid.
- Humans have a closed circulatory system called the **cardiovascular system.** The heart has atria (chambers that receive blood returning to the heart) and ventricles (chambers that pump blood out of the heart).
- The main types of blood vessels in humans are the **arteries, veins,** and **capillaries.** Arteries carry blood away from the heart and branch into smaller arterioles. Then capillaries network to form capillary beds. These capillary beds converge into venules, which converge into veins, which carry the blood back to the heart.

Concept 42.2 Double circulation in mammals depends on the anatomy and pumping cycle of the heart

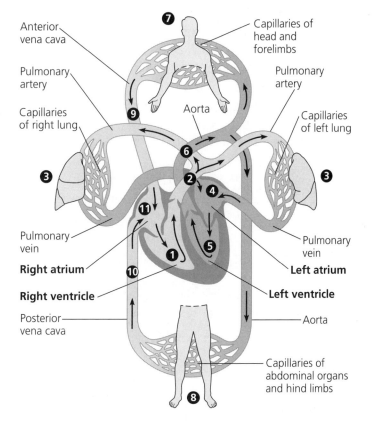

Figure 42.5   The mammalian cardiovascular system: an overview

- The steps of double circulation in mammals:

    1. Blood is pumped from the right ventricle.
    2. It enters the pulmonary arteries and is carried to the lungs.
    3. The blood flows through capillary beds in the lungs and picks up oxygen and releases CO_2.

4. The blood returns to the left atrium of the heart via pulmonary veins.
5. Then it continues to the left ventricle.
6. It leaves the heart via the aorta, which branches off and sends blood through arteries throughout the body.
7. The blood enters capillary beds in the neck, head, and arms.
8. The blood enters capillary beds in the abdomen and legs, giving up oxygen and picking up CO_2.
9. The capillaries form venules, and blood from the neck, head, and arms travels back to veins and back to the right atrium via the anterior vena cava.
10. Blood from the legs and trunk travels through the posterior vena cava back to the right atrium.
11. Blood is pumped into the right ventricle and the cycle begins again.

▮ The complete cycle of contraction and relaxation of the heart is called the cardiac cycle. The contraction phase is called **systole,** and the relaxation phase is called **diastole.**

▮ **Heart rate** is the rate of contraction per minute, and the **stroke volume** is the amount of blood pumped by the left ventricle during each contraction.

▮ An **atrioventricular (AV) valve** between each atrium and ventricle prevents the backflow of blood into the atria; there are also two **semilunar valves**—one located at the entrance to the pulmonary artery and the second at the entrance to the aorta that prevent backflow of blood.

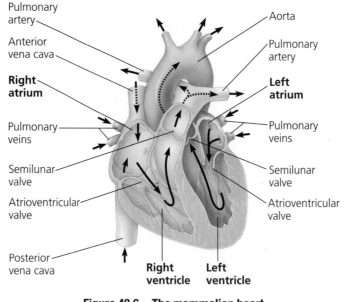

Figure 42.6   The mammalian heart

▮ The **sinoatrial (SA) node** is the pacemaker of the heart. It is located in the upper wall of the right atrium. It sets the rate at which cardiac muscle cells contract.

▮ The **AV node,** located in the lower wall of the right atrium, delays the impulses from the SA node to allow the atria to completely empty before the ventricles contract.

Concept 42.3 Physical principles govern blood circulation

▌ "**Blood pressure**" refers to the hydrostatic pressure that blood exerts against the wall of a vessel and that propels the blood. Blood pressure is measured and recorded as two numbers separated by a slash. The first number is the systolic pressure (when the heart contracts); the second is the diastolic pressure (when the heart is relaxed).

▌ **The lymphatic system** is responsible for returning lost fluid and proteins to the blood in the form of **lymph.** Along a lymph vessel are **lymph nodes** that filter lymph and attack viruses and bacteria, playing an important role in immunity.

Concept 42.4 Blood is a connective tissue with cells suspended in plasma

▌ **Plasma** is mostly water, but it also contains ions, electrolytes, and plasma proteins. It transports nutrients, metabolic wastes, gases, and hormones. In addition, blood plasma carries

1. **red blood cells (erythrocytes),** which transport oxygen via hemoglobin (an iron-containing protein).
2. **white blood cells (leukocytes),** which are part of the immune system.
3. **platelets,** which are fragments of cells responsible for blood clotting.

▌ Blood contains a soluble plasma protein called **fibrinogen,** which forms clots when it is converted to its active form, **fibrin.**

Concept 42.5 Gas exchange occurs across specialized respiratory surfaces

▌ **Gas exchange,** or **respiration,** is the uptake of molecular oxygen (O_2) from the environment and the discharge of carbon dioxide (CO_2) to the environment.

▌ **Gills** are respiratory organs in aquatic animals. Water flows through them, and blood flowing through capillaries within the wall of the gill picks up oxygen from the water. Blood flows in a direction opposite to the flow of water. This is called **countercurrent exchange,** and it maximizes the absorption of oxygen.

▌ Insects have **tracheal systems,** which are made up of air tubes that branch through the body and open to the outside. They extend to almost all cells, and gas exchange occurs directly across the epithelial membrane inside the tracheal walls.

▌ The **larynx** (voice box) is the upper part of the respiratory tract. It is a tube with cartilage-reinforced walls that leads to the trachea (windpipe). The **trachea** divides into two bronchi, each of which leads to a lung. In the lungs, the **bronchi** branch into bronchioles, and at their tips, the **bronchioles** end in clusters of air sacs called **alveoli,** the sites of gas exchange.

Concept 42.6 Breathing ventilates the lungs

▌ **Breathing** is the inhalation and exhalation of air that ventilates lungs. In mammals, breathing involves movement of the **diaphragm**—a dome-shaped muscle separating the thoracic cavity from the abdominal cavity. Lung volume increases when the rib muscles and diaphragm contract.

▌ The diffusion of a gas depends on **partial pressure.** Gases always diffuse from regions of higher partial pressure to regions of lower partial pressure.

Concept 42.7 Respiratory pigments bind and transport gases

❚ **Hemoglobin** is the respiratory pigment found in almost all vertebrates. It consists of four subunits, each of which is a heme group with an embedded iron atom. The iron atom binds O_2, so each hemoglobin can carry 4 oxygen molecules.

❚ A lowering of the pH in blood lowers the affinity of hemoglobin for oxygen, and oxygen dissociates. This is called the **Bohr shift.**

❚ CO_2 is most commonly carried in the blood in the form of bicarbonate ions. Less commonly it is transported via hemoglobin and in solution in the blood plasma.

Concept 43.1 Innate immunity provides broad defenses against infection

❚ Skin and the mucous membranes cover the surface and line the openings of the animal body, and they provide an external barrier against infectious agents.

❚ Microbes that get through the skin—for example, in a cut—encounter certain types of white blood cells called **neutrophils** that ingest and destroy them in a process called **phagocytosis.**

❚ **Monocytes** are another type of phagocytotic leukocyte. They migrate into tissues and develop into macrophages, which are giant phagocytotic cells.

❚ **Eosinophils** are leukocytes that defend against parasitic invaders such as worms by positioning themselves near the parasite's wall and discharging hydrolytic enzymes.

❚ Damage to tissue by physical injury or the entry of pathogens leads to release of numerous chemical signals that trigger the **inflammatory response.** For example, histamines are released by basophils and mast cells (two types of leukocytes) in response to injury. Histamines trigger the dilation and permeability of nearby capillaries. This aids in delivering clotting agents to the injured area.

Concept 43.2 In acquired immunity, lymphocytes provide specific defenses against infection

❚ Vertebrates have two types of lymphocytes: **B lymphocytes (B cells),** which proliferate in the bone barrow, and **T lymphocytes (T cells),** where lymphocytes mature in the thymus. They circulate through the blood and lymph, and both recognize particular microbes and are said to show specificity.

❚ **Antigens** are foreign molecules that elicit a response by lymphocytes.

❚ **Antibodies** are proteins secreted by B cells during an immune response.

❚ **Antigen receptors** are located on the antigen and allow B and T cells to recognize them. Antigen receptors on T cells are called **T cell receptors,** and they recognize antibodies specifically.

❚ When an antigen binds to a B or T cell, the lymphocyte becomes activated and forms two clones of cells. One is made up of **effector cells,** which combat the antigen, and the other consists of **memory cells,** which are long-lived and bear receptors for the same antigen. This process is called **clonal selection.**

■ When the body is first exposed to an antigen and a lymphocyte is activated, this is referred to as the **primary immune response.** Upon second exposure to the antigen, the **secondary immune response** is faster and of greater magnitude.

■ Lymphocytes and all other blood cells arise from stem cells in the bone marrow.

Concept 43.3 Humoral and cell-mediated immunity defend against different types of threats

■ Active immunity develops naturally in response to an infection; it also develops artificially by immunization (vaccination). In immunization, a nonpathogenic form of a microbe or part of a microbe elicits an immune response to an immunological memory for that microbe.

Concept 43.4 The immune system's ability to distinguish self from nonself limits tissue transplantation

■ Certain antigens on red blood cells determine whether a person has **type A, B, AB,** or **O blood.** Because antibodies to nonself blood antigens already exist in the body, transfusion with incompatible blood leads to destruction of the transfused cells and a life-threatening situation for the patient.

■ **MHC molecules** are responsible for stimulating the rejection of tissue grafts and organ transplants. The chances of successful transplantation are increased if the donor's tissue bearing MHC molecules closely matches the recipient's. The recipient also must take immunosuppressant drugs.

Concept 43.5 Exaggerated, self-directed, or diminished immune responses can cause disease

■ In localized **allergies** such as hay fever, IgE antibodies produced after first exposure to an allergen attach to receptors on mast cells. The next time the same allergen enters the body, it bonds to mast cell–associated IgE molecules, inducing the cell to release histamine and other mediators that cause vascular changes and typical symptoms.

Concept 44.1 Osmoregulation balances the uptake and loss of water and solutes

■ **Osmoregulation** is based largely on the controlled movement of solutes between internal fluids and the external environment, and the movement of water, which flows by osmosis.

Concept 44.2 An animal's nitrogenous wastes reflect its phylogeny and habitat

■ Most metabolic wastes must be excreted from the body. One of the most important types of waste products is **nitrogen-containing products** of the breakdown of proteins and nucleic acids.

■ Enzymes remove nitrogen from these compounds to create **ammonia.** Some animals excrete ammonia directly into water, where it becomes diluted. Others convert it first to **urea** in the liver, where ammonia is combined with carbon dioxide in an endergonic reaction, or to **uric acid.** Uric acid is more energetically expensive to produce, but it is insoluble in water and can be excreted as a paste or crystals.

Concept 44.3 Diverse excretory systems are variations on a tubular theme

▌ Most excretory systems produce urine in a two-step process. First, the body fluid (blood or hemolymph) is collected; then the composition of the fluid is adjusted by **selective reabsorption** of solutes.

▌ Insects and terrestrial arthropods such as the grasshopper have **Malpighian tubules** that remove nitrogenous wastes. They open into the digestive tract and dead-end at points in the hemolymph. The tubules secrete nitrogenous wastes and salts into the lumen, and water follows by osmosis.

Concept 44.4 Nephrons and associated blood vessels are the functional units of the mammalian kidney

▌ Mammals have two kidneys, and each is supplied with a **renal artery** and a **renal vein. Urine** leaves the kidneys through the **ureters,** which drain into the urinary bladder. Urine is expelled from the body through the **urethra.**

▌ The kidney has two regions, the **outer renal cortex** and the **inner renal medulla.** Each region is packed with nephrons, which are the functional units of the kidney.

▌ **Nephrons** are made up of a single long tubule and the **glomerulus,** a ball of capillaries. At one end of the tubule is the **Bowman's capsule,** a C-shaped structure that surrounds the glomerulus.

▌ The filtrate flows through the **proximal tubule,** the descending **loop of Henle,** the loop of Henle, the ascending loop of Henle, and the **distal tubule.** The distal tubule empties into a **collecting duct,** which receives wastes from many nephrons. The filtrate empties into the renal pelvis.

▌ In the human kidney, most of the nephrons are **cortical nephrons;** these are in the renal cortex. The rest are **juxtamedullary nephrons,** with long loops of Henle that extend into the renal medulla.

▌ Capillaries called **afferent arterioles** are associated with the nephrons, and as they leave the glomerulus, the capillaries converge into an **efferent arteriole.** This vessel subdivides again to form **peritubular capillaries,** which surround the proximal and distal tubules.

▌ There are five main steps in the **transformation of blood filtrate to urine,** as shown on the next page.

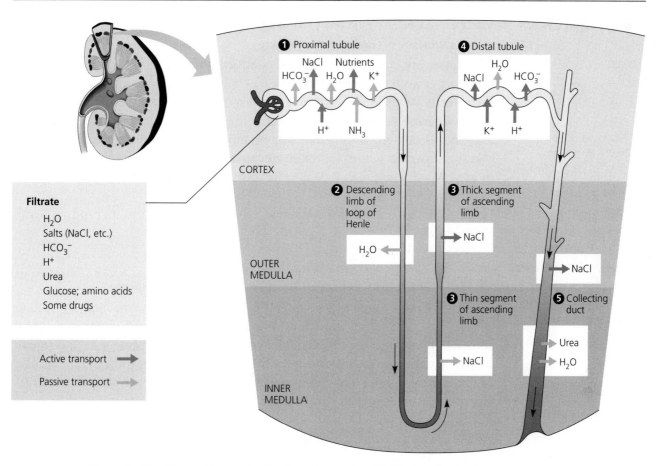

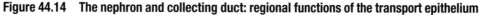

Figure 44.14   The nephron and collecting duct: regional functions of the transport epithelium

1. In the proximal tubule, secretion and reabsorption changes the volume and composition of the filtrate. The pH of body fluids is controlled, and bicarbonate is absorbed, as are NaCl and water.
2. In the descending loop of Henle, reabsorption of water continues.
3. In the ascending loop of Henle, the filtrate loses salt without giving up water and becomes more dilute.
4. In the distal tubule, K^+ and NaCl levels are regulated, as is filtrate pH.
5. The collecting duct carries the filtrate through the medulla to the renal pelvis, and the filtrate becomes more concentrated by the movement of salt.

Concept 44.5 The mammalian kidney's ability to conserve water is a key terrestrial adaptation

▍ **Antidiuretic hormone** is an important hormone in the regulation of water balance. It is produced in the hypothalamus and stored in and released from the pituitary gland. Two other hormones involved in regulation of water balance are **angiotensin** and **aldosterone.**

Concept 45.1 **The endocrine system and the nervous system act individually**
                 and together in regulating an animal's physiology

▌ **Hormones** are chemical signals released into body fluids that communicate messages around the body.

▌ **Target cells** are those cells equipped to respond to hormones.

▌ The **endocrine system** of an animal is the sum of all its hormone-secreting cells and tissues. Hormone-secreting organs are called endocrine glands.

▌ Many endocrine glands contain **neurosecretory cells,** which secrete hormones. Many chemicals act as both hormones and nervous system signals (neurotransmitters).

▌ **Feedback** is one important way by which the endocrine and nervous systems are regulated.

Concept 45.2 **Hormones and other chemical signals bind to target**
                 cell receptors, initiating pathways that culminate in specific cell responses

▌ Chemical signals may bind to receptors on the plasma membranes of certain cells, triggering a **signal transduction pathway.** A signal transduction pathway consists of a series of molecular events that initiates a response to the signal. Alternately, the signal enters the target cell and binds to a receptor in the cell. The receptor then acts as a transcription factor, causing a change in gene expression.

▌ Hormones in the body can affect one tissue, a few tissues, or most of the tissues in the body (as with the sex hormones), or they may affect other endocrine glands (these last are referred to as **tropic hormones**).

Concept 45.3 **The hypothalamus and pituitary integrate**
                 many functions of the vertebrate endocrine system

▌ The **hypothalamus** receives info from nerves throughout the body and from other parts of the brain then initiates endocrine signals in response.

▌ The **posterior pituitary** is an extension of the hypothalamus that stores and secretes two hormones (oxytocin and ADH) that are made by certain neurosecretory cells located in the hypothalamus.

▌ The **anterior pituitary** consists of endocrine cells that synthesize and secrete at least six hormones into the blood. Tropic hormones released from the hypothalamus regulate the anterior pituitary.

Table 45.1 Major Human Endocrine Glands and Some of Their Hormones

Gland	Hormone	Chemical Class	Representative Actions	Regulated By
Hypothalamus	Hormones released from the posterior pituitary and hormones that regulate the anterior pituitary (see below)			
Pituitary gland Posterior pituitary (releases neuro-hormones made in hypothalamus)	Oxytocin	Peptide	Stimulates contraction of uterus and mammary gland cells	Nervous system
	Antidiuretic hormone (ADH)	Peptide	Promotes retention of water by kidneys	Water/salt balance
Anterior pituitary	Growth hormone (GH)	Protein	Stimulates growth (especially bones) and metabolic functions	Hypothalamic hormones
	Prolactin (PRL)	Protein	Stimulates milk production and secretion	Hypothalamic hormones
	Follicle-stimulating hormone (FSH)	Glycoprotein	Stimulates production of ova and sperm	Hypothalamic hormones
	Luteinizing hormone (LH)	Glycoprotein	Stimulates ovaries and testes	Hypothalamic hormones
	Thyroid-stimulating hormone (TSH)	Glycoprotein	Stimulates thyroid gland	Thyroxine in blood; hypothalamic hormones
	Adrenocorticotropic hormone (ACTH)	Peptide	Stimulates adrenal cortex to secrete glucocorticoids	Glucocorticoids; hypothalamic hormones
Thyroid gland	Triiodothyronine (T_3) and thyroxine (T_4)	Amine	Stimulate and maintain metabolic processes	TSH
	Calcitonin	Peptide	Lowers blood calcium level	Calcium in blood
Parathyroid glands	Parathyroid hormone (PTH)	Peptide	Raises blood calcium level	Calcium in blood
Pancreas	Insulin	Protein	Lowers blood glucose level	Glucose in blood
	Glucagon	Protein	Raises blood glucose level	Glucose in blood
Adrenal glands Adrenal medulla	Epinephrine and norepinephrine	Amine	Raise blood glucose level; increase metabolic activities; constrict certain blood vessels	Nervous system
Adrenal cortex	Glucocorticoids	Steroid	Raise blood glucose level	ACTH
	Mineralocorticoids	Steroid	Promote reabsorption of Na^+ and excretion of K^+ in kidneys	K^+ in blood
Gonads Testes	Androgens	Steroid	Support sperm formation; promote development and maintenance of male secondary sex characteristics	FSH and LH
Ovaries	Estrogens	Steroid	Stimulate uterine lining growth; promote development and maintenance of female secondary sex characteristics	FSH and LH
	Progesterone	Steroid	Promotes uterine lining growth	FSH and LH
Pineal gland	Melatonin	Amine	Involved in biological rhythms	Light/dark cycles

Concept 45.4 Nonpituitary hormones help regulate metabolism, homeostasis, development, and behavior

(The maintenance of blood calcium level is one example of how homeostasis is maintained by negative feedback.)

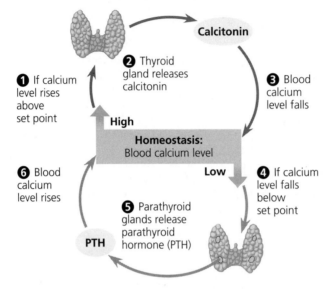

An Example of How Feedback Regulation Maintains Homeostasis

Concept 46.1 Both asexual and sexual reproduction occur in the animal kingdom

▌ **Sexual reproduction** is the creation of offspring by the fusion of haploid gametes to form a zygote. The female gamete is the ovum, and the male gamete is the sperm.

▌ **Asexual reproduction** is reproduction in which all genes come from one parent; there is no fusion of egg and sperm. Asexual reproduction can occur by fission, which is the separation of a parent into two or more individuals of about the same size.

▌ **Budding** is another form of asexual reproduction, in which new individuals "bud off" of the parent. Budding occurs, for example, in certain cnidarians and tunicates.

▌ **Fragmentation** is a form of asexual reproduction in which an individual breaks into several pieces, all of which then may form complete adults. Regeneration, the regrowth of body parts, is a necessary part of fragmentation.

▌ **Parthenogenesis** is the process in which a female produces unfertilized eggs that develop into more females.

▌ **Hermaphroditism** exists when each individual has both male and female reproductive systems.

Concept 46.2 Fertilization depends on mechanisms that help sperm meet eggs of the same species

▌ **Fertilization** is the union of sperm and egg. **External fertilization** occurs when eggs are shed by the female and fertilized by the male outside the female's body. **Internal fertilization** occurs when sperm are deposited in the female reproductive tract, and fertilization occurs within the tract.

▌ **Gonads** are the organs that produce gametes in most animals.

Concept 46.3 *Reproductive organs produce and transport gametes: focus on humans*

▌ The male's external reproductive organs are the **scrotum** and **penis,** and the internal organs are gonads (which produce gametes and hormones), accessory glands (which secrete necessary fluids), and ducts (which carry sperm and glandular secretions).

▌ The testes are made up of many highly coiled tubules surrounded by connective tissue. The tubules are **seminiferous tubules,** the sites of sperm production. In between the tubules are **Leydig cells,** which produce testosterone and other androgens. The testes are held in the **scrotum,** which is located outside the lower abdominal pelvic cavity.

▌ The sperm passes from the seminiferous tubules into the **epididymis.** During ejaculation, the sperm is propelled through the **vas deferens,** which ultimately meets up with a duct from the **seminal vesicle** and form an ejaculatory duct, which opens into the urethra.

▌ The seminal vesicles, the **prostate gland,** and the **bulbourethral gland** all contribute secretions that make up semen. These secretions supply necessary nutrients and a medium for the sperm cells.

▌ The **penis** is composed of three masses of spongy tissue derived from modified veins and capillaries.

▌ The female gonads are the two **ovaries.** Each ovary contains many microscopic follicles.

▌ **Follicles** consist of one egg surrounded by one or more layers of follicle cells, which help to develop, nourish, and protect the egg cell. One follicle matures and releases its egg cell during each menstrual cycle.

▌ The follicle cells also produce **estrogens,** the female hormones.

▌ The egg cell is released from the follicle during ovulation. The remaining follicle tissue heals and grows in the ovary to form a body called a **corpus luteum,** which secretes estrogen and progesterone. Progesterone helps to maintain the uterine wall during pregnancy. If the egg cell isn't fertilized, the corpus luteum disintegrates.

▌ The egg cell is released into the **oviduct,** and cilia lining the oviduct convey the egg cell down to the uterus. The inner lining of the uterus is called the **endometrium.**

▌ At the base of the uterus is the **cervix,** which leads to the **vagina,** the canal through which a baby is born.

Concept 46.4 *In humans and other mammals, a complex interplay of hormones regulates gametogenesis*

▌ **Spermatogenesis** is the production of mature sperm cells, and it occurs in the seminiferous tubules. The cells that give rise to sperm are called spermatogonia. They undergo meiosis and differentiation eventually to form mature, motile sperm.

▌ **Oogenesis** is the development of mature ova. **Oogonia** are the cells that develop into ova; they multiply and begin meiosis, but they stop at prophase I of meiosis I. These egg cells are called **primary oocytes,** which are quiescent until puberty. From puberty onward, FSH periodically stimulates a follicle to grow and its egg cell to complete meiosis I and begin meiosis II. This forms the **secondary oocyte.**

- Humans and other primates have **menstrual cycles.** Menstruation occurs when the endometrium is shed from the uterus through the cervix and vagina. Other mammals have **estrous cycles.**
- The **menstrual flow phase** of the female cycle is the phase during which menstrual bleeding occurs.

  - The **proliferative phase** of the menstrual cycle is that during which the endometrium begins to regenerate and thicken.
  - In the **secretory phase,** the endometrium continues to thicken, and if an embryo has not implanted in the lining by the end of this phase, menstrual flow occurs.

- The **ovarian cycle** parallels the menstrual flow cycle and begins with the follicular phase, in which several follicles begin to grow.

  - At the end of the follicular phase, ovulation occurs, during which the secondary oocyte is released from the ovary.
  - During the **luteal phase** of the ovarian cycle, endocrine walls in the corpus luteum secrete hormones.

Concept 46.5 *In humans and other placental mammals, an embryo grows into a newborn in the mother's uterus*

- In humans and other placental mammals, **pregnancy,** or **gestation,** is the condition of carrying one or more embryos in the uterus.
- Human gestation culminates in birth, or parturition, which is brought about by a series of strong rhythmic uterine contractions.

Concept 47.1 *After fertilization, embryonic development proceeds through cleavage, gastrulation, and organogenesis*

1. **Cleavage,** which is a period of rapid mitotic cell division, partitions the cytoplasm of the zygote into smaller cells called **blastomeres,** each of which has its own nucleus. Continued cleavage leads to a ball of cells called a **morula,** and then a fluid-filled central cavity called the **blastocoel** forms within the morula to produce a **blastula.**
2. **Gastrulation** is a drastic rearrangement of the cells in the blastula. In gastrulation, three (germ) cell layers are produced—the ectoderm, endoderm, and mesoderm.
3. **Organogenesis** is the development of the three germ layers into the rudiments of organs.

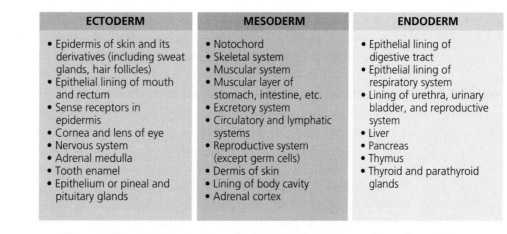

ECTODERM	MESODERM	ENDODERM
• Epidermis of skin and its derivatives (including sweat glands, hair follicles) • Epithelial lining of mouth and rectum • Sense receptors in epidermis • Cornea and lens of eye • Nervous system • Adrenal medulla • Tooth enamel • Epithelium or pineal and pituitary glands	• Notochord • Skeletal system • Muscular system • Muscular layer of stomach, intestine, etc. • Excretory system • Circulatory and lymphatic systems • Reproductive system (except germ cells) • Dermis of skin • Lining of body cavity • Adrenal cortex	• Epithelial lining of digestive tract • Epithelial lining of respiratory system • Lining of urethra, urinary bladder, and reproductive system • Liver • Pancreas • Thymus • Thyroid and parathyroid glands

Figure 47.16   Adult derivatives of the three embryonic germ layers in vertebrates

Concept 48.1 Nervous systems consist of circuits of neurons and supporting cells

▌ **Sensory receptors** collect information about the world outside the body as well as processes inside the body.

▌ The **central nervous system (CNS)** consists of the brain and spinal cord, and the **peripheral nervous system (PNS)** consists of the nerves that communicate motor and sensory signals throughout the rest of the body.

▌ **Motor output** is the conduction of signals from the CNS to **effector cells,** which are muscle or gland cells that carry out responses.

▌ The **neuron** is the functional unit of the nervous system. It is composed of a cell body which contains the nucleus and organelles; **dendrites,** which are cell extensions that receive incoming messages from other cells; and **axons,** which convey messages to other cells.

▌ Many axons are covered by an insulating fatty **myelin sheath. Synaptic terminals,** at the end of axons, relay signals from one neuron to another neuron or other cell through chemical messengers called **neurotransmitters.**

▌ A **simple nerve circuit** is the reflex arc, in which a sensory nerve receives information and passes it on to the spinal cord and then to a motor neuron, which signals an effector cell.

▌ **Ganglia** are clusters of nerve cells.

▌ **Glia** are supporting nerve cells, and they outnumber nerve cells in the body. Three important kinds of glia are **astrocytes,** which provide support for neurons; **oligodendrocytes,** which form myelin sheaths in the CNS; and **Schwann cells,** which form myelin sheaths in the PNS.

Concept 48.2 Ion pumps and ion channels maintain the resting potential of a neuron

▌ **Membrane potential** describes the difference in electrical charge across a cell membrane.

▌ The membrane potential of a nerve cell at rest is called its **resting potential.** It exists because of differences in the ionic composition of the extracellular and intracellular fluids across the plasma membrane.

■ Changes in the membrane potential of a neuron are what give rise to **nerve impulses.** A stimulus first affects the membrane's permeability to ions, and this is a graded potential with a magnitude proportional to the size of the stimulus.

Concept 48.3 Action potentials are the signals conducted by axons

■ An **action potential** (nerve impulse) is an all-or-none depolarization of the membrane of the nerve cell. It opens voltage-gated sodium channels, and Na^+ ions enter the cell, bringing the membrane potential to a positive value. The membrane potential is restored to its normal resting value by the inactivation of Na^+ channels and by opening voltage gated K^+ channels, which increases K^+ leaving the cell. A refractory period follows the action potential, corresponding to the interval when the Na^+ channels are inactivated.

■ Action potentials are propagated along the axon; **saltatory conduction,** which is the jumping of the nerve impulse between nodes of Ranvier (areas on the axon not covered by the myelin sheath), speeds up the conduction of the nerve impulse.

Concept 48.4 Neurons communicate with other cells at synapses

■ The signal is conducted from the axon of a presynaptic cell to the dendrite of a postsynaptic cell via an **electrical** or **chemical synapse.**

■ Electrical synapses occur via **gap junctions.**

■ In chemical synapses, neurotransmitters are released by the presynaptic membrane into the synaptic cleft. They bind to receptors on the postsynaptic membrane and are then broken down by enzymes, or taken back up into surrounding cells.

■ **Excitatory postsynaptic potential (EPSP)** is the electrical charge caused by the binding of the neurotransmitter to its receptor on the postsynaptic membrane.

■ **Inhibitory postsynaptic potential (IPSP)** is the voltage charge associated with chemical signaling at an inhibitory synapse.

■ **Acetylcholine** is a very common neurotransmitter, it can be inhibitory or excitatory. Other common **neurotransmitters** are epinephrine, norepinephrine, dopamine, and serotonin.

Concept 48.5 The vertebrate nervous system is regionally specialized

■ The **peripheral nervous system (PNS)** consists of paired cranial and spinal nerves and associated ganglia. The PNS is divided into the somatic nervous system, which carries signals to skeletal muscles, and the autonomic nervous system, which regulates the primarily automatic, visceral functions of smooth and cardiac muscles.

■ The **autonomic nervous system** transmits signals that regulate the internal environment by controlling smooth and cardiac muscle, including those in the gastrointestinal, cardiovascular, excretory, and endocrine systems.

■ The autonomic nervous system is composed of the **sympathetic division**—which, when activated, causes the heart to beat faster and adrenaline to be secreted (with all its effects)—and the **parasympathetic division,** which has the opposite effect when activated.

- The vertebrate brain develops from three embryonic regions: the **forebrain,** the **midbrain,** and the **hindbrain.** In humans, the most expansive growth occurs in the part of the forebrain that gives rise to the **cerebellum.**
- The **brainstem** is made up of the medulla oblongata, pons, and midbrain. The brainstem controls homeostatic functions such as breathing rate, conducts sensory and motor signals between the spinal cord and higher brain centers, and regulates arousal and sleep.
- The cerebellum helps coordinate motor, perceptual, and cognitive functions.
- The **thalamus** is the main center through which sensory and motor information passes to and from the cerebrum. The **hypothalamus** regulates homeostasis; basic survival behaviors such as feeding, fighting, fleeing, and reproducing; and circadian rhythms.
- The **cerebrum** has two hemispheres, each of which consists of a cerebral cortex overlying white matter and basal nuclei, which are important in planning and learning movements. In mammals, the cerebral cortex has a convoluted surface called the **neocortex.** A thick band of axons, the **corpus callosum,** provides communication between the right and left cortices.

Concept 48.6 **The cerebral cortex controls voluntary movement and cognitive functions**

- Each side of the cerebral cortex has **four lobes**—frontal, temporal, occipital, and parietal—which contain primary sensory areas and association areas.
- Portions of the frontal and temporal lobes, including Broca's area and Wernicke's area, are essential for generation and understanding language.

Concept 49.1 **Sensory receptors transduce stimulus energy and transmit signals to the central nervous system**

- **Mechanoreceptors** are receptors stimulated by physical stimuli, such as pressure, touch, stretch, motion, or sound.
- **Thermoreceptors** respond to either heat or cold and help maintain body temperature.
- **Chemoreceptors** transmit information about solute concentration in a solution. Gustatory (taste) receptors and olfactory (smell) receptors are two types of chemoreceptors.
- **Electromagnetic receptors** detect various forms of electromagnetic energy such as visible light, electricity, and magnetism.
- Different groups of **pain receptors** respond to excess heat, pressure, or specific classes of chemicals released from damaged or inflamed tissues.

Concept 49.2 **The mechanoreceptors involved with hearing and equilibrium detect settling particles or moving fluid**

- There are three regions in the mammalian ear.

  1. The **outer ear** is the external **pinna** and **auditory canal.** These collect sounds and direct them to the **tympanic membrane** (eardrum), which separates the outer ear from the middle ear.

2. In the **middle ear,** vibrations are conducted through three small bones (the malleus, incus, and stapes) and through the **oval window.**
3. Then the vibrations are conducted to the **inner ear,** which consists of a labyrinth of channels lined by membrane and containing fluid, all situated in bone.

▌ The inner ear contains the **cochlea,** a two-chambered organ, which is involved in hearing.

▌ The **organ of Corti,** which is in the cochlea, contains the receptors of the ear, which are hair cells with "hairs" that project into the **cochlear duct.**

▌ The cochlea transduces the energy of the vibrating fluid into action potentials, in a wave that dissipates at the **round window.**

▌ Some organs in the inner ear are responsible for detecting body position and balance. These are the **semicircular canals.**

Concept 49.3 The senses of taste and smell are closely related in most animals

▌ **Taste buds** are modified epithelial cells situated on different parts of the tongue and mouth.

Concept 49.4 Similar mechanisms underlie vision throughout the animal kingdom

▌ **Compound eyes** (in insects and crustaceans) consist of up to several thousand light detectors called ommatidia, each of which has its own lens.

▌ **Single-lens eyes** are found in vertebrates and some invertebrates.

▌ The **eyeball** in single-lens eyes is made up of two outer layers, the **sclera** and the **choroid.** At the front of the eye, the sclera becomes the **cornea,** which allows light into the eye and acts as a fixed lens. The eyeball also contains the **pupil,** which is the hole in the center of the **iris,** and the **retina,** which contains the photoreceptor cells.

▌ **Aqueous humor** fills the anterior cavity of the eye, and the **vitreous humor** fills the posterior cavity of the eye.

▌ The retina contains **rods,** which are very sensitive to light, and **cones,** which distinguish colors.

▌ **Rhodopsin** is the light-absorbing pigment that triggers a signal transduction pathway that ultimately leads to sight.

Concept 49.5 Animal skeletons function in support, protection, and movement

▌ **Locomotion** is the movement from place to place.

▌ **Hydrostatic skeletons** consist of fluid held under pressure in a closed body compartment.

▌ **Exoskeletons** are hard encasements on the surface of an animal, such as is found in the grasshopper. **Endoskeletons** consist of hard supporting elements buried within the soft tissues of an animal. An example is the human bony skeleton.

▌ **Skeletal muscle** is attached to bones and responsible for the movement of bones. It consists of long fibers, each of which is a single muscle cell. Each muscle fiber is a bundle of **myofibrils,** which in turn are composed of two kinds of myofilaments: **thin filaments** and **thick filaments.**

- **Skeletal muscle** is striated, and the basic contractile unit of the muscle is the **sarcomere.** The **Z lines** make up the border of sarcomeres, the **I band** is the area near the end of the sarcomere where only thin filament exists, and the **A band** is the entire length of the thin filaments.
- During **muscle contraction,** the length of the sarcomere is reduced.
- The **sliding-filament model** states that the thick and thin filaments slide past each other so that their degree of overlap increases. This is dependent on the interaction between the **actin** and **myosin** molecules that make up the thin and thick filaments.
- Muscle cells contract when stimulated by a **motor neuron.**
- To stimulate muscle contraction, an action potential in a motor neuron that makes a synaptic connection with the muscle cell releases acetylcholine at the **neuromuscular junction.** This depolarizes the muscle cell and triggers an action potential.
- The action potential spreads along **T tubules (transverse tubules).** This changes the permeability of the **sarcoplasmic reticulum** to calcium ions, and the newly released calcium ions bind to **troponin** and cause it to move, exposing the myosin sites on actin; the muscle contracts.
- **Fast-twitch muscle fibers** are used for fast, powerful contractions. **Slow-twitch muscle fibers** are used for slow, long-lasting contractions.

For Additional Review

Consider how the immune, digestive, nervous, circulatory, and respiratory systems and the senses all contribute to homeostasis in animals. In doing so, connect the stimuli that engage these systems with the way the systems respond to those stimuli.

Multiple-Choice Questions

1. Which of the following is required in all living things in order for gas exchange to occur?
   (A) lungs
   (B) gills
   (C) moist membranes
   (D) blood
   (E) lymph

2. In animals, all of the following are associated with embryonic development EXCEPT
   (A) gastrulation.
   (B) cleavage.
   (C) depolarization.
   (D) organogenesis.
   (E) cell migration.

3. Which of the following is most likely to result in a release of epinephrine (adrenaline) from the adrenal glands?
   (A) falling asleep in front of the TV
   (B) watching a golf tournament
   (C) doing yoga
   (D) taking a test without having studied for it
   (E) being in the kitchen while dinner is being cooked

4. Oxygen is transported in human blood by which type of cells?
   (A) erythrocytes
   (B) leukocytes
   (C) phagocytes
   (D) B cells
   (E) T cells

5. The proximal tubules in the kidney reabsorb most of which of the following compounds?
   (A) CO_2
   (B) O_2
   (C) H_2O
   (D) HCO_3^-
   (E) $C_6H_{12}O_6$

6. Salivary amylase, an enzyme secreted in saliva, begins the breakdown of which substance?
   (A) starches
   (B) proteins
   (C) lipids
   (D) nucleic acids
   (E) polypeptides

Directions: The group of questions below consists of five lettered choices followed by a list of numbered phrases or sentences. For each numbered phrase or sentence, select the one choice that is most closely related to it. Each choice may be used once, more than once, or not at all.

Questions 7–11
   (A) Ovary
   (B) Thyroid gland
   (C) Posterior pituitary gland
   (D) Adrenal medulla
   (E) Pineal gland

7. Releases hormones that raise blood glucose level, increase metabolic activities, and constrict blood vessels

8. Releases hormones that are involved in biological rhythms

9. Releases hormones that stimulate the mammary gland cells and contraction of the uterus

10. Releases hormones that stimulate growth of the uterine lining and promote the development of female secondary sex characteristics

11. Releases hormones that stimulate and maintain metabolic processes

12. Blood constitutes which of the following tissue types?
    (A) epithelial tissue
    (B) connective tissue
    (C) nervous tissue
    (D) vascular tissue
    (E) glandular tissue

13. The three types of muscle in the body are
    (A) skeletal, cardiac, and smooth
    (B) skeletal, vascular, and smooth
    (C) skeletal, cardiac, and rough
    (D) cardiac, smooth, and rough
    (E) cardiac, smooth, and vascular

14. Which of the following is an example of negative feedback?
    (A) the movement of sodium across a membrane through an antiport, and the movement of potassium in the opposite direction through the same antiport
    (B) the pressure of the baby's head against the uterine wall during childbirth stimulates uterine contractions, which causes greater pressure against the uterine wall, which produces still more contractions
    (C) the growth of a population of bacteria in a petri dish until it has used all its nutrients, and its subsequent decline
    (D) a heating system in which the heat is turned off when the temperature exceeds a certain point and is turned on when the temperature falls below a certain point
    (E) the progress of a chemical reaction until equilibrium is reached, and then the cycling back and forth of reactant to product

15. All of the following are fat-soluble vitamins EXCEPT
    (A) vitamin A.
    (B) vitamin B.
    (C) vitamin D.
    (D) vitamin E.
    (E) vitamin K.

16. Which of the following has a diet that consists solely of autotrophs?
    (A) omnivore
    (B) carnivore
    (C) herbivore
    (D) trendavore
    (E) supravore

17. The four stages of food processing are ingestion, digestion, absorption, and
    (A) incorporation.
    (B) circulation.
    (C) elimination.
    (D) filtration.
    (E) cellular uptake.

18. Hydras possess which of the following type of digestive system?
    (A) food vacuole
    (B) complete digestive tract
    (C) alimentary canal
    (D) lumen
    (E) gastrovascular cavity

19. Which of the following is the site of the production of bile?
    (A) gallbladder
    (B) small intestine
    (C) prostate
    (D) pancreas
    (E) liver

20. The primary sites of carbohydrate digestion are which of the following structures?
    (A) mouth and large intestine
    (B) mouth and stomach
    (C) stomach and small intestine
    (D) mouth and small intestine
    (E) small intestine and colon

21. Pepsin in the stomach is primarily responsible for the breakdown of which type of molecule?
    (A) starches
    (B) proteins
    (C) lipids
    (D) nucleic acids
    (E) glycogens

22. Which of the following structures is primarily responsible for reabsorbing water from the lumen?
    (A) small intestine
    (B) nephron
    (C) glomerulus
    (D) colon
    (E) cecum

23. Insects and other arthropods have which of the following circulatory fluids?
    (A) lymph
    (B) hemoglobin
    (C) blood
    (D) hemolymph
    (E) heterolymph

24. A body plan in which blood bathes the organs directly is termed
    (A) an open circulatory system.
    (B) a closed circulatory system.
    (C) a cardiovascular system.
    (D) a gastrovascular system.
    (E) a gastrovascular cavity system.

25. Which of the following carry blood away from the heart?
    (A) venules
    (B) veins
    (C) arteries
    (D) capillaries
    (E) atria

26. In the mammalian heart, the sinoatrial (SA) node is responsible for which of the following functions?
    (A) Delaying the nerve impulse to the walls of the ventricle
    (B) Controlling the atrioventricular valve
    (C) Controlling the semilunar valves
    (D) Setting the rate and timing of cardiac muscle contraction
    (E) Monitoring stroke volume

27. Fluid and proteins lost from the capillaries are returned to the blood via
    (A) the venous system.
    (B) the arteriole system.
    (C) the lymphatic system.
    (D) capillary beds.
    (E) the hemolymph system.

28. All of the following are components of blood EXCEPT
    (A) red blood cells.
    (B) white blood cells.
    (C) platelets.
    (D) leukocytes.
    (E) lymph.

29. Red blood cells are derived from which of the following tissues?
    (A) the heart
    (B) the blood vessels
    (C) bone
    (D) muscles
    (E) masses of other blood cells

30. Grasshoppers exhibit which type of respiratory system?
    (A) lungs
    (B) countercurrent system
    (C) tracheal system
    (D) Malpighian system
    (E) vessel system

31. In the blood, carbon dioxide is primarily transported in what way?
    (A) by hemoglobin
    (B) by hemocyanin
    (C) as carbon monoxide
    (D) as bicarbonate
    (E) in erythrocytes

32. All of the following are first-line barriers against infectious agents EXCEPT
    (A) skin.
    (B) nasal membranes.
    (C) saliva.
    (D) mucous secretions.
    (E) phagocytes.

33. An immune response to a specific antigen generates the production of which type of cell that launches an attack the next time that same antigen infects the body?
    (A) effector cells
    (B) memory cells
    (C) T cells
    (D) B cells
    (E) antibodies

34. All of the following are ways by which organisms exchange heat EXCEPT
    (A) transference.
    (B) conduction.
    (C) convection.
    (D) radiation.
    (E) evaporation.

35. Which of the following animals is most likely an ectoderm?
    (A) human
    (B) snake
    (C) bird
    (D) monkey
    (E) dolphin

36. The Malpighian tubules are the organs that constitute the excretory system of which of the following animals?
(A) birds
(B) humans
(C) fishes
(D) insects
(E) hydras

37. The ball of capillaries that is associated with the nephron and associated with filtration in the kidney is
(A) the Bowman's capsule.
(B) the loop of Henle.
(C) the proximal tubule.
(D) the glomerulus.
(E) the distal tubule.

Directions: The group of questions below consists of five lettered choices followed by a list of numbered phrases or sentences. For each numbered phrase or sentence, select the one choice that is most closely related to it. Each choice may be used once, more than once, or not at all.

Questions 38–42
(A) Vitreous humor
(B) Cone cell
(C) Eustachian tube
(D) Cochlea
(E) Taste bud

38. A photoreceptor

39. A coiled organ that is involved in hearing

40. Constitutes most of the volume of the eye

41. Equalizes the pressure between the middle ear and the atmosphere

42. A receptor that can be stimulated by a broad range of chemicals

43. Muscle cell contraction occurs via
(A) contraction of the A band.
(B) contraction of the I band.
(C) contraction of the Z lines.
(D) the sliding of the thin filaments by the thick filaments.
(E) the contraction of the sarcoplasmic reticulum.

44. The succession of rapid cell division that follows fertilization is called
(A) gastrulation.
(B) cleavage.
(C) morulation.
(D) involution.
(E) polarization.

45. The circuit of a sensory neuron, the spinal cord, a motor neuron, and an effector cell constitutes a
(A) presynaptic sequence.
(B) reflex arc.
(C) nerve circuit.
(D) nerve impulse.
(E) saltatory conduction system.

46. Which of the following is released into the synaptic cleft and acts as an intercellular messenger?
(A) sodium
(B) chloride
(C) neurotransmitter
(D) action potential
(E) voltage gradient

47. An egg cell surrounded by one or two layers of cells is called a
(A) follicle
(B) corpus luteum
(C) oviduct
(D) endometrium
(E) uterus

48. Sperm are formed in the
    (A) Leydig cells.
    (B) prostate gland.
    (C) seminal vesicles.
    (D) seminiferous tubules.
    (E) baculum.

49. The regulation of the internal environment in animals is referred to as
    (A) equilibrium.
    (B) stasis.
    (C) homeostasis.
    (D) regulation.
    (E) feedback.

50. Fertilization—the fusion of egg and sperm cell—results in which of the following?
    (A) embryo
    (B) zygote
    (C) gamete
    (D) ovum
    (E) follicle

Free-Response Question

1. *Muscle cells are responsible for moving parts of the skeleton by contracting. However, during muscle contraction, none of the muscle cells themselves actually contract.*

   (a) **Describe** how a muscle can contract without any of its cells contracting.
   (b) **Explain** the phenomenon of tetanus.
   (c) **Explain** why muscles become "sore" after exercise.

ANSWERS AND EXPLANATIONS

Multiple-Choice Questions

1. **(C) is correct.** The only condition listed that is necessary in all organisms that breathe is the presence of moist membranes. The movement of O_2 and CO_2 across the membranes between the environment and the respiratory surface occurs by diffusion. Respiratory surfaces are generally thin and, since living animal cells must be wet in order to maintain their plasma membranes, these respiratory surfaces must be moist.

2. **(C) is correct.** The three main stages of development in animals are cleavage, in which a multicellular embryo forms from the zygote through a series of mitotic cell divisions; gastrulation, in which cells migrate and rearrange to form three germ layers; and organogenesis, in which rudimentary organs are formed from the germ layers.

3. **(D) is correct.** Epinephrine is a hormone that is secreted by the adrenal glands, specifically the adrenal medulla. It functions in raising the blood glucose level, increasing metabolic activities, and constricting blood vessels; all of this prepares the animal for the fight-or-flight response that is elicited in the body during stressful times.

4. (A) is correct. Erythrocytes are red blood cells, and they transport oxygen around the body. They are the most numerous blood cells, and are small and disk-shaped. In mammals, erythrocytes have no nuclei. Instead they contain millions of molecules of hemoglobin, which is the iron-containing protein that transports oxygen. One molecule of hemoglobin can bind four oxygen molecules.

5. (D) is correct. The proximal tubule is the site of secretion and reabsorption that substantially changes the content and volume of the filtrate. It secretes hydrogen ions and ammonia to regulate the pH of the filtrate, and also reabsorbs about 90% of the bicarbonate, which is an important buffer.

6. (A) is correct. Salivary amylase is contained in saliva; it is an enzyme that hydrolyzes starch, a glucose polymer found in plants, and glycogen, a glucose polymer found in animals. After hydrolysis, smaller polysaccharides and maltose remain.

7. (D) is correct. The adrenal medulla secretes epinephrine and norepinephrine. The regulation of these hormones is controlled by the nervous system, and these hormones act to raise the blood glucose level, increase metabolic activity in the cell, and change blood flow patterns.

8. (E) is correct. The tiny pineal gland is located near the center of the brain. It secretes the hormone melatonin, which regulates functions related to light and seasons. Most of its functions are related to biological rhythms associated with reproduction.

9. (C) is correct. The posterior pituitary gland releases two main hormones; oxytocin, which stimulates the contraction of the uterus and mammary gland cells, and antidiuretic hormone (ADH), which promotes the retention of water by the kidney. The actions of the posterior pituitary are regulated by the nervous system and the water/salt balance in the body.

10. (A) is correct. The ovaries secrete hormones called estrogens, which stimulate the growth of the uterine lining and promote the development of secondary sex characteristics in females. They are regulated by two other hormones, FSH and LH.

11. (B) is correct. The thyroid gland releases the hormone triiodothyronine, which stimulates and maintains metabolic processes, and calcitonin, which lowers the blood calcium levels. The thyroid gland secretions are regulated by TSH and by the level of calcium in the blood.

12. (B) is correct. Blood is a connective tissue. It functions very differently from the other connective tissues, but it has an extensive extracellular matrix, which is the criterion for being considered connective tissue. The matrix is plasma, which consists of water, salts, and dissolved proteins.

13. (A) is correct. The three types of muscle in the body are skeletal muscle (responsible for voluntary movements); cardiac muscle (which forms the contractile wall of the heart); and smooth muscle (found in the walls of the digestive tract, bladder, arteries, and other internal organs).

14. (D) is correct. The traditional example of a negative feedback system is the thermostat example. In the body, one very prominent example of negative feedback is the regulation of our body temperature at about 37°C. A section of the brain is responsible for keeping track of the temperature of the blood, and if the blood is too warm, for example, it tells the sweat glands to increase production.

15. (B) is correct. The fat-soluble vitamins are vitamins A, D, E, and K. Vitamin A is found in eye pigments; vitamin D helps in calcium absorption and bone formation; vitamin E may function as an antioxidant; vitamin K is required for blood clotting.

16. (C) is correct. Herbivores are animals that eat only autotrophs (plants and algae). Some examples of herbivores are gorillas and cows. Carnivores eat other animals, and omnivores eat animals as well as plants or algae.

17. (C) is correct. The four stages of food processing are ingestion (the act of eating), digestion (the process by which food is broken down into small particles), absorption (the uptake of nutrients by the body), and elimination (the release of undigested material).

18. (E) is correct. Hydras are simple animals that contain a gastrovascular cavity, which is a pouch that functions in both digestion and the distribution of nutrients throughout the body. The gastrovascular cavity's single opening acts as both mouth and anus.

19. (E) is correct. The liver is responsible for the production of bile, which contains bile salts (which act as detergents or emulsifying agents that facilitate the digestion of fats). Bile contains pigments that are the by-products of red blood cells destroyed in the liver. These are eliminated from the body along with feces.

20. (D) is correct. The digestion of carbohydrates, such as starch and glycogen, begins in the mouth through the action of salivary amylase. In the small intestine, pancreatic amylases hydrolyze starch, glycogen, and smaller polysaccharides into monosaccharides.

21. (B) is correct. Pepsin is an enzyme in the gastric juice of the stomach. It begins the hydrolysis of proteins by breaking peptide bonds between adjacent amino acids and by cleaving proteins into smaller polypeptides. The digestion of proteins continues in the small intestine by the enzymes trypsin and chymotrypsin.

22. (D) is correct. The large intestine, also known as the colon, is responsible for recovering water from the alimentary canal. It is also responsible for compacting the wastes into feces, which are stored in the rectum and then excreted.

23. (D) is correct. Insects, many molluscs, and other arthropods have hemolymph that circulates through their bodies. In these animals, blood and interstitial fluid are mixed together, and one or more hearts pumps this fluid throughout an interconnected network of sinuses (spaces that surround organs).

24. (A) is correct. In an open circulatory system, which exists in insects and other arthropods, the blood bathes the organs directly. In closed circulatory systems, blood is contained in vessels and is separate from the interstitial fluid. In closed circulatory systems, one or more hearts pumps blood into vessels that branch and feed blood through the vessels.

25. (C) is correct. An artery is a kind of blood vessel that carries blood away from the heart, branching into arterioles and eventually into capillary beds. The capillary beds then converge into venules, which converge further into veins, which return blood to the heart.

26. (D) is correct. The role of the sinoatrial (SA) node, or pacemaker, is to control the rate and timing of the contraction of heart muscles. It generates nerve impulses just like the ones that occur in nerve cells, and the impulses spread rapidly through the walls of the atria, making them contract in unison.

27. (C) is correct. The lymphatic system collects fluid and proteins lost during regular circulation and returns them to the blood. This system is composed of a network of lymph vessels throughout the body, with lymph nodes, which are the sites at which lymph is filtered and viruses and bacteria are collected and killed.

28. (E) is correct. All of the answers listed, except lymph, are constituents of blood. White blood cells are leukocytes, and red blood cells are also called erythrocytes. Lymph is found within its vessels only in the lymphatic system.

29. (C) is correct. Erythrocytes, leukocytes, and platelets all develop from stem cells in the red marrow of bones—primarily in the ribs, vertebrae, breastbone, and pelvis. The cells that develop into blood cells have the potential to develop into any type of blood cell; they are called pluripotent cells.

30. (C) is correct. Insects have a tracheal system, which is made up of air tubes that branch throughout the body. The large tubes are called trachea, and they open to the outside, while the smallest branches reach the surface of every cell, where gas exchange takes place.

31. (D) is correct. Carbon dioxide is most commonly transported in the blood in the form of bicarbonate—it reacts with water to form carbonic acid, and a hydrogen dissociates from carbonic acid to produce bicarbonate. Less commonly, carbon dioxide is transported by hemoglobin, or transported in solution in the blood.

32. (E) is correct. All of the answers listed—except phagocytes—are examples of first-line barriers to infection by infecting agents that might attack the body. Phagocytosis constitutes the body's nonspecific internal mechanism for defending itself against infectious agents; it is the process by which invading organisms are ingested and destroyed by white blood cells.

33. (B) is correct. When a lymphocyte is activated by an antigen, it is stimulated to divide and differentiate, and it forms two clones. One clone is of effector cells that combat the antigen. One clone is of memory cells that stay in circulation, recognize the antigen if it infects the body in the future, and launch an attack against it.

34. (A) is correct. All of the answers except *A* constitute methods animals have for exchanging heat with the environment. Conduction is the transfer of heat between objects that are in direct contact. Convection is the transfer of heat by the movement of air past a surface. Radiation is the emission of electromagnetic waves by warm objects. Evaporation is heat loss through the loss of molecules as gas.

35. (B) is correct. Ectotherms are animals that have such low metabolic rates that the amount of heat they generate will not influence their body temperature. Their internal temperature is therefore determined by their environment. Ectotherms include most invertebrates; fishes; amphibians; and nonbird reptiles, including snakes. Endotherms have high metabolic rates, and this makes their bodies quite a bit warmer than the external environment. Endotherms include birds and mammals (humans, monkeys, and dolphins are mammals).

36. (D) is correct. Malpighian tubules are organs that remove the nitrogenous wastes of insects and other arthropods. They open into the digestive tract and dead-end at tips that are submerged in hemolymph. The tubules have an epithelial lining that secretes solutes into the lumen of the tubule, and water follows the solutes into the tubule by osmosis.

37. (D) is correct. The nephron, which is the functional unit of the kidney, is composed of a long tubule and the glomerulus, which is a ball of capillaries. The Bowman's capsule surrounds the glomerulus. The blood in the glomerulus is forced into the Bowman's capsule by blood pressure, and this process acts to filter the blood.

38. (B) is correct. Rods and cones are the two types of photoreceptors in the eye. They are contained in the retina and account for 70% of all the sensory receptors in the body. Cones can distinguish colors in daylight, whereas rods are sensitive to light but cannot distinguish colors.

39. (D) is correct. The cochlea is part of the inner ear that is involved in hearing. It is a coiled organ that has two large chambers—a vestibular canal and a lower tympanic canal—which are separated by a cochlear duct. The floor of the cochlear duct is home to the organ of Corti, which contains the receptors of the ear—hair cells.

40. (A) is correct. The vitreous humor is jellylike and fills the posterior cavity of the eye, constituting most of the eye's volume. The aqueous humor fills the anterior cavity of the eye and is clear and watery.

41. (C) is correct. On one end, the Eustachian tube connects to the middle ear, and on the other, the Eustachian tube connects with the pharynx. This enables it to equalize the pressure between the middle ear and the atmosphere.

42. (E) is correct. Taste buds are modified epithelial cells that act as receptors for taste. Most taste buds are on the surface of the tongue and mouth. Sweet, sour, salty, and bitter are taste perceptions detected by taste buds.

43. (D) is correct. The sliding-filament model of muscle contraction states that the thin and thick filaments do not shrink during muscle contraction. Instead the filaments slide past each other so that the degree of their overlap increases; this sliding is based on the interactions of actin and myosin molecules that make up the filaments.

44. (B) is correct. There are three successive stages of development that follow fertilization. The first is cleavage, which is rapid cell division that produces a mass of new cells that share the cytoplasm of the original cell. The new cells all have their own nuclei and are called blastomeres. The second stage is gastrulation, and the third is organogenesis.

45. (B) is correct. The reflex arc is the simplest type of nerve circuit (automatic response), and it requires just two types of nerve cells. A sensory neuron receives information from a receptor and passes it to the spinal cord and then to a motor neuron, which signals an effector cell to respond to the stimulus.

46. (C) is correct. Neurotransmitters are excreted by the synaptic vesicles and act as intercellular messengers, transmitting the nerve impulse from one neuron to the next neuron or another cell. A single postsynaptic neuron can receive signals from many neurons that secrete different neurotransmitters.

▎**47. (A) is correct.** Each of the two ovaries in the female body contains many follicles. Follicles are composed of an egg cell surrounded by one or two layers of follicle cells; these serve to nourish and protect the cell.

▎**48. (D) is correct.** Sperm is produced in the seminiferous tubules, which are coiled tightly in the testes and surrounded by connective tissue. Production of sperm cannot take place at the high temperature of the body, so the testes are held in the scrotum of the male, outside the abdominal pelvic cavity, where it is about two degrees cooler.

▎**49. (C) is correct.** Homeostasis is the ability of many animals to regulate their internal environment. They do this through thermoregulation, which is the maintenance of internal temperature in a certain range, and osmoregulation, which is the regulation of solute balance within certain parameters.

▎**50. (B) is correct.** Fertilization is the fusion of egg cell (ovum) and the sperm cell, and it results in the formation of a zygote. The zygote is diploid, whereas the egg cell and the sperm cell, both the products of meiosis, are haploid.

Free-Response Question

(a) Skeletal muscle is fibrous, and each fiber is a single long cell. The fibers are composed of myofibrils, which are, in turn, composed of two kinds of myofilaments. These are thin filaments—which are made up of two actin strands and one regulatory protein strand, coiled—and thick filaments made up of myosin molecules. The sarcomere is the basic contracting unit of the muscle. During muscle contraction, the length of the sarcomere decreases. The sliding-filament model of muscle contraction states that the thick and thin filaments slide past each other horizontally, due to the interactions of actin and myosin.

The myosin molecules look like golf clubs arranged horizontally in a group, with the heads of the golf clubs pointing up. This head region is the center of the reactions that take place during muscle contraction. Myosin binds ATP and hydrolyzes it into ADP, and its structure is changed in the process, which causes it to bind to a specific site on actin and form a cross-bridge. Myosin then releases the stored energy and relaxes to its normal conformation. This changes the angle of attachment of the myosin head relative to its tail. As myosin bends inward upon itself, tension increases on the actin filament, and the filament is pulled toward the middle of the sarcomere.

(b) In the transmission of action potentials through muscle cells, in response to a nerve impulse, a single action potential will cause an increase in tension in the muscle cell, and if a second action potential arrives within a certain short period of time, the response will be greater; the two responses are summed. If a muscle cell receives action potentials from many nerve cells surrounding it, these, too, will be summed, and the level of tension will depend on how quickly the action potentials follow one another. If the rate of stimulation is sufficiently high, the muscle twitches will blur, and tetanus will result.

(c) When oxygen is scarce, as in situations where a person is taking part in strenuous exercise, human muscle cells switch to lactic acid fermentation (which normally undergoes regular aerobic cellular respiration) to produce ATP. In lactic acid fermentation, pyruvate is reduced by NADH to form lactate with no release of CO_2. The lactate that accumulates as a result of this reaction can cause muscle fatigue and pain.

This response uses the following key terms in context, showing the writer's knowledge of their meanings and relatedness:

skeletal muscle   *cross-bridge*
myofibrils   *action potential*
myofilaments   *summation*
thin filaments   *tetanus*
actin strands   *aerobic cellular respiration*
thick filaments   *lactic acid fermentation*
myosin   *pyruvate*
sarcomere   *lactate*
sliding-filament model

It also shows knowledge of how these important biological processes take place: how muscle cells contract and ultimately cause bones to move, how tetanus is reached, and how and why strenuous exercise produces muscle pain.

CHAPTER 8

Ecology

Concept 50.2 Interactions between organisms and the environment limit the distribution of species

The **abiotic components** of an environment are the nonliving, chemical, and physical components; the **biotic components** are the living components of an environment.

▌ **Biogeography** is the study of the past and present distribution of individual species.

▌ The **dispersal** of organisms refers to their global geographic distribution. Some **abiotic factors** that affect the distribution of organisms are temperature, water, sunlight, wind, and the composition of the rocks and soil. **Biotic factors** such as parasites and pathogens, as well as the presence of pollinators and food species, also affect distribution.

▌ The components that make up the **climate** in a certain location are temperature, water, light, and wind.

▌ **Biomes** are the major types of ecosystems that occupy very broad geographic regions. Examples include coniferous forests, deserts, and grasslands.

▌ The **tropics** receive the greatest amount of sunlight annually and the least amount of solar variation through the course of the year.

▌ **Microclimates** are small-scale environmental variations—for example, under a log.

Concept 50.3 Abiotic and biotic factors influence the structure and dynamics of aquatic biomes

▌ **Aquatic biomes** make up the largest part of the biosphere, because water covers roughly 75% of Earth's surface. These biomes are classified into **freshwater biomes** and **marine biomes.**

▌ Aquatic biomes display vertical stratification; there is a **photic zone** (in which there is enough light for photosynthesis to occur) and an **aphotic zone** (where very little light penetrates).

▌ **Thermoclines** are narrow layers of fast temperature change that separate a warm upper layer of water and cold deeper waters.

▌ The **benthic zone** is located at the bottom layer of all aquatic biomes, and it is made up of sand and organic and inorganic sediments (including **detritus,** dead organic matter). Organisms that live in the benthic zone are called **benthos.**

▌ The **two types of freshwater biomes** are standing bodies of water, such as lakes, and moving bodies of water, such as streams.

- In lakes, communities are distributed according to the water's depth. The **littoral zone** (well-lit shallow waters near the shore) contains rooted and floating aquatic plants, whereas the limnetic zone (well-lit open surface waters farther from shore) is occupied by phytoplankton.
- **Oligotrophic lakes** are deep lakes that are nutrient-poor and oxygen-rich and contain sparse phytoplankton; **eutrophic lakes** are shallower, and they have higher nutrient content and lower oxygen content with a high concentration of phytoplankton.
- The prominent physical attribute of **streams and rivers** is current. A great diversity of organisms inhabits unpolluted streams and rivers. These organisms are distributed in vertical zones and from the headwaters to the mouth.
- **Wetlands** are areas covered with water deep enough to support aquatic plants.
- **Estuaries** are areas where freshwater streams or rivers merge with the ocean.
- In marine (saltwater) communities, the zone where land meets water is called the **intertidal zone,** and beyond the intertidal zone is the **neritic zone**—the shallow water over the continental shelves. Past the continental shelves is the oceanic zone. Any open water is called the **pelagic zone,** and—as in freshwater systems—the **benthic zone** lies at the bottom of the water at the ocean's floor. The **abyssal zone** refers to very deep benthic communities.
- **Coral reefs** inhabit the neritic zone. A coral reef is a biome created by a group of cnidarians that secrete hard calcium carbonate shells, which vary in shape and support the growth of other corals, sponges, and algae.

Concept 50.4 Climate largely determines the distribution and structure of terrestrial biomes

- **Savannas** are characterized by grasses, and also some trees. The dominant herbivores are insects, such as ants and termites. Fire is a dominant abiotic factor, and many plants are adapted for fire. Plant growth is quite substantial during the rainy season, but large grazing mammals must migrate during regular seasons of drought.
- **Desert** is marked by sparse rainfall, and desert plants and animals are adapted to conserve and store water. Deserts contain many CAM plants and plants with adaptations that prevent animals from consuming them, such as the spines on cacti. Temperature (either hot or cold) is usually extreme.
- **Chaparral** is dominated by dense, spiny, evergreen shrubs. These are coastal areas with mild rainy winters and long, hot, dry summers. Plants are adapted to fires.
- **Temperate grassland** is marked by seasonal drought with occasional fires, and by large grazing mammals. All these factors prevent the significant growth of trees. Grassland soil is rich in nutrients, making these areas good for agriculture.
- **Temperate broadleaf forest** is marked by dense stands of deciduous trees that require sufficient moisture. These forests are more open than (and not as tall as) rain forests. They are stratified—the top layer contains one or two

strata of trees; beneath that are shrubs; and under that is an herbaceous stratum. **Canopy** refers to the upper layers of trees in a forest. These trees drop their leaves in fall, and many enter hibernation. Many birds migrate to warmer climates.

▮ **Coniferous forest** is dominated by cone-bearing trees such as pine, spruce, and fir. The conical shape of conifers prevents much snowfall from accumulating on—and breaking—these trees' branches.

▮ **Tundra** is marked by permafrost (permanently frozen layer of soil), very cold temperatures, high winds, and little rainfall. Tundra supports no trees or tall plants. It accounts for about 20% of Earth's terrestrial surface.

▮ **Tropical forest** has pronounced vertical stratification. The canopy is so dense that little light breaks through. These forests are marked by epiphytes, which are plants that grow on other plants instead of the soil. Rainfall is varied. Biodiversity is greatest of all the terrestrial biomes.

Concept 51.1 Behavioral ecologists distinguish between proximate and ultimate causes of behavior

▮ **Behavior** is what an animal does and how it does it. Behavior is a result of genetic and environmental factors.

▮ **Behavioral ecology** is a scientific field of study that looks at how behavior is controlled and how it develops, evolves, and contributes to survival and reproductive success.

▮ There are two fundamental levels of analysis, proximate and ultimate, in the study of behavior. **Proximate** causes of behavior are the "how" questions and include the effects of heredity on behavior, genetic-environmental interactions, and sensory-motor mechanisms. **Ultimate** causes are the "why" questions and include studies of the origin of a behavior, its change over time, and the utility of the behavior in terms of reproductive success.

▮ **Ethology** is the study of animal behavior.

▮ **Innate behaviors** are developmentally fixed. A **fixed action pattern** is a sequence of innate behaviors that is largely unchangeable and usually carried to completion once it is initiated. Fixed action patterns are triggered by sign stimuli.

▮ **Imprinting** is a combination of learned and innate components that is limited to a sensitive period in an organism's life and is generally irreversible.

Concept 51.2 Many behaviors have a strong genetic component

▮ A **kinesis** is a simple change in activity in response to a stimulus, whereas a **taxis** is an automatic movement toward or away from a stimulus.

▮ A **signal** is a behavior that causes a change in the behavior of another individual. **Pheromones** are chemical signals that are emitted by animals.

Concept 51.3 *Environment, interacting with an animal's genetic makeup,*
           influences the development of behaviors

▌ **Learning** is the modification of behavior based on specific experiences.

▌ **Habituation** is a loss of responsiveness to stimuli that convey little or no information. It is a simple form of learning.

▌ A **cognitive map** is an internal representation of spatial relationships among objects in an animal's surroundings.

▌ **Associative learning** is the ability of many animals to associate one feature of their environment with another feature. **Classical conditioning** involves learning to associate certain stimuli with reward or punishment. **Operant conditioning** occurs as an animal learns to associate one of its behaviors with a reward or punishment.

▌ **Cognition** is the ability of an animal's nervous system to perceive, store, process, and use information from sensory receptors.

Concept 51.5 *Natural selection favors behaviors that increase survival and reproductive success*

▌ **Foraging behavior** includes not only eating, but also mechanisms used in searching for, recognizing, and capturing food. It represents a compromise between the benefits of nutrition and the cost of obtaining food.

▌ **Mating behavior and mate choice** include the seeking or attracting of mates, selecting a mate, and competing for a mate.

▌ **Agonistic behaviors** are often ritualized contests that determine which competitor gains access to a resource, such as food or mates.

Concept 51.6 *The concept of inclusive fitness can account for most altruistic social behavior*

▌ **Altruism** occurs when animals behave in ways that reduce their individual fitness but increase the fitness of other individuals in the population.

▌ **Inclusive fitness** is the total effect an individual has on proliferating its genes by producing its own offspring and by providing aid that enables other close relatives to produce offspring. The natural selection that favors this kind of altruistic behavior by enhancing reproductive success of relatives is called **kin selection.**

▌ **Social learning** is learning through observing others. **Sociobiology** applies evolutionary theory to the study of social behavior.

Concept 52.3 *The exponential model describes population growth in*
           an idealized, unlimited environment

▌ A **population** is a group of individuals of a single species living in the same general area.

▌ **Exponential population** growth refers to population growth under ideal conditions.

- The **carrying capacity** of a population is defined as the maximum population size that a certain environment can support at a particular time with no degradation of the habitat.

Concept 52.5 Populations are regulated by a complex interaction of biotic and abiotic influences

- When a death rate rises as population density rises, the death rate is said to be **density dependent** (competition for resources is a density-dependent factor). When a death rate does not change with increase in population density, it is said to be **density independent** (natural disasters are density-independent factors).
- Many populations fluctuate at unpredictable intervals; others undergo regular boom-and-bust cycles.

Concept 53.1 A community's interactions include competition, predation, herbivory, symbiosis, and disease

- A **community** is an assemblage of species living close enough for potential interaction.
- **Interspecific competitions** for resources occur when resources are in short supply.
- The **competitive exclusion principle** states that when two species are vying for a resource, eventually the one with the slight reproductive advantage will eliminate the other.
- An organism's **ecological niche** is the sum total of biotic and abiotic resources in its environment.
- **Predation** is an interaction between two species in which one species (the **predator**) eats the other species (the **prey**). One defense that animals have against predators is **cryptic coloration,** in which the animal is camouflaged by its coloring. Another defense is **aposematic coloration,** in which a poisonous animal is brightly colored as a warning to other animals.
- **Batesian mimicry** refers to a situation in which a nonpoisonous animal has evolved to mimic the coloration of a poisonous animal. In **Müllerian mimicry,** two bad-tasting species resemble each other, ostensibly so that predators will learn to avoid them equally.
- **Herbivory** is an interaction in which an herbivore eats part of a plant or alga. It is advantageous for an animal to be able to distinguish toxic from nontoxic plants. A plant's main protective devices are chemical toxins, spines, and thorns.
- Some **parasites** change the behavior of their hosts to aid their own life cycles. They can have a significant effect on the survival, reproduction, and density of their host population.

Concept 53.2 Dominant and keystone species exert strong controls on community structure

- The **trophic structure** of a community refers to the feeding relationships among the organisms. **Trophic levels** are the links in the trophic structure of a community.

- The transfer of food energy from plants through herbivores through carnivores through decomposers is referred to as a **food chain. Food webs** consist of two or more food chains linked together.
- **Dominant species** in a community have the highest **biomass** (the sum weight of all the members of a population).
- **Keystone species** exert control on community structure by their important ecological niches.

Concept 53.3 *Disturbance influences species diversity and composition*

- **Ecological succession** refers to transitions in species composition in a certain area over ecological time.
- In **primary succession,** plants and animals gradually invade a region that was lifeless (usually autotrophic prokaryotes, lichens, and mosses are first).
- **Secondary succession** occurs when an existing community has been cleared by a disturbance that leaves the soil intact.

Concept 53.4 *Biogeographic factors affect community biodiversity*

- The **biodiversity** of a community (its species diversity) is determined by its size and geographic location.

Concept 54.1 *Ecosystem ecology emphasizes energy flow and chemical cycling*

- **Primary producers** in an ecosystem are the **autotrophs,** and they support all the others in the ecosystem.
- Organisms that are in trophic levels above primary producers, which means they are consumers, are **heterotrophs.**
- Herbivores eat primary producers and are called **primary consumers.**
- Carnivores that eat herbivores are called **secondary consumers,** and carnivores that eat other carnivores are called **tertiary consumers.**
- **Detritivores,** or **decomposers,** get their energy from detritus, which is nonliving organic material such as the remains of dead organisms, feces, dead leaves, and wood.
- It is not uncommon for a species to feed at more than one trophic level. An animal's diet might consist of berries and fish or algae and insects. The feeding level may also change as the stage in a species' life cycle changes.

Concept 54.4 *Biological and geochemical processes move nutrients between organic and inorganic parts of the ecosystem*

- **Biogeochemical cycles** are nutrient cycles that contain both biotic and abiotic components.
- Most of Earth's nitrogen is in the form of N_2, which is unusable by plants.
- **Nitrogen fixation** occurs when microorganisms convert N_2 to usable nitrogenous compounds.
- **Nitrification** is the process by which ammonium (NH_4^+) is oxidized to nitrite and then nitrate (NO_3^-).
- **Denitrification** is the process by which some bacteria can get the oxygen they need for metabolism from nitrate rather than from O_2 under anaerobic conditions.

- The decomposition of nitrogen back to ammonium is called ammonification.
- Other important nutrient cycles involve water, carbon, and phosphorus.

Concept 54.5 *The human population is disrupting chemical cycles throughout the biosphere*

- **Nutrient enrichment** often occurs when a nutrient cycle is disrupted and nutrients are removed from one part of the biosphere and added to another, resulting in excess. It also occurs when entirely new materials, some of which are toxic, are added to ecosystems.
- **Acid precipitation** is defined as rain, snow, or fog with a pH less than 5.6. The burning of wood and fossil fuels releases sulfur oxides and nitrogen oxides into the atmosphere. These oxides react with water, forming sulfuric acid and nitric acid.
- In **biological magnification,** toxins become more concentrated in successive trophic levels of a food web.
- The **greenhouse effect** refers to the absorption of heat the Earth experiences due to certain atmospheric gases. Carbon dioxide and water vapor intercept and absorb much reflected infrared radiation, re-reflecting some back toward Earth.
- Because of the burning of fossil fuels, CO_2 levels have been steadily increasing. One effect of this increase is that Earth is being warmed significantly (**global warming**).
- The **ozone layer** reduces the amount of UV radiation penetration from the sun through the atmosphere. Chlorine-containing compounds used by humans are eroding the ozone layer. This could have disastrous effects in the future. In an attempt to curb ozone depletion, 180 countries, including the United States, signed the Montreal Protocol, calling for the elimination of ozone-depleting chemicals. As a result, many nations have stopped using CFCs (chlorofluoro-carbons).

For Additional Review

Consider the possible effects of global warming. What would happen if Earth's temperature rose by one or two degrees? How would this affect the biotic and abiotic components of Earth?

Multiple-Choice Questions

1. All of the following statements about Earth's ozone layer are false EXCEPT
   (A) It is composed of O_2.
   (B) It amplifies the amount of ultraviolet radiation that reaches Earth.
   (C) It is thinning as a result of widespread use of certain chlorine-containing compounds.
   (D) It is thickening as a result of widespread use of certain chlorine-containing compounds.
   (E) It allows green light in but screens out red light.

2. Which of the following is the major primary producer in a savanna ecosystem?
   (A) lion
   (B) gazelle
   (C) grass
   (D) snake
   (E) diatom

3. The carrying capacity of a population is defined as
   (A) the amount of time the parents in the population spend rearing and nurturing their offspring.
   (B) the maximum population size that a certain environment can support at a particular time.
   (C) the amount of vegetation that a certain geographic area can support.
   (D) the number of different types of species a biome can support.
   (E) the number of different genes a population can carry at a particular time.

4. Which of the following terms is used to describe major types of ecosystems that occupy broad geographic regions?
   (A) biome
   (B) community
   (C) chaparral
   (D) trophic level
   (E) photic zone

5. A lake that is nutrient rich and that supports a vast array of algae is said to be
   (A) oligotrophic.
   (B) abyssal.
   (C) littoral.
   (D) eutrophic.
   (E) limnetic.

6. Which of the following best describes an estuary?
   (A) An area that is periodically flooded causing its soil to be consistently damp

(B) An area where a river changes course after being diverted from its original course by an obstacle
(C) The area where a freshwater river merges with the ocean
(D) The area where a mass of cold water and a mass of warm water meet in the pelagic zone
(E) An outshoot of land that extends into the ocean

7. Which of the following is the term that refers to the layer of inorganic and organic nutrients that covers the ocean floor?
   (A) littoral zone
   (B) limnetic zone
   (C) abyssal zone
   (D) benthic zone
   (E) photic zone

Directions: The group of questions below consists of five lettered choices followed by a list of numbered phrases or sentences. For each numbered phrase or sentence, select the one choice that is most closely related to it. Each choice may be used once, more than once, or not at all.

Questions 8–12
   (A) Temperate grassland
   (B) Tropical forest
   (C) Temperate broadleaf forest
   (D) Tundra
   (E) Desert

8. Characterized by permafrost and few large plants

9. Characterized by epiphytes and significant canopy

10. Characterized by an understory of shrubs and trees that lose their leaves in the fall

11. Characterized by occasional fires, nutrient-rich soil, and large grazing animals

12. Characterized by sparse rainfall and extreme daily temperature fluctuations

13. Fixed action patterns (FAPs) are instigated by which of the following?
    (A) mating behavior
    (B) ritual behavior
    (C) innate stimulus
    (D) sign stimulus
    (E) action potential

14. One morning, a woman who usually feeds her two cats in the morning passes by the food bowl without putting food in it. The cats usually run over to the bowl as she approaches it, but after four mornings of her passing the bowl without putting food in it, the cats no longer run over to the bowl. This is an example of
    (A) maturation.
    (B) imprinting.
    (C) habituation.
    (D) foraging.
    (E) sensitivity.

15. Pavlov's dogs learned to salivate when they heard the ring of a particular bell; this is an example of
    (A) classical conditioning.
    (B) operant conditioning.
    (C) sensitivity.
    (D) imprinting.
    (E) maturation.

16. The phenomenon in which young ducks follow their mother in a line is a result of which of the following?
    (A) habituation
    (B) imprinting
    (C) maturation
    (D) foraging
    (E) conditioning

17. Altruism exists in populations because
    (A) it deprives members of the species of territory and results in agonistic behavior.
    (B) it can result in the passing on of the altruistic member's genes.
    (C) it can result in the overall success of the ecosystem.
    (D) it can result in a bond between the altruistic member and the recipient of the altruism, and the recipient might later reciprocate the altruism.
    (E) it can result in the maximizing of the altruistic member's genetic representation in a population, if the altruistic member's behavior is directed toward a close relative.

18. A bacterial colony that exists in an environment displaying ideal conditions will undergo
    (A) logistic growth.
    (B) intrinsic growth.
    (C) hyperactive growth.
    (D) exponential growth.
    (E) unbounded growth.

19. A species' specific use of the biotic and abiotic factors in an environment is collectively called the species'
    (A) habitat.
    (B) trophic level.
    (C) ecological niche.
    (D) placement.
    (E) partitioning.

20. In which type of camouflaging does a nontoxic animal mimic the appearance of a toxic animal?
    (A) Müllerian mimicry
    (B) cryptic coloration
    (C) aposematic coloration
    (D) Batesian mimicry
    (E) parasitoidism

21. The dominant species in a community is the one that
    (A) has the greatest number of individuals.
    (B) is at the top of the food chain.
    (C) has the largest biomass.
    (D) eats all other members of the community.
    (E) bears the most offspring in each mating.

22. Which statement best describes energy transfer in a food web?
    (A) Energy is transferred to consumers, which convert it to nitrogen compounds and use it to synthesize amino acids.
    (B) Energy from producers is converted into oxygen and transferred to consumers.
    (C) Energy from the sun is stored in green plants and transferred to consumers.
    (D) Energy is transferred to consumers that use it to synthesize food.
    (E) Energy moves from autotrophs to heterotrophs to decomposers, which convert it to a form producers can use again.

23. A fire cleared a large area of forest in Yellowstone National Park in the 1980s. When the first plants pioneered this burned area, this was an example of
    (A) primary succession.
    (B) secondary succession.
    (C) biological evolution.
    (D) a keystone species.
    (E) the top-down model.

24. In the nitrogen cycle, the process by which nitrogen in organic molecules is converted to ammonium is known as
    (A) ammonification.
    (B) denitrification.
    (C) nitrogen fixation.
    (D) nitrogen cycling.
    (E) nitrogenation.

25. The process in which CO_2 in the atmosphere intercepts and absorbs reflected infrared radiation and re-reflects it back to Earth is known as
    (A) global warming.
    (B) atmospheric insulation.
    (C) stratospheric insulation.
    (D) biological magnification.
    (E) the greenhouse effect.

Free-Response Question

1. *All of the organisms in a community are interrelated by the abiotic and biotic resources they use in the course of their lives.*

    (a) Describe the relationships that exist among a hawk, a mouse, a plant, and soil in a particular ecosystem.
    (b) As unlikely as it may seem, biotic components of an environment do influence the abiotic components of an environment. Give two examples of this influence.

ANSWERS AND EXPLANATIONS

Multiple-Choice Questions

▌ **1. (C) is correct.** The ozone layer is located in the stratosphere and surrounds Earth. It is composed of O_3, and it absorbs UV radiation, preventing it from reaching the organisms in the biosphere. Researchers have been observing the thinning of the ozone layer since about 1975. The destruction of the ozone layer has been attributed to the widespread use of chlorofluorocarbons.

▌ **2. (C) is correct.** In a savanna, grass constitutes the primary producer. A primary producer traps the energy of sunlight and turns it into chemical energy through photosynthesis. Primary consumers (herbivores) consume primary producers, secondary consumers (carnivores) eat herbivores, and tertiary consumers eat carnivores.

▌ **3. (B) is correct.** The carrying capacity of a population is defined as the maximum population size a particular environment can support at a particular time with no degradation of the habitat. It is fixed at certain times, but it varies over the course of time with the amount of resources that exist in an environment.

▌ **4. (A) is correct.** Biomes are major types of ecosystems that occupy broad geographic regions. Some examples of biomes are coniferous forests, deserts, grasslands, and tropical forests.

▌ **5. (D) is correct.** Lakes are classified according to how much organic matter they produce. Oligotrophic lakes are deep and generally poor in nutrients, and therefore, they have relatively little phytoplankton. Eutrophic lakes are usually shallower and have greater nutrient content, which allows the growth of more phytoplankton.

▌ **6. (C) is correct.** An estuary is an area where a running freshwater source, such as a stream or river, meets the ocean. Often estuaries are bordered by large areas of coastal wetlands, and salinity varies with location within them, as well as with the rise and fall of the ocean tides. Estuaries are one of the most biologically productive biomes, and they also are home to many of the fish and other animals that humans consume.

▌ **7. (D) is correct.** The benthic zone refers to the lowest of all the biotic zones of any aquatic biome. This bottommost layer is composed of sand and inorganic and organic sediments, and it is home to communities of organisms called benthos. These organisms derive nutrients from dead organic matter, such as dead fish and other ocean life, that fall down from the zones above.

▌ **8. (D) is correct.** Tundra is characterized by having permafrost (which is a permanently frozen layer of soil), very cold temperatures, and high winds. These factors prevent tall plants from growing in the tundra. Tundra generally does not receive much rainfall throughout the year, and what rain does fall cannot soak into the soil because of the permafrost.

▌ **9. (B) is correct.** Tropical forests generally have thick canopies that prevent much sun from filtering through. This means that in breaks in the canopy, other plants grow quickly to compete for sunlight. Tropical forests are home to epiphytes, and rainfall is frequent.

▌ **10. (C) is correct.** Temperate broadleaf forests are characterized by dense populations of deciduous trees, which drop their leaves in the fall when the weather turns cold. They do this because they won't be able to get enough water to support their leaves once the groundwater freezes.

▌ **11. (A) is correct.** Temperate grasslands are characterized by having thick grass, seasonal drought, occasional fires, and large grazing animals. Their soil is generally rich with nutrients, making them good areas for agriculture. Most of the temperate grassland in the United States is used today for agriculture.

12. (E) is correct. Deserts experience very little rainfall, so they are home to many plants and animals that have adaptations for storing and saving water. Deserts are marked by drastic temperature fluctuation; they can be very hot in the day but freezing at night. Many desert plants rely on CAM photosynthesis.

13. (D) is correct. Fixed action patterns are a sequence of behavioral acts that are virtually unchangeable and usually carried to completion once they are initiated. Sign stimuli trigger fixed action patterns. These stimuli may be a feature of another animal, such as an aspect of its appearance, or some other event.

14. (C) is correct. Habituation is one type of learning. Learning is defined as the ability of an animal to modify its behavior as a result of specific experiences. Habituation is a very simple form of learning, in which there is a loss of responsiveness to stimuli that convey very little or no information.

15. (A) is correct. Classical conditioning is a form of associative learning (the ability of animals to learn to associate one stimulus with another). It specifically refers to an animal's ability to associate an arbitrary stimulus with a reward or a punishment.

16. (B) is correct. Imprinting is a form of learning that occurs, during a sensitive period. Imprinting is generally irreversible, and the sensitive period is a limited phase in the animal's development when the learning of particular behavior can take place.

17. (E) is correct. Altruism is thought to occur in populations because if parents sacrifice their own well-being for that of their offspring, this increases their fitness by better ensuring that the genes that they passed on will make it to the next generation. Likewise, helping other close relatives increases the chances that they will survive to pass on genes that are shared between them and the altruistic member.

18. (D) is correct. A bacterial colony growing where it has limitless nutrients, and other ideal conditions, will experience what is called exponential growth. In exponential growth, all members are free to reproduce at their physiological capacity.

19. (C) is correct. A species' ecological niche is defined as the sum of its use of the abiotic and biotic factors in an environment. For instance, a particular bird's niche refers to the food it consumes, where it builds its nest, the time of day it is active, and what climate it lives in.

20. (D) is correct. In Batesian mimicry, a harmless or palatable animal evolves the same markings and/or colorings as a harmful or unpalatable animal and, in this way, can escape predation.

21. (C) is correct. The dominant species in a community has the greatest biomass, or sum weight of all of the members of a population. Dominant species are also hypothesized to be the most competitive in exploiting the resources in an ecosystem.

22. (C) is correct. Almost all organisms use solar energy stored in food to power life processes. Autotrophs convert solar energy to a form useful to both autotrophs and heterotrophs. At each successive trophic level, less energy is available because so much is converted to a form not useful to the organisms. Energy cannot be recycled.

23. (B) is correct. Secondary succession refers to a situation in which a community has been cleared by a disturbance of some kind, but the soil is left intact. The area will begin to return to its original state through the process of plants invading the area and recolonizing.

24. (A) is correct. In the nitrogen cycle, bacteria oxidize ammonium to nitrite. The bacteria then release the nitrate to be used by plants and converted to organic forms, such as amino acids in proteins. The decomposition of organic nitrogen back to ammonium, which is carried out by decomposers, is referred to as ammonification.

25. (E) is correct. The greenhouse effect is the process by which carbon dioxide and water vapor in the atmosphere intercept reflected infrared radiation from the sun and re-reflect it to Earth. Global warming is the process by which the amount of carbon dioxide in the atmosphere is increasing because of humans' combustion of fossil fuels leading to higher temperatures on Earth.

Free-Response Question

(a) The hawk, mouse, and plant in this particular ecosystem are related by the passage of energy through them. Together they comprise a food chain—the mouse is a primary consumer, and it consumes the plant, which is a primary producer (the plant is an autotroph—capable of trapping the energy of the sun and converting it into chemical energy in the form of carbohydrates). The hawk then is a predator of the mouse—and a secondary consumer. Secondary consumers eat herbivores. All of these animals are dependent on the soil in which the plant has grown because the soil provides the plant with nutrients. The plant needs a variety of organic elements to produce carbohydrate, but it also needs mineral nutrients, such as nitrogen to make proteins and nucleic acids. Most plants are incapable of using nitrogen in the form usually found in soil (ammonium), and so plants must rely on nitrogen-fixing bacteria to convert it to a usable form, nitrate.

(b) One example in which the biotic factors of the biosphere impact the abiotic factors is seen in the case of global warming. We rely on the greenhouse effect (in which atmospheric carbon dioxide acts as an insulator, trapping infrared radiation from the sun and re-reflecting it) to help maintain the hospitable temperature of Earth. Yet, due to the burning of fossil fuels—beginning during the Industrial Revolution—the concentration of carbon dioxide in the atmosphere has increased significantly, and this has led to an increase in global temperatures.

Another way in which humans (a biotic factor of the biosphere) impact abiotic processes is in the thinning of the ozone layer. Organisms are protected from ultraviolet radiation from the sun by a protective layer of ozone that surrounds Earth. However, the ozone layer has been degraded by humans' use of chlorofluorocarbons, which are chemicals used in refrigeration and other industrial processes. Many countries have stopped using these chemicals, but chlorine molecules already in the atmosphere continue to have an effect on ozone.

This response uses the following key terms in context, showing the writer's knowledge of their meanings and relatedness:

ecosystem   *nitrogen fixation*
primary producer   *herbivore*
primary consumer   *global warming*
secondary consumer   *greenhouse effect*
food chain   *ozone layer*
autotroph   *chlorofluorocarbons*
predator

This response also shows knowledge of the following important biological processes: food chains and the interaction of organisms in a community, global warming, and the depletion of the ozone layer.

Part III

Sample Tests with Answers and Explanations

On the following pages are two sample examinations that approximate the actual AP Biology Examination in format, types of questions, and content. Set aside three hours to take each test. To best prepare yourself for actual AP exam conditions, use only the allowed time for Section I and Section II.

Practice Test 1

Biology
Section 1

Time—1 hour and 20 minutes

Directions: Each of the questions or incomplete statements below is followed by five suggested answers or completions. Select the one that is best in each case, and then fill in the corresponding oval on the answer sheet.

Gene	Probability of Appearing in Gamete
P	1/4
Q	1/4
R	1/4

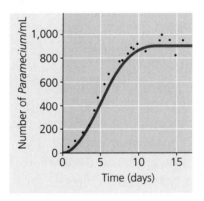

***Paramecium* Population in Lab**

1. In the diagram above, what number of paramecia best represents the carrying capacity of the environment for the population shown?
   (A) 200
   (B) 500
   (C) 600
   (D) 900
   (E) 1,000

2. Three genes—*P*, *Q*, and *R*—are not linked. The probability of each gene appearing in a gamete is shown in the table above. Which of the equations below represents the probability that all three genes will appear in the same gamete?
   (A) ¼ × ¼ × ¼
   (B) ¼ + ¼ + ¼
   (C) ¼ ÷ ¼ × ¼
   (D) (¼)⅓
   (E) 0

3. Which cellular organelle is the site of cellular respiration?
   (A) Golgi apparatus
   (B) Chloroplast
   (C) Mitochondria
   (D) Endoplasmic reticulum
   (E) Ribosomes

GO ON TO THE NEXT PAGE

4. Which term best describes how goslings recognize their mothers after they are born?
   (A) Habituation
   (B) Imprinting
   (C) Reasoning
   (D) Instinct
   (E) Maturation

5. A student using a light microscope observes a relatively small, rod-shaped cell that has no observable nucleus or other membrane-bounded organelle. What type of cell is this most likely to be?
   (A) Viral
   (B) Eukaryote
   (C) Gamete
   (D) Prokaryote
   (E) Plant

6. In a testcross, which of the following must be true?
   (A) One of the individuals is homozygous dominant.
   (B) One of the individuals is homozygous recessive.
   (C) Both individuals are heterozygous.
   (D) Both individuals are homozygous.
   (E) Both individuals have an unknown phenotype.

7. Diatoms are the major primary producers in which of the following ecosystems?
   (A) Marine
   (B) Desert
   (C) Temperate broadleaf forest
   (D) Chaparral
   (E) Tropical rain forest

8. In deer, fur length is controlled by a single gene with two alleles. When a homozygous deer with long fur is crossed with a homozygous deer with short fur, the offspring all have fur of medium length. If these offspring with medium-length fur mate, what percentage of their offspring will have long fur?
   (A) 100%
   (B) 75%
   (C) 50%
   (D) 25%
   (E) 0%

9. All of the following are types of wastes excreted by animals EXCEPT
   (A) ammonia
   (B) urea
   (C) uric acid
   (D) carbon dioxide
   (E) nitrate

10. Which of the following statements best supports the idea that certain cell organelles are evolutionarily derived from symbiotic prokaryotes living in host cells?
    (A) The process of cellular respiration in certain prokaryotes is similar to that occurring in mitochondria and chloroplasts.
    (B) Mitochondria and chloroplasts have DNA and proteins that are very similar to those in eukaryotes.
    (C) Mitochondria and eukaryotes have similar cell wall structures.
    (D) Like prokaryotes, mitochondria have a double membrane.
    (E) Mitochondria and chloroplasts have DNA and ribosomes that are similar to those of prokaryotes.

11. During the course of which type of reaction is energy consumed?
    (A) Hydrolysis
    (B) Catabolic
    (C) Oxidation-reduction
    (D) Endergonic
    (E) Exergonic

12. Consumption of CO_2 can be used as a measure of photosynthetic rate because carbon dioxide is
    (A) consumed during the light reactions of photosynthesis.
    (B) consumed during the dark reactions of photosynthesis.
    (C) used to trap photons, the form of energy in sunlight.
    (D) necessary for the production of ATP in oxidative phosphorylation.
    (E) produced when fermentation takes place.

13. Which of the following cell organelles is not bound by a membrane?
    (A) Centrosome
    (B) Golgi apparatus
    (C) Cell nucleus
    (D) Mitochondrion
    (E) Peroxisome

14. Which of the following statements is NOT part of Darwin's theory of natural selection?
    (A) Individuals survive and reproduce with varying degrees of success.
    (B) Because there are more individuals than the environment can support, this leads to a struggle for existence in which only some of the offspring survive in each generation.
    (C) The unequal ability of individuals to survive and reproduce leads to a gradual change in the population.
    (D) Members of the population that are physically weaker than others will be eliminated first by forces in the environment.
    (E) Individuals in a population vary in their characteristics, and no two individuals are exactly alike.

15. In animal development, all of the following occur EXCEPT
    (A) cleavage, a succession of rapid cell divisions, occurs just after fertilization
    (B) the zygote develops polarity
    (C) the zygote eventually develops into a hollow ball of cells called a blastula
    (D) as cleavage continues a solid ball of cells called a morula is produced
    (E) all of the genes in the zygote are activated

16. Which of the following describes a protein capable of converting related proteins to an infectious form?
    (A) Virus
    (B) Retrovirus
    (C) Prion
    (D) Spirochete
    (E) Prokaryote

17. A difference between prokaryotic and eukaryotic cells is the presence of
    (A) a membrane-bounded nucleus
    (B) genetic material in the form of DNA
    (C) cytoplasm
    (D) ribosomes
    (E) a cell membrane

18. Which plant hormone is responsible for root growth and differentiation, cell division, germination, and delaying senescence?
    (A) Auxin
    (B) Cytokinins
    (C) Gibberellins
    (D) Abscisic acid
    (E) Ethylene

19. A farmer selects one green pepper plant that has all of the most desirable traits of the species. The farmer then produces a group of offspring plants using only genetic material from this ideal parent plant. The resulting plants are genetically identical to the parent and are said to be
    (A) a community
    (B) a family
    (C) clones
    (D) a phylum
    (E) a genus

20. The domain Archaea contains prokaryotic organisms that
    (A) possess a nuclear envelope
    (B) have plantlike features
    (C) are capable of nitrogen fixation
    (D) live in extreme heat or acid environments
    (E) reproduce sexually

21. Which statement best describes the action of the hormone oxytocin in humans?
    (A) it stimulates growth
    (B) it stimulates the secretion of epinephrine
    (C) it raises blood glucose levels
    (D) it lowers blood glucose levels
    (E) it stimulates contraction of the uterus

22. In dogs, the trait for long tail is dominant (L), and the trait for short tail is recessive (l). The trait for yellow coat is dominant (Y), and the trait for white coat is recessive (y). Mating two dogs gives a litter of 3 long-tailed, yellow dogs and 1 long-tailed, white dog. Which of the following is most likely to be the genotype of the parent dogs?
    (A) $LLYY \times LLYY$
    (B) $LLyy \times LLYy$
    (C) $LlYy \times LlYy$
    (D) $LlYy \times LLYy$
    (E) $LlYY \times Llyy$

23. Which of the following can be viewed with a light microscope?
    (A) Ribosomes
    (B) Golgi apparatus
    (C) Nucleus
    (D) Lipids
    (E) Proteins

24. Which of the following areas is a site of active cell division at the tips of plant roots and shoots?
    (A) Lateral meristems
    (B) Apical meristems
    (C) Sclerenchyma cells
    (D) Cortex
    (E) Pericycle

25. Which substances are components of the plasma membrane of a cell?
    (A) Glycoproteins
    (B) Cytochromes
    (C) Nucleic acids
    (D) Phosphatidic acid
    (E) Lipoproteins

26. Mitosis in vertebrate cells occurs just after which of the following phases of the cell cycle?
    (A) G_1
    (B) S
    (C) DNA synthesis
    (D) G_2
    (E) M phase

27. Certain cells of all of the following organisms undergo meiosis EXCEPT
    (A) ferns
    (B) sponges
    (C) fungi
    (D) bacteria
    (E) nematodes

28. Water and minerals flow up through a plant through the
    (A) sieve tubes of phloem
    (B) sieve tubes of xylem
    (C) tracheids and vessel elements of phloem
    (D) tracheids and vessel elements of xylem
    (E) only vessel elements of xylem

29. In plants, change in the level of which of the following substances causes the stomata to close and conserve water during drought?
    (A) Brassinosteroids
    (B) Abscisic acid
    (C) Auxin
    (D) Cytokinins
    (E) Ethylene

30. O_2 and CO_2 diffuse from regions where their partial pressures
    (A) are higher to regions where they are lower
    (B) are lower to regions where they are higher
    (C) are zero to regions of higher partial pressure
    (D) are zero to regions of lower partial pressure
    (E) are influenced by external atmosphere changes into the cell

31. A DNA molecule that can carry foreign DNA into a cell and then replicate is called a
    (A) probe
    (B) restriction fragment
    (C) restriction enzyme
    (D) vector
    (E) transcriptase

32. It is theorized that when organisms that were capable of self-replicating originated, Earth's atmosphere contained a low concentration of
    (A) gaseous oxygen.
    (B) water.
    (C) carbon dioxide.
    (D) nitrogen.
    (E) hydrogen.

33. The composition of lymph in lymph vessels is roughly the same as which of the following?
    (A) Blood
    (B) Interstitial fluid
    (C) Glomerular filtrate
    (D) Bile
    (E) Chyme

34. In photosynthesis, most ATP is produced as a result of which of the following processes?
    (A) The light reactions
    (B) Carbon fixation
    (C) Noncyclic photophosphorylation
    (D) The dark reactions
    (E) The Calvin cycle

35. Which of the following organisms is not usually considered alive because of its dependence on other organisms for reproduction?
    (A) Nematode
    (B) Tapeworm
    (C) Mold
    (D) Virus
    (E) Lichen

36. In guinea pigs, black fur (B) is dominant to brown fur (b). No tail (T) is dominant over tail (t). What fraction of the progeny of the cross $BbTt \times BbTt$ will have black fur and tails?
    (A) 1/16
    (B) 3/16
    (C) 3/8
    (D) 9/16
    (E) 1/4

GO ON TO THE NEXT PAGE

37. A migrating flock of Canadian geese is nearly decimated by a severe storm. Only four members of the flock, which constitute the entire population of a specific region, survive and return north the next spring. These four start a new colony. This phenomenon is known as
(A) the founder effect
(B) natural selection
(C) migration
(D) polymorphism
(E) the bottleneck effect

38. Which of the following describes a drawing showing the evolutionary history among a particular species or a group of related species?
(A) Food web
(B) Punnett square
(C) Pedigree
(D) Phylogenetic tree
(E) Graph

39. Which of the following characteristics is common to all bryophytes?
(A) Large, independent gametophytes
(B) Monoecious plants
(C) Haploid spores
(D) Seed production
(E) Vascular tissue

40. The rate of flow of sugar and nutrients through the phloem is regulated by
(A) diffusion from source to sink
(B) hydrostatic pressure in the sieve tube
(C) the force of transpirational pull
(D) active transport by tracheid and vessel cells
(E) passive transport by the pith

41. Allolactose stimulates the cells of the human body to produce mRNAs that code for the enzyme β-galactosidase, which breaks down lactose into glucose and galactose. In this case, the role of allolactose can best be described as that of a
(A) DNA replication stimulator
(B) translation inhibitor
(C) stimulator of B-galactosidase secretion
(D) regulator of gene activity
(E) translation activator

42. Which of the following types of data can be used to map the locations of genes on chromosomes?
(A) Segregation frequency
(B) Rate of gene regulation
(C) Dominance patterns
(D) Rate of gene recombination
(E) Rate of gene expression

43. When the stomata of a plant leaf open, which of the following occurs?
(A) There is a decrease in CO_2 intake by the leaf.
(B) The plant shifts from C_3 photosynthesis to C_4 photosynthesis.
(C) The rate of transpiration decreases.
(D) There is an increase in the concentration of CO_2 in mesophyll cells.
(E) There is an increase in the rate of production of nucleic acids.

44. All of the following are evidence for evolution EXCEPT
(A) the presence of anatomical homologies
(B) vestigial organs
(C) the existence of molecular homologies
(D) the fossil record
(E) the existence of homologies in diet among species

45. In a certain group of iguanas, the presence of brown skin is the result of a homozygous recessive condition in the biochemical pathway producing skin pigment. If the frequency of the allele for this condition is 0.35, which of the following is closest to the frequency of the dominant allele in this population? (Assume that the population is in Hardy-Weinberg equilibrium.)
    (A) 0.15
    (B) 0.45
    (C) 0.55
    (D) 0.65
    (E) 0.85

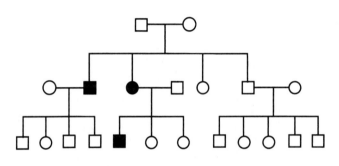

46. In the pedigree above, squares represent males, and circles represent females. Shaded figures represent individuals who possess a particular trait. Which of the following patterns of inheritance best explains how this trait is transmitted?
    (A) Partially dominant
    (B) Autosomal dominant
    (C) Autosomal recessive
    (D) Sex-linked recessive
    (E) Sex-linked dominant

47. The movement of H$^+$ across the inner mitochondrial membrane during chemiosmosis of cellular respiration, is an example of what type of movement across a membrane?
    (A) Active transport
    (B) Facilitated diffusion
    (C) The work of a symport
    (D) The work of an antiport
    (E) Cotransport

48. Which of the following is the most direct result of the presence of protein in the small intestine?
    (A) The secretion of bile by the gallbladder
    (B) The secretion of pepsin by the lining of the small intestine
    (C) The activation of the inactive form of trypsin and chymotrypsin
    (D) The activation of the inactive form of lipase
    (E) Peristalsis along the walls of the small intestine

49. During part of its life cycle, a tapeworm lives as an adult in a human's intestine. The tapeworm attaches to the intestinal lining, absorbs nutrients digested by the host, and releases eggs that are excreted in the human's feces. The feces happen to contaminate the food given to a pig, and larvae encyst in the muscles of the pig. The pig is later consumed by humans. The tapeworm is an example of
    (A) mutualistic symbiotic partner to humans
    (B) commensalistic symbiotic partner to humans
    (C) parasitic symbiotic partner to humans
    (D) mutualistic symbiotic partner to pigs
    (E) commensalistic symbiotic partner to pigs

50. Which of the following is a major food source for organisms that live in the benthic zone?
    (A) Floating aquatic plants
    (B) Phytoplankton
    (C) Zooplankton
    (D) Detritus
    (E) Cyanobacteria

GO ON TO THE NEXT PAGE

51. Which of the following cellular processes is most closely coupled with active transport?
    (A) The addition of H^+ to H_2O to produce a hydronium ion
    (B) The hydrolysis of ATP
    (C) The phosphorylation of ADP
    (D) The synthesis of G3P
    (E) The formation of peptide bonds between amino acids

52. Which of the following cells would most likely have the greatest concentration of mitochondria in its cytoplasm?
    (A) A cell lining the digestive tract
    (B) An active skeletal muscle cell
    (C) A cell in the liver
    (D) A cell in the lung
    (E) A cell in the epidermis

53. In which of the following pairs are the organisms most closely related taxonomically?
    (A) Mushroom; tulip
    (B) *E. coli*; euglenid
    (C) Lobster; spider
    (D) Shark; crayfish
    (E) Dolphin; sea star

Directions: Each group of questions below consists of five lettered choices (or five lettered items in a graph) followed by a list of numbered phrases or sentences. For each numbered phrase or sentence, select the one choice (or item) that is most closely related to it. Each choice may be used once, more than once, or not at all in each group.

Questions 54–56 refer to the following graph. Each of the curves represents one pathway for the same reaction, but one pathway is catalyzed by an enzyme.

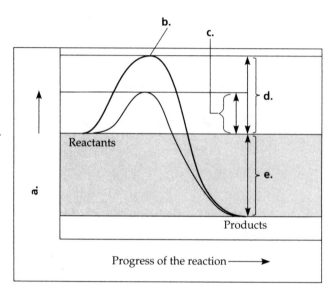

54. Represents the activation energy of the uncatalyzed reaction

55. Represents the activation energy of the catalyzed reaction

56. Represents the transition state of the uncatalyzed reaction

Questions 57–61 refer to the following diagram of the structure of a flower.

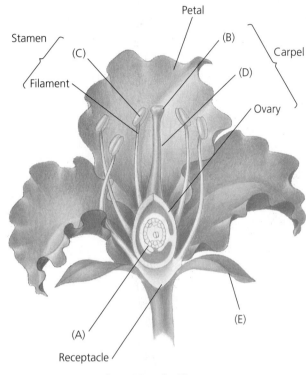

Structure of a Flower

57. Develop into seeds after fertilization

58. The site of pollen production

59. Receives pollen

60. Enclose the flower prior to its opening

61. Connects the stigma to the ovary

Questions 62–65
    (A) Follicle-stimulating hormone (FSH)
    (B) Growth hormone (GH)
    (C) Melatonin
    (D) Androgens
    (E) Endorphins

62. Secreted by the anterior pituitary gland, stimulates growth and metabolism

63. Secreted by the anterior pituitary gland, stimulates the production of ova and sperm

64. Secreted by the testes, promotes the development of secondary sex characteristics

65. Secreted by the pineal gland, involved in regulating biological rhythms

Questions 66–69
    (A) Savannah
    (B) Temperate broadleaf forest
    (C) Tundra
    (D) Chaparral
    (E) Coniferous forest

66. Possesses permafrost and is dominated by short shrubs and grasses; endures long, dark winters

67. Dominated by dense evergreen shrubs and other plants adapted to periodic fires

68. Has long, cold winters and short summers; a biome that is dominated by gymnosperms

69. Home to large herbivores and their predators, marked by grasses and scattered trees

Questions 70–73

(A) Inner mitochondrial membrane
(B) The cytosol
(C) Thylakoid membranes
(D) Ribosome
(E) Nucleus

70. Where mRNA is translated into proteins

71. Where DNA is replicated prior to cell division

72. Where chlorophyll is located

73. The location of glycolysis

Questions 74–78

(A) Rotifera
(B) Porifera
(C) Nematoda
(D) Platyhelminthes
(E) Chordata

74. Possess a notochord, a dorsal hollow nerve cord, and bilateral symmetry

75. Possess a tough exoskeleton called a cuticle, are not segmented, have a complete digestive tract but no circulatory system

76. Possess a complete digestive tract, are pseudocoelomates with a crown of cilia surrounding their mouths

77. Are hermaphrodites and suspension feeders, have no nerves or muscles, have a sac-like body

78. Possess a gastrovascular cavity with only one opening, are acoelomates, and include many parasitic species

Questions 79–82

(A) Telomere
(B) DNA polymerase
(C) Helicase
(D) Primer
(E) DNA ligase

79. DNA not made up of genes, but of multiple repetitions of short nucleotide sequences

80. Joins the sugar-phosphate backbones of the Okazaki fragments to make a complete DNA strand

81. Catalyzes elongation of new DNA at a replication fork

82. Catalyzes the unwinding of double-stranded DNA prior to transcription

Questions 83–84

A scientist is studying the cell cycles of various organisms to learn about their metabolic activities and division patterns. She kept track of the amount of time each type of cell spent in the cell cycles and collected them in the table below.

TOTAL MINUTES SPENT IN EACH CELL CYCLE PHASE				
Cell Type	G_1	S	G_2	M
Monkey liver	20	23	10	18
Plant stem	98	0	0	0

83. From the data in the table above, which of the following is the most likely conclusion about the cell from the plant stem?
(A) It is dead.
(B) This cell contains no DNA.
(C) This cell contains no mRNA.
(D) This cell has entered the G_0 phase.
(E) This cell is continually growing.

84. How long did the entire process of mitosis in the monkey liver cell last?
(A) 70 minutes
(B) 23 minutes
(C) 18 minutes
(D) 10 minutes
(E) 0 minutes

Questions 85–86

In a study of the development of chicken embryos, groups of cells in the early germ layers were stained with five different-colored dyes. After the organs of the chick developed, the location of the dyes were marked down as shown below.

Tissue	Color
Brain	Blue
Liver	Red
Mucous membranes	Green
Nerve cord	Yellow
Heart	Orange

85. Mesoderm would eventually give rise to tissues containing which of the following colors?
    (A) Yellow and purple
    (B) Red and blue
    (C) Orange and yellow
    (D) Orange and green
    (E) Red and green

86. Tissues that were stained blue were derived from
    (A) mesoderm.
    (B) ectoderm.
    (C) mesoderm and ectoderm.
    (D) ectoderm and endoderm.
    (E) mesoderm and endoderm.

Questions 87–88 refer to the following chromosome map. Letters represent gene loci and numbers represent map units.

87. Considering the possibilities of recombination, which two genes on this chromosome are most likely to segregate together into a daughter cell?
    (A) A and W
    (B) A and E
    (C) A and G
    (D) W and E
    (E) W and G

88. If the rate of recombination between gene A and W is 5%, what is the rate of recombination between gene W and gene G?
    (A) 0%
    (B) 5%
    (C) 10%
    (D) 15%
    (E) 20%

Questions 89–91 refer to the following figure, which shows a food web in a particular ecosystem. Each letter represents a species in this ecosystem, and the arrows show the flow of energy.

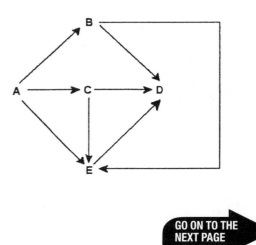

GO ON TO THE NEXT PAGE

89. Which of the species in the food web is the primary producer?
    (A) A
    (B) B
    (C) C
    (D) D
    (E) E

90. Species B and C represent which of the following?
    (A) Primary producers
    (B) Primary consumers
    (C) Secondary consumers
    (D) Tertiary consumers
    (E) Omnivores

91. Which of the following most accurately describes species E?
    (A) An herbivore, and a secondary consumer
    (B) An omnivore, and a secondary consumer
    (C) An omnivore, and both a primary and secondary consumer
    (D) An herbivore, and both a primary and secondary consumer
    (E) A cannibal

Questions 92–94 refer to the information about five organisms shown in the table below.

Environment Inhabited by Animal	Body Length	Features of Gas Exchange System	Features of Gas Exchange Surface	Percentage of Oxygen Extracted from Air
1 Terrestrial	0.01 m	Branching air tubes, large tracheae that open to the outside	Moist epithelium lining the terminal ends of the tracheal system	53%
2 Terrestrial	0.02 m	Branching air tubes, large tracheae, ventilates with rhythmic body movements	Moist epithelium lining the terminal ends of the tracheal system	48%
3 Aquatic	0.5 m	Outfoldings in the body surface suspended in water	Uses countercurrent exchange and ventilation	73%
4 Terrestrial	1.0 m	Lungs that work in conjunction with circulatory system	Gas exchange occurs across epithelium of alveoli	67%
5 Terrestrial	2.0 m	Lungs that work in conjunction with circulatory system	Gas exchange occurs across epithelium of alveoli	78%

92. Which of the above organisms is most likely to have hemolymph as its main circulatory fluid?
    (A) 1 and 2
    (B) 2 or 3
    (C) 3 or 4
    (D) 4 and 5
    (E) None of these organisms

93. In which of these organisms is hemoglobin used to transport oxygen through the blood?
    (A) 5
    (B) 4 and 5
    (C) 3, 4, and 5
    (D) 2, 3, 4, and 5
    (E) All of them

94. In which of these animals can the process of gas exchange occur without physical movement of some part of the animal?
    (A) 1 and 2 only
    (B) 1 and 3 only
    (C) 1, 2, and 3 only
    (D) 3, 4, and 5 only
    (E) All of them

Questions 95–97 refer to the following gel, which was produced from four samples of a radioactively labeled single strand of DNA that were cut with one type of restriction enzyme. The samples were separated by gel electrophoresis. Answer the questions on the basis of the bands you can visualize below.

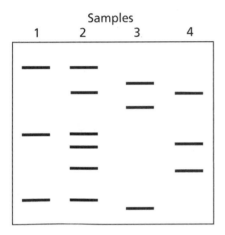

95. The DNA fragments in the gel were separated when an electric field was applied across the gel and they migrated at different speeds. The differential migration speed of the different DNA fragments was due to the
    (A) amount of radioactivity in the samples
    (B) degree to which the samples were negatively charged
    (C) degree to which the samples were positively charged
    (D) size of the fragments within the samples
    (E) polarity of the samples

96. Which of the following is true about the DNA samples that were loaded onto the gel?
    (A) The DNA strand of sample 2 was originally the longest.
    (B) The DNA strand of sample 4 was originally the shortest.
    (C) Samples 2 and 4 are the same DNA sample.
    (D) Sample 2 was cut at more restriction sites than was sample 4.
    (E) Sample 4 was cut at more restriction sites than was sample 2.

97. What was the purpose in radioactively labeling the DNA fragments in this experiment?
    (A) To visualize them
    (B) To make them travel through the gel
    (C) To hydrolyze them into fragments
    (D) To get rid of contaminants
    (E) To destroy their polarity

Questions 98–100 refer to an experiment in which there is an initial setup of a U-tube with its two sides separated by a membrane that permits the passage of water and NaCl but not molecules of glucose. The U-tube is filled on one side with a solution of 0.4 M glucose and 0.5 M NaCl, and on the other, 0.8 M glucose and 0.4 M NaCl.

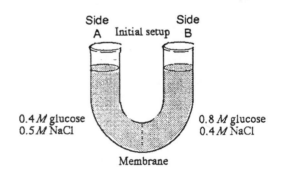

98. When this U-tube was set up, at time = 0 in the experiment, which of the following was true?
    (A) The solution on side A was more concentrated than the solution on side B.
    (B) The solution on side B was more concentrated than the solution on side A.
    (C) The two solutions had equal concentration.
    (D) There was more salt on side B than on side A.
    (E) There was more glucose on side A than on side B.

99. Which of the following is most likely to occur after two hours of the U-tube being undisturbed? (Assume that both sides are at atmospheric pressure.)
    (A) The water levels of sides A and B will remain the same.
    (B) The amount of NaCl on side B will have increased.
    (C) The amount of NaCl on side A will have increased.
    (D) The amount of glucose on side B will have increased.
    (E) The amount of glucose on side A will have increased.

100. After two hours, which of the following would probably be true of the level of water on each side of the U-tube?
    (A) There would be no change in the water levels on either side of the U-tube.
    (B) The water column in side A would be slightly higher.
    (C) The water column in side B would be slightly higher.
    (D) The water columns on both sides would be slightly lower.
    (E) The water columns on both sides would be slightly higher.

Biology
Section II

Time—10 minutes to plan responses; 1 hour and 30 minutes for writing

Answer all questions. Number your answer as the question is numbered below.

Answers must be in essay form. Outline form is NOT acceptable. Labeled diagrams may be used to supplement discussion, but in no case will a diagram alone suffice. It is important that you read each question completely before you begin to write. After reading the questions thoroughly, allow yourself 10 minutes to organize your thoughts and plan your responses.

1. Birth control pills are chemical contraceptives that are made up of estrogen and progestin (which is a progesterone-like substance). They act through a negative feedback loop to stop the secretion of GnRH by the hypothalamus, and of FSH and LH by the pituitary.
   (a) **Explain** how a negative feedback loop works.
   (b) **Explain** how the effects of the birth control pill described above make pregnancy highly unlikely when taken as prescribed.

2. Gene expression in a cell is influenced by a variety of factors. Not all genes on the eukaryotic chromosome are expressed, and in fact, only a small fraction of the genes are transcribed into working proteins.
   (a) **Discuss** three ways in which gene control works in the cell.
   (b) **Describe** three laboratory procedures you could employ in order to determine how much transcription and translation is going on in a cell at a given time.

3. It has been determined that, evolutionarily, the closest relative of humans is the chimpanzee. Other somewhat close relatives are the gibbon and the orangutan.
   (a) **Describe** the relationships among these four species—taxonomically and through phylogeny.
   (b) **Describe** three kinds of evidence that were used to determine the relationship among these four species.
   (c) **Describe** the general structure of the ancestor of *Homo sapiens*, relative to that of other anthropoids.

4. A flowering plant in a ceramic pot is placed in a window that has light shining through most of the day, and it is given adequate water and soil nutrients.
   (a) **Describe** the daily and nightly events in the plant's metabolism.
   (b) **Describe** the changes in the plant that would be induced by rotating the plant 180°.

END OF EXAMINATION

ANSWERS AND EXPLANATIONS

Multiple-Choice Questions

1. (D) is correct. The carrying capacity of a population is defined as the maximum population size that a certain environment can support without itself being degraded. If you look at the graph, you can see that the population increases in number until it reaches about 900 members, and at that point it stabilizes. The number 900 therefore represents the carrying capacity.

2. (A) is correct. This is a simple probability question. In order to calculate the chance that two or more independent events will occur together in a specific combination, you can use the multiplication rule. Take the probability that gene *P* will segregate into a gamete ($\frac{1}{4}$), and multiply it by the probability that gene *Q* will segregate into a gamete ($\frac{1}{4}$). Then multiply that by the probability that gene *R* will segregate into a gamete to get $\frac{1}{4} \times \frac{1}{4} \times \frac{1}{4} = \frac{1}{64}$.

3. (C) is correct. The mitochondria of the cell is the site of cellular respiration and produces the most ATP by extracting energy from sugars, fats, and other fuels. Mitochondria are found in almost all eukaryotic cells, and are enclosed by two membranes—a smooth outer membrane and an inner membrane with many infoldings called cristae. The inside of the inner membrane is called the mitochondrial matrix. There are two processes that occur in the mitochondria to produce energy. One is the citric acid cycle, and the other is chemiosmosis.

4. (B) is correct. Imprinting is defined as a type of learning that is generally irreversible and that is limited to a certain period in an animal's life (usually when the animal is very young). The phenomenon of mother-offspring bonding in geese is an example of this type of learning. If this imprinting does not happen, the mother will not take care of the offspring, and the goslings will die.

5. (D) is correct. This is most likely a prokaryotic cell. Most prokaryotes are about one-tenth the size of eukaryotic cells, and the most common shapes of prokaryotic cells are spherical, rod-shaped, and helical. Finally, prokaryotes lack membrane-bound organelles, including nuclear membranes; instead they have nucleoid regions, which are a complex of DNA and fibers in a certain region of the cell.

6. (B) is correct. A testcross is the breeding of an organism that has an unknown genotype with one that is homozygous recessive, in order to determine the genotype of the unknown parent. The phenotypic ratio of the offspring will reveal the unknown genotype.

7. (A) is correct. Diatoms are single-celled algae that reproduce asexually by mitosis. They live in both freshwater and marine environments, and they are very numerous in those environments. They are major primary producers in marine environments.

8. (D) is correct. If you consider that the homozygous long-hair deer is *HH*, and the homozygous short-hair deer is *hh*, then crossing them would give all offspring with the genotype *Hh* and medium-length hair phenotype. Crossing the heterozygotes would give you offspring in the ratio of 1:2:1—*HH:Hh:hh*. This means that 25% of the offspring would have long hair (*HH*), 25% of them would have short hair (*hh*), and 50% of them would have medium-length hair (*Hh*).

■ **9. (E) is correct.** Nitrate is the only answer listed that does not represent a form of waste secreted by some kind of animal. Ammonia is the waste product secreted by many aquatic species; urea is the common waste form of mammals, most amphibians, and many fishes; and birds and reptiles secrete uric acid. Carbon dioxide is a waste product of respiration.

■ **10. (E) is correct.** Among these answers, the one that best supports the idea that certain cell organelles, such as mitochondria and chloroplasts, were once symbiotic prokaryotes living inside larger cells is answer E, which states that mitochondria, chloroplasts, and bacteria have similar DNA and chromosomes.

■ **11. (D) is correct.** An endergonic reaction is a nonspontaneous chemical reaction; in order for the reaction to begin, free energy must be absorbed from the surroundings. During the course of an endergonic reaction, energy is released.

■ **12. (B) is correct.** The Calvin cycle—often referred to as the dark reactions of photosynthesis—occurs in the stroma of the chloroplast. In the course of the cycle, the enzyme rubisco combines carbon dioxide with a five-carbon sugar, consuming NADPH and ATP, and ultimately producing glyceraldehyde-3-phosphate. Since carbon dioxide is consumed in the course of the Calvin cycle, the rate of its consumption can be used to determine the rate of photosynthesis.

■ **13. (A) is correct.** All of the cell organelles listed, except centrosomes, are contained by a membrane composed of phospholipids. Centrosomes are areas that are present in the cell cytoplasm only during cell division; they are the sites at which the centrioles containing microtubules comprising the spindle apparatus are organized.

■ **14. (D) is correct.** The only one of the statements not included in Darwin's theory of natural selection is answer *D*. Darwin's theory stated that the individuals that are least well suited will not leave behind as many offspring, but physical weakness does not necessarily lead to an individual's being unsuited for its environment.

■ **15. (E) is correct.** All of the answers list events in the embryonic development of an animal except *E*. During development, certain genes are turned on at certain points in the process, but at no point are all of the genes in a cell activated.

■ **16. (C) is correct.** Prions are proteins that are the cause of diseases such as "mad cow" disease; they are misfolded proteins that are capable of converting normally folded proteins into misfolded forms (like themselves), triggering a chain reaction that vastly increases their numbers. These proteins exist primarily in the brain, which is why their misfolding has such serious negative effects.

■ **17. (A) is correct.** Prokaryotic cells are very simple cells that have no membrane-bound nucleus—instead they have a nucleoid region, at which the genetic material is concentrated. They do, however, share the remaining characteristics with eukaryotes—they are bound by a membrane, they have genetic material that is translated into proteins on ribosomes, and they have cytoplasm.

18. (B) is correct. Cytokinins enhance the growth and development of plant cells; they are produced primarily in actively growing tissues such as roots, embryos, and the fruits of a plant. They act in concert with auxins to cause cell division and differentiation. They are also responsible for retarding the aging process of some plant organs.

19. (C) is correct. Asexual reproduction is a form of reproduction in which just one parent contributes genetic material to the offspring, which are clones of the parent and of each other. On the other hand sexual reproduction, in which two parents contribute genetic material to the offspring, results in offspring that differ from each other and their parents.

20. (D) is correct. The domain Archaea, possesses members that are known for their extreme hardiness. Many Archaea are extremophiles: they thrive in extreme environments such as hot-water geysers in Yellowstone Park. Extreme halophiles live in very saline places; extreme thermophiles live in very hot environments.

21. (E) is correct. Oxytocin is produced in the posterior pituitary gland and is regulated by the nervous system. It stimulates the powerful contractions of the smooth muscles in the uterine wall that occur during childbirth. Oxytocin also stimulates the placenta to secrete prostaglandins, which also contribute to contractions.

22. (D) is correct. The ratio of offspring produced is 3:1. Answer *A* can be eliminated because it would produce all dogs with long tails and yellow coats, since only the dominant alleles are present. First, figure out the gametes that the resulting parents in each answer would produce, and do a Punnett square to figure out the resulting offspring proportions. For answer *D*, the gametes produced by parent 1 are *LY, Ly, lY,* and *ly.* For parent two, the possible gametes are *LY* and *Ly.*

23. (C) is correct. A light microscope can be used to view structures that are no smaller than 0.2 μm. This means that they can be used to see most plant and animal cells, cell nuclei, and certain large organelles such as mitochondria. They can also be used to view some bacterial cells.

24. (B) is correct. Apical meristems are located at the roots and shoots of plants, and they supply cells that enable the plant to grow in length. The elongation of plants is called primary growth (as opposed to secondary growth, when plants grow in diameter). Meristems are perpetually embryonic tissues that exist in a plant's areas of growth.

25. (A) is correct. Glycoproteins are complexes of carbohydrate and protein that are associated with the cell membrane and that function in cell-cell recognition—a cell's ability to determine the function of a neighboring cell—for example. Glycoproteins vary from species to species and from individual to individual.

26. (D) is correct. Mitosis, or the M phase of the cell cycle, occurs just after the G_2 phase in the cell cycle. In the G_1 phase, the cell grows. In the S phase, the cell continues to grow and also copies its chromosomes. In the G_2 phase, again the cell grows, and it begins to prepare for cell division. It divides finally in the M phase.

27. (D) is correct. Bacteria, which are the only prokaryotes listed, reproduce by an asexual reproductive process called binary fission. In binary fission, the bacterial cell chromosome (which consists of a single circular DNA molecule) replicates itself, and the cell grows with the plasma membrane growing inward and eventually pinching off to form two cells. The organisms in all of the other answers produce gametes, and gametes are produced by meiosis.

28. (D) is correct. The water-conducting elements of xylem (which is the plant tissue that carries water upward from the roots toward the shoots of the plant) are the tracheids and vessel elements. These cells are elongated and dead when they reach functional maturity. When the cell dies, its interior disintegrates. This leaves only the hard cell wall, which forms a conduit for the movement of water and dissolved minerals.

29. (B) is correct. Abscisic acid is a plant hormone that prompts seeds to enter a dormant phase until conditions are favorable for germination. Abscisic acid also acts as the primary hormonal signal in times of drought. When a plant begins to wilt, abscisic acid accumulates in leaves and causes the stomata to close, which prevents water loss through transpiration.

30. (A) is correct. Gases in general, including carbon dioxide and oxygen, diffuse down a pressure gradient from regions where their partial pressure is higher to regions where it is lower. This means that if cells in one location are depleting their supply of oxygen, the partial pressure of oxygen in that area will drop, and more oxygen will be unloaded at the site of the depletion.

31. (D) is correct. A vector is an important component of genetic engineering; it is a plasmid (a circular piece of DNA) in which a foreign piece of DNA can be inserted. The vector can then be injected into a bacterial cell, causing transformation, and can then be replicated (along with the DNA fragment that it carries) by the cell's machinery.

32. (A) is correct. It is theorized that diatomic oxygen levels in the atmosphere were quite low around the time when the first self-replicating organisms were appearing on Earth. Oxygen began to accumulate in the atmosphere when photosynthesis evolved.

33. (B) is correct. Lymph is the fluid that is inside the lymphatic system, and the composition of lymph is similar to that of interstitial fluid. Fluids and proteins that are lost as they pass through the capillaries are picked up by the lymph vessels and returned to the blood. The lymphatic system drains into the circulatory system near the junction of the venae cavae and the right atrium.

34. (C) is correct. In noncyclic photophosphorylation, ATP is generated by chemiosmosis; the redox reactions of the electron transport chain create an H^+ gradient across the thylakoid membrane, and this gradient is used to power an ATP synthase. This ATP synthase makes ATP.

35. (D) is correct. Viruses are usually not considered to be alive, because they depend on host cells in order to reproduce. Invading viruses use the host cell's machinery to produce its proteins and replicate itself.

36. (B) is correct. Crossing guinea pigs with genotype *BbTt* gives a ratio of offspring of 9:3:3:1; this is a dihybrid cross between two independently assorting characters. Nine-sixteenths of the offspring will display both of the dominant traits; $\frac{3}{16}$ of the offspring will display one of the dominant traits and one recessive one; $\frac{3}{16}$ of the offspring will display the other dominant trait and the other recessive trait; $\frac{1}{16}$ of the offspring will display both recessive traits. This question asks how many of the offspring will display one of the dominant traits (black fur) and one of the recessive traits (tail); the answer is $\frac{3}{16}$.

37. (E) is correct. This is an example of the bottleneck effect—a type of genetic drift. Genetic drift is defined as a change in the allelic frequencies of a population due to chance, and the bottleneck effect occurs when a large part of a certain population is destroyed by a disaster such as an earthquake, drought, or fire. The surviving members may not be representative of the population's gene pool.

38. (D) is correct. A phylogenetic tree shows the hypothetical evolutionary history of a species or a group of related species. Systematists create phylogenies in order to study the path of evolution on Earth and to better understand relationships among species that live on Earth today.

39. (A) is correct. The gametophyte is the dominant generation in bryophytes and typically is a plant that is large enough to be noticed. Bryophytes produce diploid spores that land on suitable environments and divide by mitosis to eventually grow into gametophytes. Most bryophytes lack vascular tissue, which limits their ability to grow tall. Some common bryophytes are mosses, liverworts, and hornworts.

40. (B) is correct. The flow of sap from the leaves to the other parts of the plant body is driven by hydrostatic pressure that develops inside the sieve tube, as phloem unloading creates a high solute concentration at the source end of the sieve tube—in contrast with a low solute concentration at the sink end. Water flows through the tube because the pressure is greatest at the tube's source end.

41. (D) is correct. Regulatory genes are those that code for a protein—either a repressor or an inducer—that controls the transcription of another gene or a group of genes. In this case, allolactose is an inducer. When it is present in the cell, it causes the genes that transcribe for β-galactosidase to be turned on and to produce the enzyme. This represents an example of an inducible operon.

42. (D) is correct. Scientists can use the rate of genetic recombination between two genes in order to build a genetic map, which is an ordered list of the genetic loci along the length of a chromosome. The closer two linked genes are (linked genes are those located on the same chromosome), the less likely it is that they will be separated during crossing over. The rate of recombination is proportionate to the distance between genes on a chromosome.

43. (D) is correct. The opening of the stomata in the leaves of a plant results in CO_2 being taken in from the atmosphere. This, in turn, results in photosynthesis when light energy can also be captured by the leaf. Another result is an increase in transpiration, or water loss by the leaf, by evaporation through the stomata.

44. (E) is correct. All of the answer choices are proof of the process of evolution except the existence of homologies among different species' diets. Since all living organisms require certain nutrients in order to survive—and since there are only so many consumable organic substances on Earth—the fact that two species might have similar components in their diet does not necessarily imply evolutionary relatedness.

45. (D) is correct. Since the frequency of the recessive allele is 0.35, we know that the frequency of the other allele is $1 - 0.35$, which equals 0.65. The Hardy-Weinberg equation states that if a population contains just two alleles for a given trait, and if the frequency of one of the alleles is known, the frequency of the other allele can be calculated using the equation $p + q = 1$. If you designate the frequency of the occurrence of the recessive allele as q, and use its value of 0.35, you can rearrange the equation to read $p + 0.35 = 1$. Then, $1 - 0.35 = 0.65$, which is equal to p, or the frequency of the other (in this case, the dominant) allele.

46. (C) is correct. This is an autosomal recessive trait. If it were sex-linked, it would be expressed in only one of the sexes—usually the male, since males have only one X chromosome. We know it is recessive because it does not appear in every generation; only dominant traits appear in every generation. Also, the first generation does not show the trait, but they have children who do.

47. (B) is correct. In facilitated diffusion, the transport of certain substances across a membrane is aided by transport proteins that span the membrane. These transport proteins are specialized for the solute that they transport. In the case of chemiosmosis, an H^+ gradient is established across the inner mitochondrial membrane by the electron transport chain, which moves H^+ against its concentration gradient into the mitochondrial matrix. As these ions move back to the matrix, diffusion is facilitated by ATP synthase proteins.

48. (C) is correct. When protein enters the small intestine, the enzymes that are responsible for breaking down proteins go to work. Trypsin and chymotrypsin are secreted by the pancreas in inactive form. They must be activated by an intestinal enzyme called enteropeptidase before beginning to break down the peptide bonds between the amino acids.

49. (C) is correct. This is an example of parasitic symbiosis, between the human and the tapeworm. The tapeworm gains nutrients from the human, whereas the human is harmed by the symbiotic relationship. The tapeworm causes intestinal blockage when it grows to its maximal length, and it can rob nutrients from the human to the extent that the human can develop nutritional deficiencies.

50. (D) is correct. The benthic zone in the ocean is the bottom of all aquatic zones; it is made up of sand and organic nutrients and is occupied by bacteria, fungi, seaweeds, algae, invertebrates, and some fishes. These organisms receive nutrients from the detritus that rains down from the ocean levels above it, where animals produce various metabolic wastes and die.

51. (B) is correct. Active transport involves the movement of substances across membranes against their concentration gradient. In this process, the cell must expend energy, usually in the form of ATP. One example of active transport in the cell is the sodium-potassium pump, in which three sodium ions are pumped out of the cell and two potassium ions are pumped in. In the process, ATP is hydrolyzed—it transfers one of its phosphate groups to the transport protein.

52. (B) is correct. An active skeletal muscle cell would be the most likely to have a high concentration of mitochondria in its cytoplasm because mitochondria are the sites of cellular respiration, and cellular respiration is the source of ATP in the cell. Muscle cells use ATP in the process of contraction, and since they store only enough ATP for a few contractions, they must have many functional mitochondria to keep up the flow of ATP production when muscle contraction is continuous.

53. (C) is correct. The two most closely related organisms are the lobster and the spider. Both are arthropods, which are characterized by having segmented bodies, exoskeletons, and jointed appendages. Both organisms also have an open circulatory system.

54. (D) is correct. The activation energy of a reaction is the initial energy investment required in order for the reaction to proceed. It is the energy required in order to break the bonds of the substrate enough for the substrate to reach the highly unstable transition state. You can tell that answer *D* is the reaction energy of the uncatalyzed reaction (because the presence of a catalyst would decrease the overall energy of the reaction), so the taller curve must be the uncatalyzed reaction.

55. (C) is correct. The activation energy of the catalyzed reaction is represented by answer *C*. The overall energy of this reaction is significantly lower than that of the uncatalyzed reaction. This is because enzymes speed up the course of reactions by lowering the energy of activation so that the transition state is much easier to reach.

56. (B) is correct. The transition state of a reaction is the highest-energy, most unstable form of the reactants in the reaction. The energy put into the reaction in order to make it "go"—also known as the activation energy—must be sufficient to enable the reactants to reach this transition state.

57. (A) is correct. The ovules are structures that develop in the plant ovary, and they contain the female gametophyte.

58. (C) is correct. The anther is the site of pollen production in the plant, and pollen grains contain the immature male gametophyte of a plant.

59. (B) is correct. The stigma is the sticky structure located at the end of the carpel. It is responsible for catching pollen grains.

60. (E) is correct. The sepals are usually green, and they are a whorl of modified leaves that enclose and protect the flower bud before it opens.

61. (D) is correct. The style is the stalk of the carpel of a flower; the ovary is at the base of the stalk; the stigma is at the top of the style.

62. (B) is correct. Growth hormone (GH) is secreted by the anterior pituitary gland and affects many different target tissues. It promotes growth and stimulates the production of growth factors.

63. (A) is correct. Follicle-stimulating hormone, or FSH, is secreted by the anterior pituitary. It stimulates the production of ova and sperm in the gonads.

64. **(D) is correct.** Androgens are the male sex hormones, and the main androgen is testosterone. Androgens are synthesized in the testes, and they stimulate the development and maintenance of the male reproductive system.

65. **(C) is correct.** Melatonin is secreted by the pineal gland (in the brain); it is a modified amino acid that is secreted at night. The amount of melatonin secreted depends on the length of the night.

66. **(C) is correct.** The tundra is characterized by having a permafrost, which is a permanently frozen subsoil, and bitterly cold temperatures. Because of the frozen subsoil, little precipitation, and high winds plants do not grow very tall.

67. **(D) is correct.** The chaparral is home to many dense, spiny evergreen bushes. The summers are long, hot, and dry; and the winters are mild and rainy. Plants in the chaparral are adapted for the periodic fires that ravage these biomes.

68. **(E) is correct.** The coniferous forest biome is characterized by frequent snowfall, harsh winters, short summers, and the presence of gymnosperms.

69. **(A) is correct.** Savannas are home to grazing herbivores and their predators. They contain tall grasses with sporadic clusters of trees. There is a considerable rainy season interrupted by periods of seasonal drought in areas containing savannas.

70. **(D) is correct.** Ribosomes are cell organelles that are constructed of rRNA and protein and function as the site of protein synthesis in the cytoplasm.

71. **(E) is correct.** DNA replication occurs in the nucleus of the cell. The genetic material is replicated prior to mitotic or meiotic cell division.

72. **(C) is correct.** Light reactions generate ATP by powering the addition of a phosphate group to ADP, a process called photophosphorylation. In the chloroplast, chlorophyll is embedded within the thylakoid membranes.

73. **(B) is correct.** Glycolysis takes place in the cytosol of the cell. In glycolysis, glucose is split into two molecules of pyruvate. This metabolic pathway occurs in all living cells, and it is the starting point for fermentation or cellular respiration.

74. **(E) is correct.** The phylum Chordata contains two groups of invertebrates plus all animals with backbones. All chordates possess a notochord, a dorsal hollow nerve cord, pharyngeal clefts, and a post-anal tail as an embryo.

75. **(C) is correct.** Nematodes are found in aquatic habitats and have unsegmented bodies with a tough exoskeleton called a cuticle. They have a complete digestive tract but lack a circulatory system, and they reproduce sexually.

76. **(A) is correct.** Rotifers have a complete digestive tract, with a separate mouth and anus, and a ring of cilia around their mouths, which draws in water. They are pseudocoelomates.

77. **(B) is correct.** Porifera are sponges that have a sac-like body and are suspension feeders with no nerves or muscles. They draw water into a central cavity and filter it for nutrients. Sponges are also hermaphrodites.

78. **(D) is correct.** Platyhelminthes are flatworms that live in marine environments and other wet habitats. They include many parasitic species, and they have a gastrovascular cavity with just one opening. They are also acoelomates.

79. (A) is correct. Telomeres are regions found at the tips of chromosomes, and they are made up not of genes but of repeating short sequences of DNA. These parts of chromosomes are copied by a special enzyme called telomerase.

80. (E) is correct. DNA ligase is an enzyme that is necessary for the replication of DNA; it catalyzes the covalent bonding of the $3'$ end of the new DNA fragment to the $5'$ end of the growing chain.

81. (B) is correct. DNA polymerase is another enzyme involved in DNA replication—it catalyzes the elongation of new DNA at the replication fork by adding nucleotides to the existing chain.

82. (C) is correct. Helicase is an enzyme that untwists the double helix of DNA at replication forks prior to DNA replication.

83. (D) is correct. The plant cell is probably in G_0 phase (G_0 phase is a nondividing phase). In many cells, there exists a G_1 checkpoint, and if at this checkpoint the cell is made to exit the cycle, it enters this nondividing G_0 phase. Because this plant cell has spent no time in any other phase besides the G_1, it is most likely arrested in G_0.

84. (C) is correct. The process of mitosis in the monkey liver cell took 18 minutes. The M phase of the cell cycle is the mitotic phase, and it is the phase in which the cell divides the nucleus and partitions the cytoplasm and organelles, plus the newly replicated DNA, to two new daughter cells.

85. (D) is correct. The mesoderm eventually gives rise to most organs and tissues in the body, including the kidney, heart, and inner layer of the skin (including mucous membranes). Therefore, mesoderm would have given rise to the heart, which was stained orange, and the mucous membranes, stained green in this example.

86. (B) is correct. The tissue stained blue was the brain, and the brain is derived from the ectoderm. Also arising from ectoderm is the rest of the nervous system, and the outer epidermal layer of skin.

87. (D) is correct. The genes most likely to travel together and end up in the same daughter cell are W and E. This is because they are located close together on the chromosome. The closer two genes are on the chromosome, the less likely it is that crossing over will occur between them—and that they would be recombined.

88. (D) is correct. If the rate of recombination between A and W is 5%, and the distance between gene A and gene W is 5 map units, and the distance between gene W and gene G is 15 map units, then you can calculate the rate of recombination between W and G by multiplying the 5% by 3, to get a 15% recombination rate.

89. (A) is correct. Species A is autotrophic and the primary producer of the ecosystem. This species is capable of capturing solar energy and converting it into the chemical energy contained in the bonds of organic compounds, which are used by the other organisms in this ecosystem. It also is the only one that has arrows flowing only from it, indicating that it is not a consumer.

90. (B) is correct. Species B and C represent primary consumers—they consume only the autotrophs in this ecosystem, which are the primary producers. They are presumably herbivores since their only food source is the primary producer.

91. (C) is correct. Species E consumes species A (presumably a plant), species C (presumably an animal), and species B (also presumably an animal). This means that species E is an omnivore—it eats both plants and animals. Species E is also both a primary consumer (because it consumes species A) and a secondary consumer (because it consumes species B and C).

92. (A) is correct. The most likely of these organisms to have hemolymph as its circulatory fluid are the smallest organisms, which are presumably insects. These insects have open circulatory systems, in which no distinction is made between blood and interstitial fluid, and hearts that pump the hemolymph directly into the sinuses, which are open cavities for chemical exchange.

93. (C) is correct. In all of these animals, hemoglobin (an iron-containing molecule) is used to transport oxygen. It is contained in the red blood cells, or erythrocytes, which are a component of the blood of each of these animals. Animals 1 and 2 have hemolymph, which in most circumstances does not contain hemoglobin.

94. (B) is correct. The two organisms in this chart in which gas exchange can occur without movement of some part of the animal are the small insect (#1) and the fish (#3). If insects are small enough, gas exchange simply takes place across the moist membranes of their trachea. Some fishes can sit still in water and have the water flow across their gills, with gas exchange taking place.

95. (D) is correct. The DNA fragments migrated along the gel at rates according to their size—the smaller DNA fragments migrated more quickly through the dense gel and can be found near the bottom of the gel, whereas the larger fragments migrated more slowly and can be found closer to the top.

96. (D) is correct. Sample 2 must have been cut at more restriction sites than was sample 4 because more DNA fragments of different sizes were produced. This is shown by the greater number of bands on the gel in the lane of sample 2.

97. (A) is correct. The purpose of radioactively labeling these DNA samples was to make them visible when the gel was done running. After the gel is finished, and the DNA samples have migrated to a sufficient position to be distinguishable, the radiation is detected by radiography.

98. (B) is correct. The solution on Side A is hypotonic to the solution on Side B—it is less concentrated than the solution on Side B, at the time this experiment began.

99. (B) is correct. After two hours, the amount of NaCl on side B will have increased. The membrane separating the two sides allows the passage of NaCl and not glucose, so there will be no movement of glucose—thus, no change in its concentration—but NaCl will travel down its concentration gradient to Side B.

100. (C) is correct. After two hours, the water column in Side B would be slightly higher. If the concentration of NaCl had equalized on both sides of the tube, the solution on Side B would still be hypertonic to that on Side A; thus, water would flow through the membrane in an attempt to equalize its concentration on both sides of the tube until gravitational pressures exerted an equal force to prevent it from rising farther.

Free-Response Questions

1. (a) Negative feedback loops are very important in maintaining homeostasis, through factors such as hormone secretion. Negative feedback loops work much the same way as thermostats do in houses. A receptor somewhere in the body detects a change in some factor in the animal's internal environment, and it transmits this information to a control center. The control center processes the information and directs a response to an effector, which carries out the response. In negative feedback, a change in the variable triggers the control center to prevent further change in the same direction.

(b) The birth control pill blocks the secretion of GnRH by the hypothalamus, and FSH and LH by the pituitary. Together, GnRH, LH, and FSH all work in an elaborate feedback loop that synchronizes the ovarian cycle and the menstrual cycle. During the ovarian cycle, the hypothalamus releases GnRH which stimulates the pituitary to release FSH and LH. FSH stimulates the follicle to grow, and the follicle cells secrete estrogen, which in negative feedback keeps the secretions of FSH and LH relatively low. Later in the cycle, the follicles begin to secrete estrogens rapidly, which has the effect of suddenly causing the increased secretion of FSH and LH. The sudden increase in the secretion of LH is what stimulates ovulation. By blocking the release of GnRH, birth control pills also back LH, which prevents ovulation and FSH, which prevents the follicle from maturing. Ovulation is the release of the egg from the ovaries, and this is the time in the ovarian cycle when fertilization can occur if sperm are present.

This is a good free response answer because it shows working knowledge of the following terms:

negative feedback loop	*LH*
hormone	*pituitary gland*
receptor	*follicle*
control center	*estrogens*
effector	*ovarian cycle*
GnRH	*menstrual cycle*
hypothalamus	*ovulation*
FSH	*fertilization*

This response also demonstrates an understanding of the following important biological processes—a negative feedback loop and the female menstrual/ovarian cycle.

2. (a) Three ways in which gene expression in a cell is controlled are through chromatin packing, DNA methylation, and histone acetylation. In chromatin packing, when the genetic material is in heterochromatin form, it is highly condensed and proteins involved in transcription do not have access to the DNA. In DNA methylation, methyl groups are attached to specific regions of

DNA immediately after it is synthesized. In some cases, this is thought to be responsible for these genes' long-term inactivation. Finally, in histone acetylation, acetyl groups are attached to certain amino acids of histone proteins, and when the histones are acetylated, their shape alters so that they are less tightly bound to DNA; this enables the proteins involved in transcription to move in and begin work. When histones are deacetylated, DNA transcription is impossible.

(b) In order to tell how actively a certain cell is transcribing its DNA and translating its mRNA into protein, you could do a few things in the laboratory. You could monitor the rate of relaxation of the heterochromatin in the cell nucleus; the more relaxed the chromosomes are, the more DNA is being transcribed. Then you could monitor the amount of uptake of cytosine, guanine, uracil, and adenine in the cell; the rate at which these bases are taken up would be an indicator of the rate at which they are being incorporated into mRNA in transcription. Finally, you could monitor the rate at which free amino acids are being consumed in the cell. This would indicate the rate at which they are being incorporated into growing peptide chains in translation.

This is a good free-response answer because it shows working knowledge of the following key terms:

chromatin packing	*cytosine*
DNA methylation	*adenine*
histone acetylation	*uracil*
histones	*guanine*
transcription	*amino acids*
heterochromatin	*peptides*

The response also shows an understanding of the following important biological processes: control of gene expression in eukaryotes and the process of transcription and translation.

3. (a) Humans, gibbons, orangutans, and chimpanzees are primates, so all have an opposable thumb and feet that can grip. Living primates consist of three groups—the lemurs, lorises, and pottos; the tarsiers; and the anthropoids. All four of these species are anthropoids, and they are all hominoids. Evidence suggests that humans and chimps are two divergent branches of the hominoid tree that evolved from a common ancestor (that was neither human nor chimp) about 5 million years ago. The phylogenetic tree on the next page could be used to show the relationships between the primates.

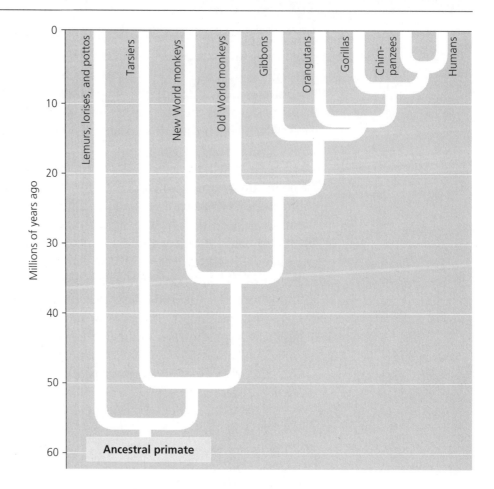

(b) One of the three kinds of evidence that was used to determine relationships among these species is fossil evidence. Fossils are impressions or parts of organisms that are preserved in rock. Most fossils are found in sedimentary rock, and the age of fossils can be determined to a certain extent by the depth of the rock layer in which they are found. Another type of evidence that is used to determine relationships among the anthropoids is the existence of structural homologies. Homologies are shared characteristics that are the result of two species having evolved from a common ancestor. The third type of evidence is molecular homologies in DNA or proteins. The likeness of two species' DNA or proteins tells how closely they are related evolutionarily.

(c) Some of the characteristics of the ancestors of *Homo sapiens* are a relatively large brain (which is associated with the use of language and with other cultural aspects), a longer jaw and certain resulting changes in the teeth, bipedal posture, and a reduced difference in the sizes of the two sexes—males and females were more nearly the same size.

This is a good free-response answer because it shows a working knowledge of the following key terms:

primates   *phylogenetic tree*
anthropoids   *fossils*
hominoids   *homologies*

The response also shows an understanding of these key biological concepts: evolution, the relatedness of primates, and how humans are similar and different from other primates.

4. (a) In the morning, the stomata in the leaves of the plant would open and allow the intake of carbon dioxide and the release of oxygen. The plant would then begin to use the light energy from the sun to convert carbon dioxide and water into sugar molecules, which it will use as food, and oxygen. The process of transpiration is a critical one. Transpiration is the loss of water through the stomata. There must be a balance between the intake of carbon dioxide and the loss of water. Therefore, the plant must keep its stomata open during the day in order to use the sun's energy for photosynthesis, while risking loss of water through transpiration. When night falls, the plant will close its stomata to prevent unnecessary water loss. Because it can no longer get energy from the sun for photosynthesis, it doesn't need carbon dioxide.

Plants are generally bound to follow a biological clock that controls their circadian rhythms. The amounts of transpiration and enzyme synthesis fluctuate during the course of the day. Some of this is in response to changes in humidity and temperature that occur during the course of the day, but even without those external changes, the biological clock functions. Since this is a flowering plant, it will flower when the night length reaches a critical length; this is how a plant determines the time of season.

(b) If this plant is rotated 180°, plant hormones will act to start its growth in the direction facing the sun. This is thought to be because a plant responds to light by an asymmetrical distribution of auxin going down from the tip of the plant, which causes the cells on the darker side of the plant to elongate (not divide) more than the cells on the brighter side of the plant. Growth of a plant toward a light source is known as positive phototropism.

This is a good free-response answer because it shows knowledge of the following terms:

stomata   *circadian rhythm*
transpiration   *auxin*
photosynthesis   *phototropism*
biological clock

The response also shows an understanding of the following important biological processes: the daily metabolic cycle of plants and plant responses to light.

Practice Test 2

Biology
Section 1

Time—1 hour and 20 minutes

Directions: Each of the questions or incomplete statements below is followed by five suggested answers or completions. Select the one that is best in each case, and fill in the corresponding oval on the answer sheet.

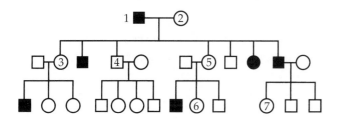

1. Which of the following patterns of inheritance best explains the transmission of the trait in the pedigree above?
   (A) Sex-linked dominant
   (B) Sex-linked recessive
   (C) Autosomal dominant
   (D) Autosomal recessive
   (E) Incompletely dominant

2. A geneticist crosses two rabbits, both of which have brown fur. In rabbits, brown fur is dominant over white fur. Six of the eight offspring produced have brown fur, and the other two have white fur. The genotypes of the parents were most likely which of the following?
   (A) $BB \times bb$
   (B) $BB \times Bb$
   (C) $Bb \times bb$
   (D) $Bb \times Bb$
   (E) $bb \times bb$

3. Which of the following is an example of simple diffusion across a membrane?
   (A) The movement of H^+ across the thylakoid membrane during photosynthesis
   (B) The uptake of neurotransmitters by the postsynaptic membrane during the transmission of a nerve impulse
   (C) The movement of oxygen in the alveoli across the epithelial membrane and into the bloodstream
   (D) The exchange of sodium and potassium across a cell membrane through the Na^+-K^+ pump
   (E) The movement of glucose across the body cell membranes and the cells of the liver, which stores it as glycogen

GO ON TO THE NEXT PAGE

4. Which of the following correctly represents the order of the tissues through which water and minerals will pass on their way up from a plant's roots?
   (A) Root hair, endodermis (Casparian strip), epidermis, cortex, stele
   (B) Root hair, cortex, epidermis, endodermis (Casparian strip), stele
   (C) Root hair, stele, cortex, endodermis (Casparian strip), epidermis
   (D) Root hair, epidermis, stele, cortex, endodermis (Casparian strip)
   (E) Root hair, epidermis, cortex, endodermis (Casparian strip), stele

5. Which of the following evolved before algae?
   (A) Bacteria
   (B) Hydras
   (C) Cnidarians
   (D) Fungi
   (E) Protists

6. Insertions and deletions may cause which of the following types of mutation?
   (A) Missense mutation
   (B) Nonsense mutation
   (C) Gene substitution
   (D) Base-pair substitution
   (E) Frameshift mutation

7. The stomata—the openings on the underside of a plant leaf through which carbon dioxide is taken up and oxygen is expelled—are opened as a result of
   (A) movement of mesophylls away from the stomatal opening
   (B) increased turgidity in the guard cells
   (C) decreased turgidity in the guard cells
   (D) growth of the guard cells toward the mesophyll
   (E) elongation of the guard cells toward the mesophyll

8. Which characteristic is NOT required of a population in Hardy-Weinberg equilibrium?
   (A) The population must be very large.
   (B) There must be no migration into or out of the population.
   (C) The members of the population must be mating randomly.
   (D) There must be only two alleles present for each characteristic in the population.
   (E) Natural selection must not be operating in the population.

9. The mitotic spindle consists of microtubules and which structure?
   (A) Centromere
   (B) Centrosome
   (C) Cytoplasm
   (D) Kinetochore
   (E) Metaphase plate

10. In plants that undergo alternation of generations, the gametophyte stage is always
    (A) a large visible plant
    (B) a seed
    (C) diploid
    (D) haploid
    (E) unicellular

11. Bacteria reproduce by which of the following processes?
    (A) Mitosis
    (B) Meiosis
    (C) Binary fission
    (D) Binary division
    (E) Cleavage

12. All of the following are factors contributing to the ascent of water through the xylem in plants EXCEPT
    (A) transpiration
    (B) low water potential at one end
    (C) cohesion of water to the vessel walls
    (D) adhesion of water to the vessel walls
    (E) sources and sinks

13. In plants, the abscission, or dropping, of leaves is triggered by changes in
    (A) cytokinin
    (B) ethylene
    (C) abscisic acid
    (D) gibberellins
    (E) brassinosteroids

14. Near the lungs, a branch from the pulmonary artery would contain which of the following?
    (A) Oxygen-rich blood
    (B) Oxygen-poor blood
    (C) Dissolved nutrients from the stomach
    (D) Blood rich in carbon monoxide
    (E) Lymph

15. Gel electrophoresis can be used for which of the following laboratory procedures?
    (A) Determining the molecular weight of proteins and nucleic acids
    (B) Determining the charge of proteins and nucleic acids
    (C) Separating nucleic acids and proteins on the basis of their size
    (D) Separating nucleic acids and proteins on the basis of their charge
    (E) Breaking up proteins and nucleic acids into their monomers

16. In humans, if red hair (R) is dominant to brown hair (r), and freckles (F) are dominant to no freckles (f), what fraction of the progeny of the cross $RrFf \times RRff$ will have red hair and no freckles?
    (A) $\frac{9}{16}$
    (B) $\frac{1}{2}$
    (C) $\frac{3}{8}$
    (D) $\frac{3}{16}$
    (E) $\frac{1}{16}$

17. Which of the following can be observed best by using a compound light microscope?
    (A) Atoms and molecules
    (B) Proteins
    (C) Ribosomes
    (D) Bacteria
    (E) Viruses

18. The phenomenon by which plants will bend toward or away from a light source is known as
    (A) photoaffinity
    (B) taxis
    (C) phototropism
    (D) thigmotropism
    (E) photophilia

19. All of the following are functions of microtubules in the cell EXCEPT
    (A) components of cilia, used for locomotion
    (B) components of flagellum, used for locomotion
    (C) involvement in the movement of chromosomes during cell division
    (D) components of the cytoskeleton, function in cell support
    (E) part of the nuclear membrane

20. Which of the following organelles is the site of macromolecule hydrolysis in the cell?
    (A) Mitochondria
    (B) Centrosome
    (C) Lysosome
    (D) Golgi apparatus
    (E) Ribosome

GO ON TO THE
NEXT PAGE

21. Which of the following describes how a dog that is prodded while asleep will respond to the touch initially, but will eventually ignore repeated prodding?
    (A) Habituation
    (B) Imprinting
    (C) Reasoning
    (D) Instinct
    (E) Trial and error

22. Which of the following is characteristic of a plant cell but not of an animal cell?
    (A) Rough endoplasmic reticulum
    (B) Cell membrane
    (C) Ribosomes
    (D) Large central vacuole
    (E) Golgi apparatus

23. When a species is split into two populations, separated by a geographic barrier that makes breeding between the populations impossible, this could eventually lead to
    (A) sympatric speciation
    (B) allopatric speciation
    (C) adaptive radiation
    (D) polyploid speciation
    (E) exaptation

24. The fact that pairs of alleles will segregate randomly during gamete formation describes which of the following laws?
    (A) The law of segregation
    (B) The law of independent segregation
    (C) The law of equal inheritance
    (D) The law of independent assortment
    (E) The law of equal segregation

25. In cows, eye color is controlled by a single gene with two alleles. When a homozygous cow with brown eyes is crossed with a homozygous cow with green eyes, cows with blue eyes are produced. If the blue-eyed cows are crossed with each other, what fraction of their offspring will have brown eyes?
    (A) 0
    (B) ¼
    (C) ½
    (D) ¾
    (E) 1

26. Which of the following is NOT an adaptation for gas exchange?
    (A) Lungs
    (B) Tracheal system
    (C) Gills
    (D) Moist epidermis
    (E) Sinuses

27. Which of the following best characterizes the reaction represented below?
    $A + B \rightarrow AB + energy$
    (A) Exergonic reaction
    (B) Endergonic reaction
    (C) Oxidation-reduction reaction
    (D) Catabolism
    (E) Hydrolysis

28. During prophase of mitosis, nuclear DNA is in which of the following forms?
    (A) Daughter chromosomes
    (B) Chromatin
    (C) Chromosomes consisting of two sister chromatids
    (D) Single sister chromatids
    (E) Single linear chromosomes

29. One way to measure the metabolic rate of a cell would be to measure the rate at which
    (A) CO_2 is consumed by the cell
    (B) O_2 is consumed by the cell
    (C) water is consumed by the cell
    (D) O_2 is produced by the cell
    (E) glucose is consumed by the cell

30. Which of the following is a site of translation in the cell?
    (A) The nucleus
    (B) The Golgi apparatus
    (C) Smooth ER
    (D) Rough ER
    (E) Mitochondria

31. In certain plant cells, the synthesis of ATP occurs in which of the following?
    (A) Ribosomes and mitochondria
    (B) Ribosomes and chloroplasts
    (C) Mitochondria and chloroplasts
    (D) Mitochondria and the cytoplasm
    (E) Chloroplasts and the cytoplasm

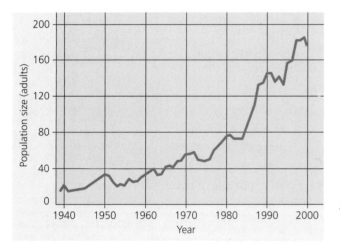

32. The graph above shows the rate of growth of a population of squirrels in a certain geographic area in Connecticut during the past several decades. This population is most closely exhibiting which of the following types of growth?
    (A) Logistic growth
    (B) Probable growth
    (C) *r*-selected growth
    (D) *K*-selected growth
    (E) Exponential growth

33. Genes *M* and *N* are located on different chromosomes, and the probability of their undergoing crossing over is quite low. If the probability of allele *M* segregating into a gamete is ⅙, and the probability of allele *N* segregating into a gamete is ¼, then the probability that both of them will segregate into the same gamete is
    (A) ¹⁄₁₂
    (B) ¼
    (C) ⁵⁄₁₂
    (D) ¾
    (E) 1

34. Two individuals who are carriers for cystic fibrosis (a recessively inherited disorder) have 3 children together. None of the children have cystic fibrosis. What is the probability that the couple's fourth child will be born with cystic fibrosis?
    (A) 0%
    (B) 25%
    (C) 50%
    (D) 75%
    (E) 100%

35. Which of the following groups comprise a strand of DNA?
    (A) Phosphate groups, deoxyriboses, and nitrogenous bases
    (B) Phosphate groups, riboses, and nitrogenous bases
    (C) Phosphate groups, deoxyriboses, and amino acids
    (D) Phosphate groups, riboses, and amino acids
    (E) Deoxyriboses and nitrogenous bases

GO ON TO THE NEXT PAGE

36. The statement that evolutionary changes are composed of rapid bursts of speciation that alternate with long periods in which species do not change significantly is known as
(A) gradualism
(B) punctuated gradualism
(C) punctuated equilibrium
(D) sympatric speciation
(E) allopatric speciation

37. Which of the following vertebrates lacks an amnion during its development?
(A) Bird
(B) Human
(C) Lizard
(D) Frog
(E) Alligator

38. Which of the following is capable of reverse transcription, with an RNA → DNA information flow?
(A) Viruses
(B) Retroviruses
(C) T cells
(D) B cells
(E) Ciliates

39. Compared with prokaryotic cells, eukaryotic cells are generally
(A) smaller but more complex
(B) larger and more complex
(C) smaller and less complex
(D) larger but less complex
(E) the same size but more complex

40. Which of the following plant hormones is responsible for stimulating stem elongation, root growth, and cell differentiation?
(A) Ethylene
(B) Abscisic acid
(C) Cytokinin
(D) Gibberellin
(E) Auxin

41. In terms of evolution, which of the following is closest to fungi?
(A) Plants
(B) Animals
(C) Archaea
(D) Bacteria
(E) Viruses

42. In humans, which of the following glands is responsible for secreting several hormones involved in reproduction?
(A) Thyroid gland
(B) Adrenal cortex
(C) Adrenal medulla
(D) Anterior pituitary
(E) Posterior pituitary

43. Which is thought to have been the first self-replicating genetic material?
(A) DNA
(B) RNA
(C) cDNA
(D) mRNA
(E) tRNA

44. When a break in the epidermal layer of humans occurs, which type of blood cell travels in great numbers to the break and releases clotting factors?
(A) Leukocytes
(B) Erythrocytes
(C) Helper T cells
(D) Helper B cells
(E) Platelets

45. In photosynthesis, the functional product(s) of the light reactions
(A) are ATP and NADPH
(B) are ATP and NADH
(C) is glyceraldehyde
(D) is glucose
(E) are carbohydrates

46. Which group is best characterized as being eukaryotic and saprophytic with hyphae?
    (A) Protista
    (B) Plantae
    (C) Archaea
    (D) Fungi
    (E) Animalia

47. In humans, color blindness is a sex-linked recessive trait. If a man and a woman have a son who is color blind, which of the following must be true?
    (A) The father is color blind.
    (B) Both parents carry the allele for color blindness.
    (C) Neither parent carries the allele for color blindness.
    (D) The father carries the allele for color blindness.
    (E) The mother carries the allele for color blindness.

48. If a horse breeds with a donkey, a mule is produced. Mules are not capable of breeding with either parental species, or each other. This is an example of what type of postzygotic barrier?
    (A) Reduced hybrid viability
    (B) Hybrid sterility
    (C) Hybrid breakdown
    (D) Mechanical isolation
    (E) Gametic isolation

49. Radioactive isotopes can be used to date fossils. The amount of time it takes for half of a radioactive isotope to decay is also known as the substance's
    (A) release rate
    (B) radioactive decay rate
    (C) half-life
    (D) time scale
    (E) decay rate

50. The female gametophytes of a plant develop in the ovaries of the plant, whereas the male gametophyte develops in which plant structure?
    (A) Stigma
    (B) Style
    (C) Carpel
    (D) Anther
    (E) Sepal

51. Which of the following is the most direct result of the presence of salivary amylase in the mouth?
    (A) The breakdown of proteins
    (B) The breakdown of polypeptides
    (C) The breakdown of lipids
    (D) The breakdown of carbohydrates
    (E) The breakdown of nucleic acids

52. The leaves of a plant appear green to us because
    (A) chlorophyll reflects green light
    (B) chlorophyll absorbs green light
    (C) chlorophyll reflects red light
    (D) chlorophyll reflects blue light
    (E) chlorophyll is green, and plants contain hundreds of chlorophyll molecules

53. What bonds are responsible for ice being less dense than liquid water and water being a good insulator?
    (A) Ionic
    (B) Covalent
    (C) Polar covalent
    (D) Hydrogen
    (E) Double

GO ON TO THE NEXT PAGE

54. Which of the following is the insulating layer wrapped around nerve cells that increases the speed of nerve impulse transmission?
    (A) Axons
    (B) Dendrites
    (C) Synaptic terminal
    (D) Myelin sheath
    (E) Nodes of Ranvier

55. Which of the following is the substrate in the citric acid cycle?
    (A) Carbon dioxide
    (B) Acetyl CoA
    (C) Citrate
    (D) Oxaloacetate
    (E) Glucose

56. Insects, spiders, and crustaceans are all classified in which phylum?
    (A) Arthropoda
    (B) Annelida
    (C) Chordata
    (D) Nemertea
    (E) Cnidaria

Directions: Each group of questions below consists of five lettered choices followed by a list of numbered phrases or sentences. For each numbered phrase or sentence, select the one choice (or item) that is most closely related to it. Each choice may be used once, more than once, or not at all in each group.

Questions 57–59
    (A) Meiosis II
    (B) Meiosis I
    (C) Binary fission
    (D) Mitosis
    (E) Interphase

57. The process during which prokaryotes reproduce

58. The process during which the diploid chromosome number is reduced by half

59. The process during which the genetic material of the cell is replicated

Questions 60–64
    (A) Amphibia
    (B) Reptilia
    (C) Echinodermata
    (D) Chordata
    (E) Chondrichthyes

60. Members have cartilaginous skeletons and include sharks and sea rays.

61. Members have a water vascular system and include sea stars and sea cucumbers.

62. Members have eggs without shells, and some have a moist epithelium that participates in gas exchange.

63. Members have scales, lungs, and amniotic eggs.

64. Members have a notochord and pharyngeal clefts and include humans.

Questions 65–69
    (A) Electron transport chain
    (B) Chemiosmosis
    (C) Glycolysis
    (D) The citric acid cycle
    (E) Light reactions of photosynthesis

65. Drives the synthesis of ATP through a hydrogen ion gradient

66. Occurs in all living cells and is the starting point for aerobic respiration and fermentation

67. Is part of cellular respiration and completes the breakdown of glucose into carbon dioxide

68. Shuttles electrons and releases energy that is used to make ATP

69. Photoexcited electrons pass from one photosystem to the next via an electron transport chain.

Questions 70–73
(A) Population
(B) Community
(C) Species
(D) Niche
(E) Biome

70. Members are capable of interbreeding and are anatomically similar.

71. The biotic and abiotic resources a species uses in its environment

72. Individuals of one species that live in a discrete geographic area

73. All the organisms that live within a discrete geographic area

Questions 74–78
(A) Antigens
(B) Antibodies
(C) Histamines
(D) Eosinophils
(E) Macrophages

74. Large phagocytotic cells that engulf microbes

75. A type of white blood cell that damages invaders with destructive enzymes

76. Proteins that bind antigens

77. Foreign molecules that elicit an immune response

78. Chemical signals released in response to injury

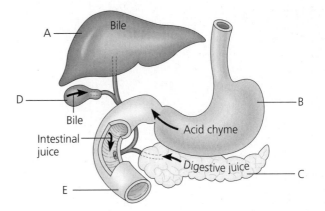

Questions 79–83
Identify the letter pointing to each organ.

79. Stomach

80. Gallbladder

81. Duodenum

82. Pancreas

83. Liver

Questions 84–86
Identify the letter that points to each description.

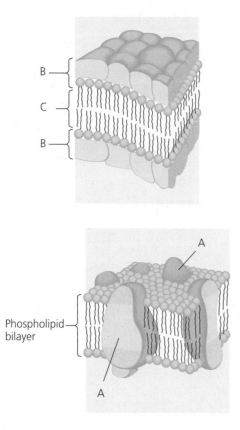

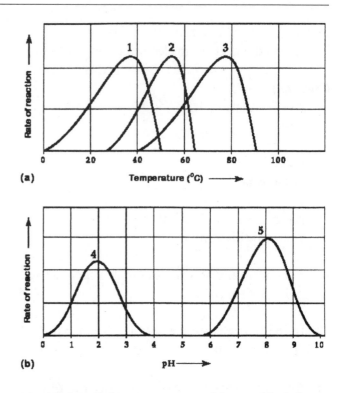

(a) Temperature (°C) →

(b) pH →

84. The hydrophilic zone of the plasma membrane

85. The hydrophobic zone of the plasma membrane

86. Allows for facilitated diffusion across the membrane

Directions: Each group of questions below concerns an experimental or laboratory situation or data. In each case, first study the description of the situation or data. Then choose the one best answer to each question following it.

Questions 87–89
The rate of reaction for 3 enzymes was calculated at different temperatures, and the rate of reaction for 2 additional enzymes was calculated at different pH levels. The results are shown in the following graphs. Assume that the *y*-axes share the same scale.

87. Which of the enzymes would most likely be able to function in the human bloodstream?
(A) 1 and 4
(B) 1, 2, and 4
(C) 1, 2, and 5
(D) 3 and 4
(E) 3 and 5

88. Which of the enzymes would be most likely to function in the geysers of Yellowstone National Park?
(A) 1
(B) 2
(C) 3
(D) 4
(E) 5

89. Which of these enzymes is most efficient—that is, has the highest rate of reaction?
(A) 1
(B) 2
(C) 3
(D) 4
(E) 5

Questions 90–92
A scientist studying the mammalian heart is experimenting on a white rat. She injects different radioactive elements into different sections of the rat's heart. The chart below lists where she injected each substance.

Heart chamber	Radioactive Isotope Used
Right ventricle	^{32}P
Right atrium	^{3}H
Left ventricle	^{14}C
Left atrium	^{238}U

90. Just after its injection, where would the radioactive isotope ^{238}U be detected first?
   (A) Left ventricle
   (B) Right ventricle
   (C) Right atrium
   (D) Systemic capillaries
   (E) Pulmonary capillaries

91. Just after its injection, the blood injected with ^{14}C would be detected performing which of the following tasks in the body?
   (A) Picking up oxygen from the systemic capillaries
   (B) Transporting oxygen to systemic capillaries
   (C) Picking up oxygen in the capillaries of the lungs
   (D) Dropping off carbon dioxide in the capillaries of the lungs
   (E) Delivering oxygen to the capillaries of the lungs

92. Just after its injection of ^{32}P, the blood injected with ^{32}P would be detected performing which of the following tasks in the body?
   (A) Picking up oxygen from the systemic capillaries
   (B) Delivering oxygen to the systemic capillaries
   (C) Picking up oxygen in the capillaries of the lungs
   (D) Dropping off carbon monoxide in the capillaries of the lungs
   (E) Delivering oxygen to the capillaries of the lungs

Questions 93–94 refer to the graph shown below.

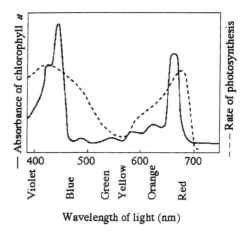

Wavelength of light (nm)

93. A biologist would use which of the following terms to refer to the solid line in the graph?
   (A) Action spectrum
   (B) Absorption spectrum
   (C) Photostimulation curve
   (D) Electromagnetic spectrum
   (E) Visible light spectrum

94. Which of the following is the best reason the curve for the absorbency of light by chlorophyll *a* does not perfectly match the rate of photosynthesis?
   (A) The rate of photosynthesis is always fractionally slower than the rate of absorbency by chlorophyll *a*.
   (B) The rate of photosynthesis is always fractionally faster than the rate of absorbency by chlorophyll *a*.
   (C) There are fewer chlorophyll *a* molecules in the cell than the other molecules involved in photosynthesis, so chlorophyll *a* is the rate-limiting reagent.
   (D) Chlorophyll *a* is not the only photosynthetically important pigment in chloroplasts.
   (E) Light of about 550 nm inhibits all photosynthesis.

GO ON TO THE NEXT PAGE

Questions 95–98
An ecologist studying a certain biogeographic area has sketched the following food web for the community that lives there. The arrows represent energy flow, the letters represent species.

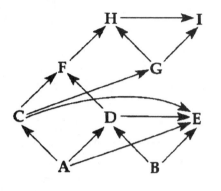

95. Which of the following is most likely to be autotrophic?
 (A) E
 (B) A
 (C) I
 (D) G
 (E) D

96. Which members of the food web are secondary consumers?
 (A) D, E, and F
 (B) A, B, and C
 (C) G, H, and I
 (D) E, F, and G
 (E) B, D, and E

97. Which of the species in the food web are exclusively carnivores?
 (A) E, F, G, H, and I
 (B) F, G, H, and I
 (C) C, D, and E
 (D) F and G
 (E) H and I

98. If this were a savanna ecosystem, what organisms are species A and B most likely to represent?
 (A) Two species of small low-growing bushes
 (B) Two species of lichen
 (C) Two species of insects
 (D) Two species of rodent
 (E) Two species of grasses

Questions 99–100 refer to the following table, which shows the temperature at which the DNA of various species has been found to denature.

Species	Temperature at Which DNA Denatures
A	25°C
B	80°C
C	72°C
D	58°C
E	57°C

99. Which of the species in this table are most likely to be related most closely evolutionarily?
 (A) A and B
 (B) B and C
 (C) C and D
 (D) D and E
 (E) A and E

100. What other experimental method besides heating could be used to denature DNA strands in order to obtain the same type of information?
 (A) Adding a buffer to the DNA samples
 (B) Adding a solvent to the DNA samples
 (C) Slowly lowering the pH of the DNA samples
 (D) Slowly adding free bases to the DNA samples
 (E) Freezing the samples

END OF SECTION I

Biology
Section II

Time—10 minutes to plan responses; 1 hour and 30 minutes for writing

Answer all questions. Number your answers as the questions are numbered below.

Answers must be in essay form. Outline form is NOT acceptable. Labeled diagrams may be used to supplement discussion, but in no case will a diagram alone suffice. It is important that you read each question completely before you begin to write.

1. The cell membrane is one of the most important parts of a cell; it allows the selective passage of materials into and out of the cell, thereby maintaining a constant, desired internal composition.
   (a) **Discuss** the components of a typical animal cell membrane, as well as the roles each of these components plays in regulating the cell's internal environment.
   (b) **Discuss** the ways in which the following can enter an animal cell, including:
      • viral DNA.
      • hormones.
      • water molecules.

2. It is thought that the terrestrial plants we see around us today evolved from aquatic algae.
   (a) **Discuss** three obstacles to the movement of plants to land.
   (b) **Discuss** three adaptations that have evolved in terrestrial plants that combat the obstacles above.

3. **Describe** the process of cell division in a typical plant cell, including:
   (a) the cell cycle of a plant cell.
   (b) the process of mitosis.
   (c) cytokinesis.

4. It is theorized that glycolysis was the first metabolic pathway for the production of ATP.
   (a) **Provide** three pieces of evidence that support this point.
   (b) **Describe** how the citric acid cycle is related to chemiosmosis and oxidative phosphorylation.

END OF EXAMINATION

ANSWERS AND EXPLANATIONS

Multiple-Choice Questions

1. **(B) is correct.** The trait is sex-linked and recessive. Two sets of unaffected parents in the second generation have a child that is affected. You can tell that the trait is sex-linked because five out of the six people affected by the trait are males.

2. **(D) is correct.** Because both parents have brown fur, but they produce some white offspring, you have to conclude that both rabbits were heterozygous. Each parent must have a recessive allele to pass on.

3. **(C) is correct.** The movement of oxygen from the clusters of alveoli at the tips of the bronchioles in the lung, across the epithelial walls, and into the bloodstream is an example of passive diffusion. Carbon dioxide moves from the bloodstream back into the lungs, to be expelled during exhalation in the same way—through diffusion. All of the answers except *C* are examples of active transport.

4. **(E) is correct.** The order of tissues through which water and certain minerals will pass as they travel from the roots to the xylem (then to be transported through the entire plant) is as follows: into the root hair cell, through the epidermis, through the cortex, through the endodermis (where the Casparian strip acts as a filter), and then into the stele (which contains the xylem vessels).

5. **(A) is correct.** Bacteria are the only living organisms among the answers to evolve before algae; bacteria are prokaryotes, whereas algae are eukaryotes. The earliest eukaryotes were single-celled algae, and they are thought to have evolved about a half billion years after prokaryotes.

6. **(E) is correct.** Insertions and deletions are point mutations that occur when one nucleotide pair is added or lost in a gene. They have a detrimental effect on the protein product of the gene, because they often affect the reading frame of the gene—all of the codons downstream of the insertion or deletion will be grouped incorrectly and will be misread.

7. **(B) is correct.** The stomata open as a result of increased turgidity of the guard cells that flank them. As a result of this increased turgidity, they become turgid and buckle, causing a space to open between them. The change in turgidity in the guard cells is influenced by uptake and loss of potassium ions.

8. **(D) is correct.** All of the answers listed are conditions that must be met for a population to be in Hardy-Weinberg equilibrium—except the criteria that there must be only two alleles present for each characteristic. Any population that is not in Hardy-Weinberg equilibrium will evolve, and natural populations rarely achieve this type of equilibrium for extended periods of time.

9. **(B) is correct.** During mitosis and meiosis, the microtubules begin to be assembled at the centrosome, which is a cell organelle that organizes the microtubules. Animal cells have a pair of centrioles at the center of their centrosomes. Together, the centrosomes and microtubules form a spindle.

10. **(D) is correct.** The two forms that alternate in plants undergoing alternation of generations are the sporophyte and the gametophyte. The sporophyte is

the diploid form (cells with two sets of chromosomes), and the gametophyte is the haploid form (cells with one set of chromosomes).

- ▌ **11. (C) is correct.** Bacteria reproduce by a process called binary fission. Most bacteria contain a single, circular chromosome that also contains associated proteins. They start to replicate this circular chromosome. One of the copies moves toward one end of the cell. At the end of replication, the plasma membrane pinches inward and a new cell wall is formed, resulting in two identical daughter cells.

- ▌ **12. (E) is correct.** Sources and sinks do not contribute to the movement of water and minerals up through the xylem of the plant. The movement of sugars from sources to sinks occurs through the phloem, which distributes the products of photosynthesis from the leaves throughout the plant.

- ▌ **13. (B) is correct.** The plant hormone responsible for promoting leaf abscission, or the loss of leaves each fall, is ethylene. This practice prevents trees from dehydrating in winter when the ground is frozen and water is unavailable. Ethylene is also responsible for fruit ripening and for controlling the growth of roots, leaves, and flowers.

- ▌ **14. (B) is correct.** A branch from the pulmonary artery located near the lungs would be oxygen poor. The branches from the pulmonary artery carry oxygen-poor blood away from the heart to the lung's alveoli for oxygenation. Pulmonary veins return oxygenated blood to the heart, which then pumps the oxygenated blood to the rest of the body.

- ▌ **15. (C) is correct.** Gel electrophoresis is a procedure used in a laboratory to separate proteins and nucleic acids on the basis of their size—essentially, the rate at which they move through a gel when an electric field is applied. Larger segments of DNA move through gel at a slower pace than smaller segments.

- ▌ **16. (B) is correct.** The answer is ½. In order to deduce this, you should first determine the gametes that each of the parents could produce. The first parent could produce the gametes *RF*, *Rf*, *rF*, and *rf*; the second parent would produce only *Rf* gametes. Use a Punnett square to help you figure out the proportions of offspring based on these gametes.

- ▌ **17. (D) is correct.** Most bacteria can be seen with a compound light microscope, whereas all of the other structures listed are too small to be seen with this type of microscope. They must be viewed with an electron microscope.

- ▌ **18. (C) is correct.** Phototropism refers to a plant's growth in response to a light source. Negative phototropism occurs when a shoot grows away from a light source, and positive phototropism occurs when a shoot grows toward the light source.

- ▌ **19. (E) is correct.** Microtubules are involved in all of the cell functions listed except as a component of the nuclear membrane. The nuclear membrane, as all the other membranes of the cell, is composed mainly of phospholipids and associated proteins. Microtubules in the cell function in the roles of support and movement.

- ▌ **20. (C) is correct.** Lysosomes are digestive compartments in the cell. They are membrane-bound sacs containing hydrolytic enzymes that can digest macromolecules such as proteins, sugars, fats, and nucleic acids; the lysosomal interior has a low pH that aids in the breakdown of these large molecules.

21. (A) is correct. Habituation is one of the simplest types of learning; it is a loss of responsiveness to a stimulus that conveys limited information or no information at all. If the dog learns that the prodding is not associated with any type of outcome—soon it will learn to ignore the sensation.

22. (D) is correct. One difference between plant cells and animal cells is that plant cells have a large central vacuole. This vacuole is important to the plant because it acts as a stockroom for necessary organic compounds and is a repository for inorganic ions. The vacuole can make up about 80% of a plant's total volume.

23. (B) is correct. One of the two general types of speciation is allopatric speciation. In allopatric speciation, two populations are geographically separate, with no link between the two populations. The other type of speciation is sympatric speciation. In this case, two populations are in the same geographic area, but biological factors (such as chromosome changes and nonrandom mating) reduce gene flow.

24. (D) is correct. Mendel's law of independent assortment states that during gamete formation, each pair of alleles will segregate independently of one another; which allele travels to which gamete is independent of the actions of the other alleles.

25. (B) is correct. If you say that the brown-eyed homozygous cow has genotype $E^B E^B$ and the green-eyed homozygous cow has genotype $E^G E^G$, then all of their offspring would be genotype $E^B E^G$ (blue-eyed). With a Punnett square, you can see that crossing two individuals with genotype $E^B E^G$ would give you offspring in the following ratio: 1 $E^B E^B$:2 $E^B E^G$:1 $E^G E^G$. So ¼ of the offspring would have genotype $E^B E^B$, or brown eyes.

26. (E) is correct. The only adaptation listed that is not used for gas exchange is the sinuses, which are basically just spaces surrounding the organs of the body of animals that have open circulatory systems. Fish have gills, many insects have tracheal systems, many vertebrates have lungs, and some amphibians such as frogs also exchange gases across their moist epithelium.

27. (A) is correct. In reactions that are exergonic, energy is given off—often in the form of heat—during the course of the reaction. Conversely, endergonic reactions require the input of energy in order to proceed. In written reactions, the reactants are generally written on the left side of the arrow, and the products are written on the right side of the arrow.

28. (C) is correct. During prophase of mitosis, the DNA exists in the form of chromosomes consisting of two sister chromatids. During interphase, the DNA exists as chromatin, which is loose DNA and protein. As mitosis begins, the newly replicated DNA condenses into chromosomes composed of the two newly formed sister chromatids.

29. (B) is correct. O_2 receives electrons from the electron transport chain and forms water during the process of oxidative phosphorylation, and the cell makes ATP through the oxidative phosphorylation. So measuring the rate of consumption of O_2 by the cell is a good way to determine its metabolic rate.

30. (D) is correct. Transcription (the process by which DNA is transcribed into mRNA) takes place in the nucleus, whereas translation (the process by which mRNA is translated into the amino acid sequence of a polypeptide) takes place at ribosomes. Some ribosomes are associated with the rough endoplasmic reticulum, a series of continuous membranes in the cell. Smooth ER is not associated with ribosomes.

31. **(C) is correct.** In plant cells, both chloroplasts and mitochondria produce ATP by chemiosmosis. The thylakoid membrane of the chloroplasts and the inner mitochondrial membrane of the mitochondria and electron transport chain pump protons across the membrane. This energy is used to power an ATP synthase that produces ATP.

32. **(E) is correct.** This population is exhibiting exponential growth. Exponential growth can occur when the conditions in an environment are ideal—when there is enough of, or an excess of, required resources in an environment. The population then grows at its maximum rate until it reaches its carrying capacity.

33. **(C) is correct.** According to the addition rule, the probability that an event will occur in two or more different ways can be calculated by adding the separate probabilities of those two ways. In this case, you can figure out the probability of alleles *M* and *N* segregating into the same gamete by adding the probabilities that either will segregate into a gamete: $\frac{1}{4} + \frac{1}{6} = \frac{5}{12}$.

34. **(B) is correct.** The carrier parents would each have the genotype *Aa*. This means that their children would have a 25% chance of inheriting both of the recessive genes, with the genotype *aa*. The fact that their first three children do not have cystic fibrosis in no way affects the probability of the fourth child having cystic fibrosis—these events are unrelated.

35. **(A) is correct.** The groups that comprise a strand of DNA are phosphate groups, deoxyriboses, and nitrogenous bases. The four nitrogenous bases contained in DNA are adenine, thymine, guanine, and cytosine.

36. **(C) is correct.** Punctuated equilibrium is the term used for the idea that evolutionary change in a species occurs in rapid bursts alternating with long periods of little or no change. Gradualism is the model of evolution in which species evolve gradually and diverge more and more as time passes.

37. **(D) is correct.** The frog is the only animal listed that does not have an amnion at some stage in its development. An amnion is the innermost of the four extraembryonic membranes; it contains a fluid-filled sac in which the embryo is suspended. Frog eggs can develop without this protective sac because they are laid in aquatic environments.

38. **(B) is correct.** Retroviruses are viruses that are capable of reverse transcription—they use an enzyme called reverse transcriptase to transcribe DNA from an RNA template. This newly made cDNA integrates into the chromosome of an animal cell and is copied along with the animal cells' DNA.

39. **(B) is correct.** Eukaryotic cells are generally larger than prokaryotic cells, and they are more complex. Unlike eukaryotes, they have no nucleus (their genetic material is concentrated in a nucleoid region); they also lack many of the cell organelles that eukaryotes have. They are very simple cells.

40. **(E) is correct.** Auxins are plant hormones that are responsible for stimulating stem elongation (when they are present in low concentration), root

growth, cell differentiation, and shoot branching. They also regulate the development of fruits, and they function in gravitropism and phototropism.

41. (B) is correct. In several important characteristics, such as nutritional mode, structural organization, growth, and reproductive technique, the fungi are more similar to animals than to plants. Molecular studies have also supported this finding.

42. (D) is correct. The anterior pituitary is responsible for the secretion of some hormones that are involved in the human reproductive cycle, such as follicle-stimulating hormone (which stimulates production of sperm and ova) and luteinizing hormone (which stimulates the ovaries and testes).

43. (B) is correct. The first genetic material may have been short pieces of RNA that served as templates for aligning amino acids in polypeptide synthesis and for aligning nucleotides in a primitive form of self-replication. Early protobionts with self-replicating, catalytic RNA would have been more effective at using resources and would have increased in number through natural selection.

44. (E) is correct. Platelets are small, enucleated blood cell fragments that are derived from bone marrow. They travel to the site of a break in the skin and release clotting factors, which through a complex set of reactions transform fibrinogen to fibrin, which in turn aggregates into threads that form a framework for a clot, sealing the break.

45. (A) is correct. The light reactions of photosynthesis convert solar energy to chemical energy in the form of ATP and NADPH. They do this when light is absorbed by various pigments in the thylakoid membrane of the chloroplasts; the pigments pass the energy down a chain of electron acceptors, and in the process, ATP and NADPH are produced.

46. (D) is correct. Fungi are eukaryotes that are decomposers—also known as saprobes. They absorb nutrients from nonliving organic material such as decomposing plants, dead animals, or wastes from living animals. The bodies of fungi are composed of hyphae—tiny filaments that form a mat called a mycelium.

47. (E) is correct. If a sex-linked trait is recessive, the female will express it only if she is homozygous for it, whereas a male needs only to receive the affected allele from his mother in order to be affected. If this couple produces a color-blind son, then the mother must carry the allele for color blindness. If the father is color blind, he cannot pass the trait on to a son because all sons inherit a Y chromosome from their father, rather than an X.

48. (B) is correct. This is an example of hybrid sterility—if two species mate and produce offspring, they can still be reproductively isolated if their offspring cannot reproduce.

49. (C) is correct. The half-life of a radioactive isotope is the amount of time it takes for half of the original sample to decay. The half-life is useful because it is unaffected by temperature, pressure, or any other changes in environment.

50. (D) is correct. Pollen grains are the male gametophytes of flowering plants. In the anthers of the plant are microspores, which divide by mitosis to produce a generative cell nucleus and a pollen tube cell nucleus. A pollen grain consists of these two nuclei enclosed in a thick wall.

51. (D) is correct. Salivary amylase is an enzyme that is found in human saliva and secreted into the oral cavity. It is capable of hydrolyzing starch (a glucose polymer found in plants) and glycogen (a glucose polymer in animal tissues). Salivary amylase breaks down these carbohydrates into maltose and other disaccharides.

52. (A) is correct. We perceive the leaves of plants to be green because chlorophyll absorbs blue and red light while reflecting and transmitting green light.

53. (D) is correct. Because water molecules can form relatively strong hydrogen bonds between them, many unique characteristics of water result. These characteristics include good insulation properties with a high specific heat, greater density in liquid form than solid form, and high surface tension.

54. (D) is correct. In the nervous system, some nerve cells (neurons) are covered by Schwann cells, which are wrapped in myelin. As the nerve impulse travels the length of the nerve cell, it jumps along the gaps between Schwann cells. These gaps are called nodes of Ranvier.

55. (B) is correct. In cellular respiration, the pyruvate that is produced in glycolysis is converted to acetyl CoA, which then enters the citric acid cycle. In each "turn" of the citric acid cycle, acetyl CoA is oxidized, CO_2 is reduced, and the following are produced: 1 ATP, 3 NADH, and 1 $FADH_2$.

56. (A) is correct. All of the listed animals are part of the phylum Arthropoda. Arthropods are characterized by their segmentation, hard exoskeleton, and jointed appendages. The exoskeleton of arthropods is composed of protein and chitin—and in order to grow, arthropods must shed their hard exoskeleton in a process called molting.

57. (C) is correct. Binary fission is the process by which bacteria reproduce. The bacterium replicates its DNA, and the DNA migrates to opposite ends of the cell. Then the plasma membrane infolds, and a cell wall begins to divide the two daughter cells.

58. (A) is correct. In meiosis II, the chromosome number of the cell is reduced by half. The parent cell is diploid, with a chromosome number of $2n$; the daughter cells are haploid, or n.

59. (E) is correct. Interphase of the cell cycle is the phase during which the cell grows and replicates its genetic material. Mitosis, which is divided into several phases, is the part of the cell cycle during which the cell divides.

60. (E) is correct. Sharks and rays are in the class Chondrichthyes; they have cartilaginous skeletons as well as jaws and paired fins.

61. (C) is correct. Sea stars and sea cucumbers are both part of the phylum Echinodermata. These animals are slow moving and have a radial body plan. Echinoderms have a water vascular system, which is a network of canals that function in movement, feeding, and gas exchange.

62. (A) is correct. These are characteristics of the class Amphibia, which includes frogs and salamanders. Amphibians are characterized by being both aquatic and terrestrial, as well as by laying eggs that have no exterior shell (which would dehydrate quickly if not laid in water).

63. (B) is correct. Reptiles such as snakes and lizards have several adaptations for land that amphibians don't have, such as scales and lungs. Reptiles are ectotherms; they absorb external heat instead of regulating their internal body temperature.

64. (D) is correct. Chordates such as humans are characterized by having a notochord; pharyngeal clefts (at some point in their development); a post-anal tail (again at some point in their development); and a dorsal, hollow nerve cord.

65. (B) is correct. Chemiosmosis is an energy-coupling reaction. The energy created by a hydrogen gradient formed across a membrane is used to drive the synthesis of ATP.

66. (C) is correct. Glycolysis is the process by which glucose is split into two molecules of pyruvate. It is a metabolic pathway that occurs in all living cells and is the first part of cellular respiration and fermentation.

67. (D) is correct. The citric acid cycle completes the breakdown of glucose started in glycolysis. In the citric acid cycle, acetyl CoA is broken down completely into carbon dioxide. It occurs in the mitochondria and is the second part of cellular respiration.

68. (A) is correct. An electron transport chain is composed of a series of electron carriers (which are proteins) embedded in a membrane. They shuttle electrons and, in the process, release energy that is used to make ATP.

69. (E) is correct. In the light reactions of photosynthesis, solar energy is converted to the chemical energy of ATP. One step of this occurs when photoexcited electrons are passed from one photosystem to the next in an electron transport chain that functions similarly to the one in cellular respiration.

70. (C) is correct. A species is defined as a population or group of populations whose members can interbreed with one another to produce viable, fertile offspring.

71. (D) is correct. An organism's ecological niche is the sum total of its use of biotic and abiotic resources in its environment.

72. (A) is correct. A population is defined as a group of individuals of one species that live together in a certain geographic area.

73. (B) is correct. A community consists of all of the populations of organisms that live in a particular geographic area.

74. (E) is correct. Monocytes develop into macrophages—phagocytic cells found in many tissues that function in innate immunity by destroying microbes and in acquired immunity as antigen-presenting cells.

75. (D) is correct. Eosinophils are leukocytes that act against large parasitic invaders; they position themselves against the wall of a parasite and inject destructive enzymes into the invader.

76. (B) is correct. Antibodies are secreted by B cells. They are proteins that are specific to antigens. They represent the effectors in an immune response.

77. (A) is correct. Antigens are foreign particles in the body that elicit a response from the immune system.

78. (C) is correct. Histamines are chemical signals that are released by cells of the body in response to an injury; they are stored in and released by mast cells.

79. (B) is correct. The stomach is an elastic muscular sac that stores and starts to digest food. It secretes gastric juice, which contains enzymes that start the initial digestion of proteins. The churning motion of the stomach walls also facilitates digestion.

- **80. (D) is correct.** The gallbladder is an organ found near the liver that stores bile and releases it into the small intestine when needed to emulsify fats.
- **81. (E) is correct.** The duodenum is the first section of the small intestine, where acid chyme from the stomach mixes together with digestive juices from the pancreas, liver, gallbladder, and walls of the small intestine.
- **82. (C) is correct.** The pancreas secretes digestive enzymes—as well as an alkaline solution—into the small intestine.
- **83. (A) is correct.** The liver produces bile, and bile is stored in the gallbladder. It acts as a detergent, aiding in the digestion of fats.
- **84. (B) is correct.** The phospholipid bilayer is made up of phospholipids, which have a hydrophilic head group and two hydrophobic, fatty acid chains. The head group points inward to the cytoplasm and outward to the interstitial fluid.
- **85. (C) is correct.** The hydrophobic fatty acid tails of the phospholipids point toward each other, avoiding contact with the cytoplasm and the watery environment outside of the cell.
- **86. (A) is correct.** Proteins are both embedded in the phospholipid bilayer (these are integral proteins) and associated with the cytosol face of the cell membrane (these are called peripheral proteins).
- **87. (C) is correct.** The enzymes that would be able to function in the bloodstream of humans according to this data are 1, 2, and 5. The temperature of the human body is about 36–38 degrees Celsius, so enzymes 1 and 2 would be somewhat functional; the pH of the bloodstream is about 7.4. Only enzyme 5 would function at that pH.
- **88. (C) is correct.** The enzyme most likely to function in the hot springs of Yellowstone National Park is enzyme 3, which has an optimal activity at a temperature of about 80 degrees Celsius. Enzymes of thermophilic (heat-loving) bacteria work best at very high temperatures.
- **89. (E) is correct.** Enzyme 5 is the most efficient enzyme in this example—it has the highest rate of reaction. This means that its optimal rate is faster than that of any of the other enzymes depicted, assuming a standard measurement for the y-axes of both graphs.
- **90. (A) is correct.** Just after the ^{238}U was injected into the left atrium, it would travel to the left ventricle. Blood enters the heart through the right and left atria; next it travels to the right or left ventricle.
- **91. (B) is correct.** Just after it was injected, the blood carrying the radioactive carbon would be detected dropping off oxygen in the systemic capillaries. Blood leaves the left ventricle, enters the aorta, and then travels through the body, dropping off oxygen to active metabolic tissues.
- **92. (C) is correct.** Just after it was injected, the blood carrying ^{32}P would be found in the lung capillaries, where it would be picking up oxygen and dropping off carbon dioxide before returning to the heart through the left atrium. Oxygen-depleted blood is pumped through the right side of the heart on its way to the lungs.
- **93. (B) is correct.** An absorption spectrum is a graph plotting a particular pigment's light absorption—that is, the fraction of light not reflected or transmitted

versus the wavelength of light. This is a plot of the absorbency of the chlorophyll a pigment versus light wavelength.

94. **(D) is correct.** The reason the action spectrum for photosynthesis doesn't match the absorption spectrum for chlorophyll *a* is because chlorophyll *a* is not the only photosynthetically important pigment in the chloroplast. Two other photosynthetically important pigments are chlorophyll *b* and carotenoids.

95. **(B) is correct.** Species A is most likely to be autotrophic—autotrophs convert light energy from the sun into chemical energy of organic molecules. As you can see, species A does not consume any other species (likewise with B), so it must produce its own food by obtaining energy from the sun.

96. **(D) is correct.** Species E, F, and G are all secondary consumers in this food web. Secondary consumers consume primary consumers, and primary consumers consume primary producers. In this case, for example, species F eats species C and D, which in turn consume primary producers A and B.

97. **(B) is correct.** The carnivores in this food web are represented by species F, G, H, and I. Carnivores are generally secondary, tertiary, and quaternary consumers, and they are distinct from omnivores, which eat both plants and animals. Species E is an example of an omnivore.

98. **(E) is correct.** If this were a food web drawn to represent the ecosystem of a savanna, species A and B most likely would represent two species of grasses, since grasses are the predominant primary producers of the savanna biome. Insects are also predominant as primary consumers, so species C, D, and E could represent different species of insects.

99. **(D) is correct.** The two species that are likely to be most closely related evolutionarily are species D and E. Because their DNA denatures at about the same temperature (57°C and 58°C, respectively), one could hypothesize that the composition of their DNA is similar.

100. **(C) is correct.** Another way to denature DNA is to lower the pH of its environment—DNA denatures at low pH, and keeping track of the pH at which each of the DNA samples degraded would give you the same kind of data as the table above. DNA that degraded at relatively higher pH would be less tightly bound than DNA that degraded at lower pH.

Free-Response Questions

1. (a) The cell membrane of a typical animal cell is composed of three main components: phospholipids, which are two fatty acids joined to two glycerol hydroxyl groups and a phosphate group connected to the third glycerol hydroxyl group; proteins, both integral (embedded in the cell membrane) and peripheral (associated with the outside of the membrane); and membrane carbohydrates and glycolipids, which are small carbohydrates associated with the outside of the membrane.

   Phospholipids form a semisolid foundation for the rest of the molecules in the cell membrane. Some very small molecules and ions can pass through the lipid membrane unaided. This type of movement across the membrane is called passive diffusion, because energy is not needed to move the substance across the membrane.

The function of the proteins is multifold, but one important function is to facilitate the passive transport of water and certain other solutes across the membrane. The proteins that serve this function are called transport proteins. Proteins can also participate in the active transport of certain substances across the membrane; they can act as pumps that use ATP energy to transport substances against their concentration gradient. Proteins can also act as important cell-surface receptors.

Membrane carbohydrates and glycolipids on the cytosolic surface of the cell membrane are important in cell-cell recognition; these carbohydrates and glycolipids vary from species to species, and from cell type to cell type, so they function in cell-cell recognition.

(b) Glycoproteins found on viral envelopes bind to specific receptor molecules on the surface of a host cell. This promotes entry of the capsid and viral genome into the cytoplasm where cellular enzymes digest the capsid and release the genetic material. Viral reproduction follows, but the specific steps differ depending on the type of virus.

Hormones are the chemical messengers of the body. They travel through the bloodstream to their target cells. There are two ways by which hormones can gain entry into a target cell. Lipid-soluble hormones diffuse through the cell membrane, then through the cytoplasm, and then bind to a specific receptor protein in the nucleus. Water-soluble hormones bind to a specific receptor protein found on the target cell membrane. This binding signals a series of biochemical signal transduction pathways.

Water enters the cell through a process called facilitated diffusion. This means that water crosses the cell membrane down its concentration gradient, but with the help of specific transport proteins. Transport proteins are specific for the molecules they assist across the membrane, but they do not require the input of energy.

This is a good free-response answer because it shows knowledge of the following important biological terms:

phospholipid	*passive diffusion*
fatty acid	*facilitated diffusion*
glycerol	*active transport*
integral protein	*hormones*
peripheral protein	*target cell*
carbohydrate	*signal transduction pathway*
glycolipid	*receptor*
capsid	

The response also shows knowledge of the following important biological processes: the importance and function of the cell membrane; how molecules get across the cell membrane, how viruses infect cells; and mechanisms of hormonal signaling.

2. (a) Three major obstacles the plants faced for living on land were dehydration, reproduction, and support. Aquatic plants do not require adaptations for *conserving* water (because water is all around them and available at all times), but land plants are in danger of losing water through evaporation. Plants faced a reproductive obstacle—fertilization—as well. In water, the gametes could float from one plant to another, allowing for fertilization. On land, however, there is no watery environment for these gametes to float in. Also even after fertilization occurs, what will stop the zygote from desiccating? A third obstacle to plants' living on land was structural. In aqueous environments, plants are supported by water. On land, they would need to develop mechanisms for support.

(b) The problem of dehydration was solved by the development of a waxy epidermal layer on the outside of leaves called the cuticle. Plants also have stomata, which allow for gas exchange. Stomata can open and close to control excessive transpiration. Vascular tissues (xylem and phloem) also evolved for the transport of water and other nutrients around the plant body. Xylem transports water from the roots up to the leaves, and phloem carries sugar from the leaves (source) to other parts of the plant (sink).

The problem of how to reproduce on land was solved in part by the evolution of the seed. A seed consists of a plant embryo combined with a food supply and encased in a protective coat. This protective coat prevents the embryo from dehydrating even if the seed sits on dry ground for a relatively long period of time. Another adaptation to aid in plant reproduction on land was the spore. Spores are reproductive cells that can develop into a mature plant without fusing with another cell. They are generally lightweight and can travel significantly far from the parent through the air and grow into a new plant.

Plants adapted to living on land without the structural support of water. They developed hard, stiff shoots that enabled them to grow to great heights. The shoots of plants are made up of several types of plant tissues, including the vascular tissues xylem and phloem. Both xylem and phloem are made up of dead water-conducting cells joined together to form long, stiff tubes that help support the plant in its growth.

This is a good free-response answer because it shows a working knowledge of the following important terms:

fertilization	*seed*
gametes	*xylem*
epidermis	*phloem*
cuticle	*spores*
stomata	

The response also shows a working knowledge of the important biological concept of the evolutionary adaptations of plants that enabled them to colonize terrestrial environments.

3. The cell cycle of a plant cell, much like the cell cycle of most other types of cells, includes two main phases: interphase and mitosis. Interphase is divided into three phases: the G_1 (gap 1), S (synthesis), and G_2 (gap 2). The cell undergoes a tremendous amount of biochemical activity during the G_1 phase, in which the plant cell grows and produces new organelles. In the S phase, synthesis of new DNA material takes place. During the G_2 phase, there is continued growth, and organelles needed for cell division or mitosis are replicated. There are several checkpoints in the cell cycle of a plant cell, the most crucial of which is the G_1 checkpoint. If the plant cell gets the go-ahead signal at this checkpoint, it will be committed to divide. If not, it will enter the G_0 phase, which is a nondividing phase.

In late interphase, just before the mitotic phase, the nucleus is intact and the chromosomes are not well defined in the nucleus. When the plant enters the first mitotic phase (prophase), the chromatin fibers become more condensed into visible chromosomes, each of which has two sister chromatids. In the cytoplasm, the mitotic spindle forms, and the centrosomes move away from each other and toward the opposite poles of the cell. The next phase that the plant cell would enter is prometaphase, in which the nuclear envelope would fragment and the microtubules would attach to the kinetochores of the chromatids. In metaphase, all of the chromosomes would line up on the metaphase plate at the equator of the cell, and microtubules would be attached to the kinetochores of every sister chromatid. When the plant cell enters anaphase, the sister chromatids are "dragged" apart from each other to opposite ends of the cell by the retracting microtubules.

The final stages of plant cell mitosis are telophase and cytokinesis. In telophase, two new nuclei begin to form around the groups of sister chromatids that have now migrated to opposite ends of the cell. The chromosomes becomes less condensed, and the cell plate—which divides the cytoplasm in two—starts to grow at the center of the cell, eventually growing all the way to the perimeter of the parent cell and effectively dividing the cell in two.

Following the outline above, this response deals with the following important terms:

cell cycle	chromatin fibers
G_1 phase	sister chromatids
S phase	mitotic spindle
G_2 phase	prometaphase
G_1 checkpoint	metaphase
G_0 phase	nuclear envelope
nondividing phase	microtubules
interphase	kinetochores
mitotic phase	telophase
centrosomes	cytokinesis
prophase	cell plate

The response also describes thoroughly the following processes: the cell cycle including its checkpoints, plant cell mitosis, and cytokinesis.

4. (a) There are three convincing reasons the theory that glycolysis was the first ATP-producing metabolic pathway to evolve is probably true. The first reason is that long ago, Earth's atmosphere contained almost no oxygen, and only relatively recently have the current atmospheric levels of gases come to be what they are. Glycolysis does not require oxygen, so it is possible that prokaryotes (which evolved before eukaryotes) used this method for making ATP.

The second substantiating clue is that glycolysis is a very common method for making ATP; in fact, almost all living organisms use it. This commonality implies that it originated very early in the evolution of metabolic pathways.

The final reason has to do with the site of glycolysis—that is, it takes place in the cytosol, and not in an organelle. Prokaryotic cells, which evolved first, are much simpler than eukaryotic cells, and they contain no membrane-bound organelles (not even a nucleus). Therefore, if glycolysis were to take place in an early prokaryotic cell, it would have to evolve such that it was capable of taking place in the cytosol—for instance, it would have to evolve such that it did not rely on a specialized membrane in order to function.

(b) In the course of the citric acid cycle, acetyl CoA is first joined to oxaloacetate to form citrate, and then the molecule is manipulated extensively to finally re-form a molecule of oxaloacetate. In the course of these reactions, the citric acid cycle produces 1 ATP molecule, 3 NADH molecules, and 1 $FADH_2$ molecule (per turn).

The way that the citric acid cycle is related to oxidative phosphorylation is that the NADH and $FADH_2$ molecules produced during the citric acid cycle donate electrons to the electron transport chain, which is embedded in the wall of the inner mitochondrial membrane. This electron transport chain shuttles the electrons down its length, in an exergonic reaction. The energy produced in this series of electron transfers is used to power an enzyme called ATP synthase, which is also embedded in the wall of the inner mitochondrial membrane; ATP synthase catalyzes the phosphorylation of ADP to form ATP.

This is a good free-response answer because it knowledgeably uses the following key terms:

glycolysis	*oxaloacetate*
prokaryotes	*citrate*
eukaryotes	*citric acid cycle*
ATP	*NADH*
cytosol	*FADH$_2$*
organelle	*inner mitochondrial membrane*
nucleus	*phosphorylation*
acetyl CoA	

The response also shows a working knowledge of the following important biological concepts: the origin of life and ancient Earth, relationships among living organisms, glycolysis, the citric acid cycle, and the electron transport chain.